industry and government

ivan allen, jr. department of science

The Human Rights Handbook

The HUMAN RIGHTS Handbook

A guide to British and
American international
human rights organisations

Compiled by
Marguerite Garling
for the
WRITERS AND SCHOLARS
EDUCATIONAL TRUST

Facts On File
119 West 57th Street, New York, N.Y. 10019

First published 1979 by

FACTS ON FILE INC.
New York

Library of Congress Cataloging in Publication Data

Garling, Marguerite.
  The human rights handbook.

  Bibliography: p.
  Includes index.
  1. Civil rights—Societies, etc. I. Title.
JC571.G32   323.4'06'2   78-26169
ISBN 0-87196-403-1

Contents

Part D INTERNATIONAL (Inter-Governmental Organisations)

Preface

The Writers and Scholars Educational Trust (WSET) is an independent charitable body set up to gather information about censorship and restraints on free expression. Many of the results are published in the Trust's associated magazine, *Index on Censorship*, which is published bi-monthly and includes banned literature and personal testimonies. Other research studies published separately include: *The Emergency, Censorship and the Press in India 1975-7*, published in London by WSET and in India by Central News Agency (PVT) Ltd; *Unofficial Art from the Soviet Union*, published in London by Secker and Warburg and in the United States by Random House; *Television and Political Life, Studies in Six European Societies*, published in London by Macmillan and in the United States by St Martin's Press; *Human Rights Research Guide*, a guide to library holdings in London, published by WSET. We also hope to publish more studies: *The Greek Press Under the Dictatorship and After, 1967-77*; *The Press in Argentina, 1973-8*; *Censorship in Brazil*.

The British section of the present study was compiled by Marguerite Garling and completed in September 1977. Inevitably there will have been changes in some organisations since then; the editors have tried to keep abreast of the latest news and they apologise if they have overlooked important developments. In fact the editors would be grateful for corrections or additions which readers manage to send in.

Particular thanks are due to Laurie Wiseberg of the Human Rights Internet, for help in compiling a number of entries on the USA organisations and for providing suggestions and contacts; to the Meiklejohn Civil Liberties Institute, for permission to use several of the entries in their *Human Rights Organisations and Periodicals Directory*; to the Members of Congress for Peace Through Law (MCPL) Education Fund, for permission to use several of the entries in their *Directory of Human Rights Organisations*; and to those organisations who responded to the questionnaire. Thanks are also due to Daniela von Bethlenfalvy and Jane Spender. Finally, the *Handbook* owes its existence to a grant from the Ford Foundation, to which the Trust is most grateful.

Readers should note the existence of a book which complements this one — Glenda da Fonseca's *How to File Complaints of Human Rights Violations*, a practical guide to inter-governmental procedures, published by the World Council of Churches, Geneva. This deals with the UN Commission on Human Rights, the International Labour Organisation, the European Commission on Human Rights and the Inter-American Commission on Human Rights.

Michael Scammell, *Director*
Writers and Scholars Educational Trust

London 1978

Introduction

The phrase 'human rights' has now entered into common currency, and is constantly on the lips of newscasters, pundits and presidents – which, some fear, may prove to be the kiss of death for the authenticity of the human rights movement. But, however much the human rights industry has become a standby of hardpressed editors and politicians, the movement in defence of basic human rights has always been solidly based on the largely voluntary and self-motivated initiatives of ordinary, unofficial individuals working to express their anxiety and concern. This has been the strength of the human rights movement, and is likely to remain so.

This handbook aims to provide basic background information for two groups of people: those already involved in human rights activities who need to know what other organisations are doing; and those who seek assistance in respect of particular human rights cases. And perhaps also for potential donors, who will need little prompting to realise that human rights organisations, almost by definition, never have sufficient money to meet their needs.

The information given here is mainly practical: where to turn for assistance, what each organisation does, the scope and nature of its resources. I hope that the handbook can also fulfil a secondary purpose, which is to give an idea both of the quantity and of the quality of human rights work in Britain and the USA; and, with regard to Britain, to consider the problems confronting the voluntary and professional organisations, the financial and structural restrictions on their work, the direction of recent thinking, and the new initiatives taken.

The present handbook grew out of a project on aid-giving agencies commissioned by the Writers and Scholars Educational Trust in London. It became clear from the outset that the definition of 'aid-giving agencies' could not be confined to organisations providing financial assistance alone. Only a few of the humanitarian, charitable and professional organisations covered by this survey dispose of any significant reserves of financial aid; the bulk of their assistance takes the form of advice, counselling, information, lobbying and other forms of moral and practical support, which they would argue are ultimately more important to the recipients than simple financial awards.

The categories of beneficiaries also required definition. I confined my attention to those deprived of certain basic freedoms – of speech, opinion, political and religious belief, of association and of movement – as defined by the UN Universal Declaration of Human Rights. (See the Appendix.)

I also chose to include individuals forcibly deprived of those rights or threatened with their loss, and those driven into exile as a result.

The survey is centred on voluntary and professional organisations within the United Kingdom and the USA which deal with international and not just domestic issues, and also includes certain international agencies. It was at first expected that we would deal only with British-based organisations, but later the sections on the USA and the international agencies were brought in. This has produced a temporary imbalance, but we think readers will prefer to have the extra information. Our intention is to expand the US and international sections in any future edition of the *Handbook.*

Three categories of organisation have been distinguished: voluntary human rights and related humanitarian organisations; professional associations; and organisations providing help for refugees arriving in the United Kingdom. I have not included national bodies concerned with the protection of internal civil liberties, except where they are involved with human rights cases outside their own country. The limitation was prompted by the number and variety of organisations now in existence and by the recognition that greater emphasis was now being put on human rights activities by other institutions.

It is one of the primary aims of this survey to stimulate an increased exchange of the sort of information which often circulates only within specialised networks. Thus, work undertaken on behalf of refugees is covered because there is a scarcity of practical information on this important field of activity, where human rights problems overseas are brought home, quite literally, to the host community. There is a need for closer cooperation at the level of information and mutual support between refugee agencies and those organisations working on behalf of individuals overseas who may share with the refugees a 'well-founded fear of persecution' in their own country. I have also attempted to show how, in particular, the international relief and development agencies can fulfil an important function in their awareness and support of groups and individuals at risk overseas. I have tried to give examples of how professional bodies can intervene successfully in support of the counterparts at risk overseas. Lastly, I have listed in outline some of the numerous committees and *ad hoc* bodies involved in campaign and support work; these too may provide essential first-hand information about human rights violations in their particular area of concern.

Marguerite Garling

Part A

The United Kingdom

I Voluntary Organisations

Chapter 1

HUMAN RIGHTS ORGANISATIONS

The human rights lobby in the United Kingdom has never had a strong centre. It is only in the last few years that the label 'human rights' has come to be applied, with varying degrees of relevance, to a disparate collection of humanitarian organisations, most of them small, all of them independent, which have campaigned over the years for the recognition of fundamental rights. Indeed, some of them began to do so long before these rights were formulated by the United Nations in its 1948 Universal Declaration (see Appendix). Most, however, are of post-war origin, subsisting on a shoestring until the human rights explosion of the 1970s. And it is only since 1974 that a loose 'network' has existed under the aegis of the United Nations Association and the National Council for Social Service, to serve as an informal forum for their widely ranging viewpoints.

The impulse that led to the formation of what has been called the human rights industry in recent years has been essentially international in character. To describe human rights work in this country as a 'lobby' is in fact misleading, since in essence this work is directed beyond the interests of the British government to the international community at large. Nor are its aims political in a partisan sense (although frequently misinterpreted as such by outside bodies, including the Charity Commissioners). They may be defined as seeking observance by governments and institutions of universally acknowledged rights, duties and standards of behaviour which are, if far from universally observed in practice, enshrined in international treaties, covenants and laws.

The growth of this human rights industry and its recognition as a legitimate sphere of concern are well illustrated by the rapid growth of Amnesty International from its modest British beginnings 15 years ago to a vast international complex coordinating local voluntary action with high-level diplomatic initiatives and a worldwide network of information on political imprisonment, torture and related questions. Amnesty, like the other human rights organisations, has had an uphill job establishing its non-political credentials: governments are still only too ready to view external attempts to gain observance of basic rights as politically-inspired interference in their internal affairs. As an international mass movement, Amnesty has largely succeeded in establishing the legitimacy of non-governmental concern with human rights violations wherever, and in whichever circumstances, they occur, but recognition of this legitimacy is far from universal.

The international framework of human rights actions is too complex to describe in this survey, though a selected list of important American, European and international organisations is to be found in Appendix II. The international human rights lobby involves complex diplomacy both amongst concerned non-governmental organisations (NGOs) and in relation to a multiplicity of power centres, in particular, the United Nations and its agencies, and that Mecca of international bureaucracies, Geneva. It is sufficient to note here that contact and information-flow between the British voluntary organisations and the international human rights lobby is largely under-developed, and tends to be confined to international parent-bodies and a few counterpart committees and organisations overseas. In some areas, the British voluntary community seems to be just emerging from a long twilight of parochialism. In many instances, human rights issues have provided the impetus for a resurgence of internationalism in the post-Vietnam years.

In addition to international organisations like AI or the Geneva-based International Commission of Jurists, a number of British-based organisations are involved in work whose scope and impact are international. The doyen of these is the 140-year-old Anti-Slavery Society, which has successfully adapted its abolitionist objectives to more subtle modern forms of slavery, and almost singlehanded has kept the issues alive at an international level. The Minority Rights Group and Survival International are well on their way to establishing a similar international lobby on behalf of minority groups and aboriginal peoples respectively.

The third category of human rights organisations covered in this section includes non-specialist British groups with a broad interest in human rights issues and an international angle to their work. Although many of the organisations listed throughout this survey would answer this description, we have listed in this section those *primarily* concerned with human rights, whether from a juridical viewpoint, or as animators of the human rights lobby in this country.

Given this wide diversity of aims, levels of approach and access to information, any attempt to describe the internal workings of the human rights lobby is fraught with difficulties. Organic rather than mechanical figures of speech are called for: grapevines, branches and roots, rather than circuits and systems. Any individual attempting to beat a pathway through this jungle of committees, working-groups, contacts, delegations, bulletins and backlogs is likely to conclude that human rights work is a matter of a relatively small number of harassed and overworked altruists (usually underpaid, if paid at all) trying desperately to keep pace with events. And if some of them may uncharitably be described as prima donnas, this is perhaps an indication of the lengthy struggles many of them have waged in defence of individual freedoms against governments, institutions, entrenched habits of mind, and throttling bureaucracy. Human rights workers as a whole are a hard-headed lot — far removed from the woolly-minded idealists of popular legend — and well versed in the art of cutting through bureaucratic obfuscation; but the increasing need to coordinate their activities means that they are in danger of being engulfed in it themselves.

A few organisations, new as well as old, are jealous guardians of their territorial prerogatives and tend to resent any incursions into their own demarcated field of action. These purely institutional tendencies may be exacerbated by excessive security considerations, political defensiveness, or domination by powerful individual personalities. But nobody, as the saying goes, has a monopoly of conscience, and it is both sad and ironic that these inhibitions should operate so persistently in the field of human rights work.

By its very nature, human rights work is individual and *ad hoc*. Any attempts at systematisation go against this grain. Yet there is a widely recognised need for more efficient flow of information and more systematic referral of individual casework. The most satisfactory means to date of reconciling these divergent demands in Britain has been the informal contact provided by the Human Rights Network, which has proved flexible enough to encompass the varying interests of the human rights 'adhocracy'. Further progress is likely to depend on how far coordination can be reconciled with the autonomy of the individual organisations.

Amnesty International
International Secretariat
Tower House, 10 Southampton Street
London WC2E 7HF
Tel: (01) 836 7788
International Chairman: Thomas Hammarberg
Secretary General: Martin Ennals
British Section: Tel: (01) 836 1851
Director: David Simpson

Over the sixteen years of its existence, Amnesty International has built up a formidable reputation in the field of human rights work. An international non-governmental organisation with sections in over thirty countries and a 168,000-strong (and still growing) membership, it constitutes the strongest organised international pressure-group for the respect of human rights.

Amnesty International is a voluntary organisation working for the release of persons imprisoned or otherwise detained by reason of their political, religious or other conscientiously-held beliefs, or on the grounds of their ethnic origin, race, sex or cultural background. Provided they have neither used nor advocated violence, their cases may be taken up individually or collectively as 'Prisoners of Conscience'. The reservation against violence only applies to formal adoption of Prisoners of Conscience: Amnesty campaigns for the abolition of torture and capital punishment and for the implementation of the United Nations' Standard Minimum Rules on the Treatment of Prisoners, regardless of whether or not the prisoners are charged with the use or advocacy of violence.

The strength of Amnesty's appeal can be ascribed to a combination of factors.

— Its aims are specific and incontrovertible. It bases its action on internationally-agreed norms, embodied in the international conventions to which the majority of states subscribe — at least in the form of lip-service, since they are more often honoured in the breach than in the observance. By approaching governments from the angle of their own prior commitments, Amnesty International has a moral leverage through which to press for the release of individuals or the redress of particular injustices. (Little wonder that many governments are acutely annoyed by such reminders.)

— The essential back-up for this moral leverage is that Amnesty has the force of international public opinion behind it. Not a single-minded public opinion, naturally enough, for there is plenty of criticism, both internal and external, of its overall strategy, particularly in the use of publicity. But because it invokes support for each of its initiatives on a worldwide basis and across a wide range of political viewpoints and personal interests, Amnesty underscores the political impartiality of its approach, and the universal character of its demands.

— The nature of this support is entirely voluntary. Amnesty International is frequently taken to task by governments as the tool of international political movements of the Left or Right, but the conspiratorial overtones of these charges are entirely inappropriate. It ignores the sense of individual commitment and responsibility for the fate of others which impels individuals to join Amnesty. And it is Amnesty's strength that it has been able to channel this concern through practical action with individuals participating in local groups.

— Amnesty International accordingly recognises no restrictions or frontiers when working for the release of individual prisoners. It rejects charges that such action is 'interference in the internal affairs' of the state in question, just as it rejects any attempted justification of torture and other forms of ill-treatment on grounds of governmental expediency. By upholding the right of private individuals to question the behaviour of governments, bureaucracies and prison authorities, Amnesty

International has largely succeeded in establishing the validity of this mode of action — through its relative success and its now widespread acceptance.

Against this, it can be argued that Amnesty's universal approach is far from being realised. Its membership is concentrated overwhelmingly in the Western European welfare democracies and North America. Its humanitarian ideals are frequently dismissed as a rich man's privilege by Third World governments intent on achieving social and economic goals with a minimum of political inconvenience to themselves. And there are clear risks for Amnesty's work inherent in its very success, both in terms of coping with the fast-growing new membership, and with the dangers of appearing too closely identified with specific elements in Western foreign policies.

Activities

Amnesty International was the first major human rights organisation to employ the practice of case-adoption by local groups. These groups of private individuals work on behalf of up to three political prisoners — always selected from contrasting backgrounds and never from the group's own country — writing letters on their behalf, making personal representations to officials, publicising details of each case, and enlisting further support within their own community. The appeal of direct action on each case, coupled with a degree of personal identification with the prisoner's plight, has provided the answer for many individuals whose concern and indignation about political imprisonment had been aroused, but who had felt helpless to act upon it. (Amnesty's group actions are occasionally criticised as a form of group therapy for the alienated Western middle classes, but this attack does not stand up to close consideration of the group's activities and motivation.) Many hundreds of such groups now exist in the 33 countries where Amnesty has a national section.

The corollary of such massive local-level involvement is that a degree of supervision needs to be exercised over the conduct of the groups in handling each case — advice on how to approach the authorities, whether to contact families and lawyers (who may also be at risk), guidelines on publicity, follow-up on new developments, joint actions with other groups, and so on. Loose supervision and coordination are exercised from the central Secretariat in London, by each national office, and through a number of *ad hoc* national coordination groups.

Each case-history is carefully assessed by the Research Department in London before being allocated to a group, to ensure that the case concerned falls within Amnesty's classification as a 'Prisoner of Conscience'. Where doubts persist, the case will be investigated by the group in an effort to obtain confirmation: only then can the group press for the prisoner's release. It will maintain close contact with the International

Secretariat on developments in the case — including, on occasion, news of a release.

In addition to the individual's fundamental right to go unpunished for what he thinks, says, or is, the group is concerned with his rights while awaiting trial, on trial, under sentence, and in prison. According to the nature of the case it will press for freedom from pre-trial intimidation or torture; access to legal advice and family visits; the right to a fair trial and adequate defence; the right to appeal against sentence; and while in prison, adequate conditions, access to medical care, exercise, study facilities, and so on. The group may in come cases raise money for the prisoner's family and provide moral support by sustaining friendly contact with them.

Amnesty International adoption groups are of necessity involved in work on a wide range of topics related to the essential fact of imprisonment. Some may, through their experience of particular cases, choose to act as coordinators for other groups, specialising in the problems of one particular country. Others may opt for campaign work, within the context of Amnesty's international programmes against torture (launched by an international conference in 1973) and against the death penalty (1976-7). One particular feature of this work has been the setting-up of an Urgent Action network, spreading beyond Amnesty's formal membership, to initiate an immediate response in the form of letters and cables on behalf of those whose lives may be in acute danger.

Owing to Amnesty International's rapid growth in membership in recent years, and the consequent difficulties in keeping pace with group demands for prisoner cases (not for want of prisoners, or of case-sheet supply, which is higher than ever before), discussion currently centres on the expansion of group work into these other areas of action, with greater stress on public education and campaign work.

Structure

One essential feature of Amnesty's work lies in its combination of grass-roots activity and initiatives at all national and international levels. The concerted work of so many individual groups in such varied countries and on so many issues requires a degree of back-up at national and international level, which is supplied by the national sections and from the International Secretariat in London. Group actions are conceived within the context of national approaches — to embassies, national organisations and parliamentary bodies, and in nationwide public education campaigns; and within an overall international strategy — initiatives at diplomatic levels, missions and trial observations, published statements and reports.

Amnesty International's national sections provide a focal point for Amnesty actions within their own country, and a two-way liaison between their member groups and the International Secretariat. A strong degree of national autonomy means that Amnesty's international work can be readily translated by each national section into modes of action – campaigns, press contacts, lobbying – appropriate to the national arena. Thus the British Section of Amnesty represents Amnesty's overall viewpoint within the British human rights community, while maintaining its own particularly British identity, and launching its own fund-raising and campaigning initiatives.

The International Secretariat in London, through its own staff, the national sections and groups, implements the strategy of the organisation, which is formulated in overall terms by an annual International Council Meeting representing the sections, and throughout the year by an International Executive Committee. The interim is assured by the organisation's Secretary General, whose office is also responsible for international diplomatic contacts. The specialised research staff scan, sift and evaluate the small mountain of information which arrives on Amnesty's London doorstep each morning; they keep a watching brief on developments in all countries – including the 'closed' societies, from which information rarely filters through; individual prisoner-dossiers are prepared for allocation to the groups, missions despatched, and detailed reports drawn up on particular topics of concern. Standards of impartial assessment are high, and a significant amount of time is spent on covering events in areas which rarely give rise to large-scale international publicity. (Amnesty's 1975 campaign on events in Uruguay served to bring the tragic situation in that country to public attention at a time when it was heavily overshadowed by events in Chile.) The Programme Department translates the Research Department's findings into campaign and group-work through the national sections, coordination groups and individual local groups.

Finance

Amnesty International is entirely self-financing. Its income derives from individual membership fees, donations, fund-raising campaigns, sale of publications, public events, and contributions by the groups. In the British Section, each local group is asked to contribute up to and beyond a target sum set for the year: in 1977-8 this will be in the region of £250. The national section in turn contributes to the financing of international action through the International Secretariat in London:[1] the national contributions vary according to targets set by the sections themselves and reflecting their expected funding capacity for each coming year.

Amnesty's *Prisoner of Conscience Fund* channels relief money – over £100,000 annually – to Prisoners of Conscience and their families. Distribution is through local contacts, which may be a local church aid or development aid office, or an established charitable body. The Fund is financed by private donations from a wide variety of sources;

---

[1] The organisation's international budget for 1977-8 has been stepped up to £829,000, and will increase to about £1.2 million for 1978-9.

no governmental funding is permitted and the Fund avoids over-reliance on any single source by the wide diversity of its contributors.

Anti-Slavery Society for the Protection of Human Rights
60 Weymouth Street
London W1N 4DX
Tel: (01) 935 6498
Chairman: Jeremy Swift
Secretary: Col J.R.P. Montgomery, MC

The Anti-Slavery Society, whose work goes back to the abolitionist movement of the 1830s, is the sole research and pressure group concerned with identifying and reporting on slavery in all its persistent forms throughout the world. This work, like that of Survival International, may be termed human rights work – in the narrow definition adopted for the purpose of this survey – where subject, endebted and enslaved groups have no means of pressing for their rights and liberty other than through such external agencies. The Anti-Slavery Society commissions reports, based on detailed fieldwork, which are presented on completion to the government concerned for comment; depending on the response, the Society will proceed by quiet diplomacy or publicity as the case demands. Examples of recent enquiries undertaken by the Society include: child labour in Morocco, enforced prostitution in Hong Kong, the decimation and debt-bondage of South American tribes.

The Anti-Slavery Society is an international non-governmental organisation which provides an international lobby on slavery. As a result of its pressure, in 1975 the United Nations set up an Expert Group on Slavery, to which the Society makes regular well-documented submissions on the persistence of forms of slavery in many areas of the world, such as forced labour in Africa, and the dispossession, oppression and killing of peasants in Central America. The Society, which has consultative status with the United Nations (ECOSOC), works for the observance of the UN Supplementary Convention of 1956, which binds signatory states to the elimination of slavery and related forms of bondage.

Finance

The Society operates on a budget of around £12,000, which is drawn largely from voluntary donations. Its recent publications have included studies of tribes of the Amazon Basin (1972), of the fight for self-determination in Western Sahara (1976), and of forced labour and political murder in Equatorial Guinea (1976).

British Institute of Human Rights
Charles Clore House
17 Russell Square
London WC1B 5DR
Tel: (01) 636 5802
Chairman: Professor James Fawcett, DSC
Director: Mr A.B. McNulty, CBE

The British Institute of Human Rights initiates research projects on the legal aspects of human rights questions and, in particular, sets these projects in a European context. The Institute has also organised international meetings on Detention and a British Bill of Rights, and has co-sponsored with the Council for Science and Society the handbook *Scholarly Freedom and Human Rights*.[1] It gave evidence to the House of Lords Select Committee on a Bill of Rights for the United Kingdom in July 1977.

The Institute (a registered charity) and its associated Human Rights Trust were set up in 1970. The Institute's Board of Governors includes distinguished public figures, with particular emphasis on the law. Its approach to human rights questions is essentially juridical, and it stresses a strict political impartiality. It does not consider itself in any way a pressure group. Because of this, it tends to confine its work to creating a human rights information centre and to launching various research projects.

The Institute's main information source is the Reference Centre, a retrieval index of the sources of human rights law, financed by a grant from the Leverhulme Trust Fund. As a compilation of source material on the interpretation of the international instruments pertaining to Human Rights (the UN Covenants primarily and the European Convention), the Reference Centre enables lawyers and others to ascertain the state of implementation both on the international and national levels and the common standards which are emerging from their implementation. The Reference Centre covers the following: the Strasbourg Human Rights Commission and the Committee on Human Rights; the Luxembourg Court of Justice; national decisions from those countries where the terms of the European Convention have been incorporated into national law.

The Institute's work is not widely publicised, and there would appear to be wide scope for more explanatory outlines of legal machinery for the layman, on the lines of *Scholarly Freedom and Human Rights*. To this end, closer cooperation with the campaigning organisations might help establish where the major information gaps occur, without in any way compromising the impartiality of the legal approach.

---

[1] Barry Rose, London, 1977.

United Kingdom

Finance

The British Institute for Human Rights is funded through its associated Human Rights Fund, set up in 1970. The Trust has attracted donations from charitable foundations, notably the Leverhulme Trust Fund. In November 1977, an appeal was launched for further funding, in order to further the research work undertaken by the Institute.

Centre for Human Rights and Responsibilities
Nansen House
64 Millbank
London SW1
Tel: (01) 834 6326; (01) 834 2457 (after office hours)
President: Rt Hon Philip Noel-Baker
Chairman: Yehudi Menuhin

The Centre for Human Rights and Responsibilities works to promote education and research into the far-reaching social issues behind human rights violations, which are viewed as symptomatic of changes within society felt by many to be beyond control. Apathy, alienation and sporadic or institutionalised violence are viewed as forms of response to the breakdown in the earlier reliance on a paternalistic order. 'We therefore see the principle of Human Rights and Responsibilities as a minimum base of values and behaviour patterns below which one must not allow oneself or others, be it as victims or victimisers, to sink.'

Within the framework of this philosophy, the Centre has initiated a number of studies covering local community programmes, social issues and trans-national projects focusing on situations of conflict and minority groups. Amongst projects falling within the scope of this survey are: proposals for a Bill of Rights in Britain, help to Kurdish minorities, contacts with persecuted minorities in South and South-East Asia.

The Centre is the British affiliate of the Fédération Internationale des Droits de l'Homme, a union of the Western European Ligues des Droits de l'Homme, for many years dormant and which the French, Belgian, Swiss and British sections are now trying to reanimate as a working federation at international level. The Secretary of the British Centre is interim Vice-President of the International Federation; the interim President is from the Belgian League (1 avenue de la Toison d'Or, B-1060 Brussels).

Finance

The Centre for Human Rights and Responsibilities has an annual budget of £20,000–£25,000 which is financed from donations and foundation grants

14

it hopes eventually to become self-supporting. It employs a permanent staff of eight and is assisted by some 30-40 part-time volunteers.

Human Rights Network
National Council of Social Service (NCSS)
26 Bedford Square
London WC1B 3HU
Tel: (01) 636 4066
Secretary: Bill Seary

The Human Rights Network — essentially a mailing list and an occasional forum — came into being in December 1974, as the brainchild of the UNA Human Rights Committee, in response to the multitude of charities and pressure groups with a human rights angle to their work. It was decided not to impose a strict definition of what constituted 'human rights' — which is anyway not possible — in order to attract the widest range of interested parties. These now number over 60, and new adherents are still coming forward. The Network thus includes human rights organisations, i.e. those working to secure observance of internationally-agreed norms at international level — and also those groups which have become involved due to a less easily defined humanitarianism (the numerous pacifist and church-related groups would come under this heading). A further category would include a number of organisations which are strictly speaking civil rights organisations seeking the redress of particular injustices under British law.[1] A glance at the Network membership will illustrate the number of interests involved.

Representatives of these organisations meet a few times a year to exchange notes on campaigns, techniques and new developments in their field. They may make appeals for support in joint initiatives, such as circulating petitions, or offer available facilities such as mailing-lists. The National Peace Council (29 St James Street, London WC1N 3ES, tel: 01-242 3228) provides a 'date-clash avoidance calendar' to assist in planning campaign work.

The philosophy behind the Network's informal and wide-ranging approach is to promote a cross-fertilisation of ideas and greater pooling of scarce resources, while avoiding duplication of effort. If it has one drawback, it is in the great variety of interests present. There is a clear

---

[1] While all civil rights cases — concerning, for example, educational rights or women's rights — are of course also 'human rights' cases, we are here adopting the current rule-of-thumb which distinguishes between internal and international issues.

15

disparity between those organisations which are international in outlook and those whose attention is confined to purely British issues, each requiring a quite distinct formulation of strategy.

Where major issues require full discussion, special working groups may be set up for those directly interested. One recent development has been the setting-up of a *Task Force for Cooperative Action on Southern Africa*, to pool information, ideas and support amongst interested Network members and external pressure groups.[1] The co-ordination of approaches on British foreign aid policies in relation to human rights issues is another such area of pressing concern. Others may include cooperation on refugee and immigration questions, which are frequently raised at Network meetings. Neither the development aid agencies nor the refugee organisations are strongly represented in the Network;[2] there is a strong case for establishing closer regular contact with them.

Finance

The cost of servicing the Network is borne by the National Council for Social Service. Member organisations contribute £3 each year towards the circulation costs.

Minority Rights Group
Benjamin Franklin House
36 Craven Street
London WC2N 5NG
Tel: (01) 930 6659
Director: Ben Whitaker

The Minority Rights Group exists as an international research and information centre to make known the plight of persecuted ethnic, religious, and cultural minorities which are, in many instances, not able to speak out for themselves. The definition of a 'minority' is, accordingly, defined in part by the fact of its persecuted or disadvantaged status, even though it might technically constitute a majority of the population.

The work of the Minority Rights Group rests on the premise that thorough and well-researched information is the essential prerequisite for any effective human rights action on behalf of those persecuted, and that publication of such research, calling attention to their plight,

---

[1]   Rev. John Hastings, Methodist Relief Fund, 1 Central Buildings, Matthew Parker Street, London SW1H 9NH. See page 89.

[2]   Only BCAR, JCWI, UKIAS and War on Want are to date Network members.

contributes to the cessation of persecution and discrimination. The leverage of informed opinion, though intangible (and though many repressive governments profess themselves impervious to it), is a powerful weapon, the more so as governments are increasingly called to account for their behaviour in the international arena. By publicising the facts as widely as possible, MRG considers its work to be remedial, preventive and educative.

MRG Reports, commissioned from outside specialists, such as academics and journalists, and verified by authorities on the subject in question, have built up a depressingly predictable catalogue of exploitation, discrimination and the cultural repression of minorities in every corner of the world. Reports are sent out to the world's press, media and educational establishments, and are sold widely to individuals and libraries in 89 countries. MRG has also recently published the first volume of a two-volume directory of minorities, (*World Minorities* ed. G. Ashworth, London, 1977), and it organises conferences on minority issues.

It has been granted consultative status with the United Nation's Economic and Social Council (ECOSOC). MRG's Director is also the British member of the UN Human Rights Sub-Commission in Geneva.

Finance

The Minority Rights Group is not a membership organisation and subsists through donations and sales of its reports. It operates on an annual budget of £25,000, which covers administration, research (including fieldwork) and publications.

Parliamentary Human Rights Group
c/o Lord Avebury
House of Lords
Westminster
London SW1
Chairman: Lord Avebury
Honorary Secretaries: Philip Whitehead MP and John Hunt MP

The Parliamentary Human Rights Group is an all-party group set up in 1976 with the support of a number of NGOs concerned with human rights. The UNA Human Rights Committee services it and helps to coordinate its activities with the other interests. As yet, it is an informal arrangement, bringing together interested MPs with expert speakers and human rights workers. Topics raised to date include: the abuse of psychiatry in the Soviet Union; human rights violations in Brazil, Argentina, Chile; human rights and the Press; Namibia; human rights and the UN;

17

Uganda; human rights and international relations.

The Parliamentary Group aims at mustering a core of around 100 MPs who can be called upon to provide support when human rights issues arise in the course of debates. It maintains contact with various human rights organisations and raises Parliamentary questions. Recognising that many MPs are still all too frequently ill-informed about human rights issues (despite some determined lobbying by human rights groups), the Parliamentary Human Rights Group seeks to stimulate interest and debate on these matters within both Houses, as well as promote action on them.

The example afforded by the US House Sub-Committee on Foreign Affairs ('the Fraser Sub-Committee') in focusing attention on human rights issues in connection with US foreign aid policies is considered particularly relevant to the work of the Parliamentary Group; Congressman Fraser has been a guest speaker at a Parliamentary Group meeting. The British Parliamentary Group hopes to work on building up concerted pressures together with the Fraser Sub-Committee, although unlike the American body it has no money or staff to arrange major hearings on special issues of concern.

Survival International
Benjamin Franklin House
36 Craven Street
London WC2N 5NG
Tel: (01) 839 3267
Director: Barbara Bentley

Survival International was founded in 1972 to publicise the problems and aspirations of aboriginal peoples and to extend the area of international responsibility and recognition of these needs. Beyond publicity and pressure on their behalf, the organisation administers a wide-ranging programme of fieldwork amongst aboriginal groups whose existence is directly threatened, whether by natural and environmental factors, or by aggressive government policies. Survival International publishes details of this work in its quarterly, *Survival International Review*, and may on occasion submit evidence to the United Nations Human Rights Commission.

Survival International is an international organisation, with support groups in the United Kingdom, Canada and W. Germany. Its British membership totals around 1,000. Together with the Anti-Slavery Society's Committee for Indigenous Peoples, it operates a Joint Projects Committee, which commissions research, acts as a clearing-house for development project proposals, and provides legal, medical and technical advice to workers in the field.

Finance

Survival International's projects are funded separately by outside organisations in Europe and America. Its own budget is drawn from donations and subscriptions (of £5 per annum); like many other independent voluntary organisations, it has been experiencing acute financial difficulties in recent years.

United Nations Association
3 Whitehall Court
London SW1A 2EL
Tel: (01) 930 2931
Chairman: Rt Hon Jeremy Thorpe MP
Director: Rev David J. Harding
The Human Rights Committee Secretary: Leah Levin

The UNA Human Rights Committee works to promote a better functioning of the human rights machinery both in this country and internationally, having been set up to continue the work started during International Human Rights Year (1968).[1] To this end, it was instrumental in bringing into being the **Human Rights Network** in 1974, following a human rights seminar which had brought into the open a general concern amongst human rights workers at the fragmentation, compartmentalisation and duplication of their work. The Committee also helped to set up the **Parliamentary Human Rights Group**, to focus attention within Parliament on particular issues of concern.

Reflecting the viewpoint of its international federation, the World Federation of United Nations Associations (WFUNA – see p. 251), the British UNA takes part in lobbying activities on matters affecting British policy towards the United Nations, implementation of UN programmes, and the improvement of UN Human Rights machinery. In its approach to these structural questions, the UNA Human Rights Committee favours a flexible *ad hoc* response, with the emphasis on a strong information back-up; it has sought ways to break down territorial barriers and increase collaboration between voluntary organisations, but is fully aware that over-systematisation in these areas can go against the grain of traditional working methods.

The UNA Human Rights Committee is not involved in casework and

---

[1] Its work is described in a leaflet 'A Lead for Human Rights'.

does not dispose of any funds. However, it does on occasion offer advice and assistance on individual cases brought to its attention (usually in the form of referral to specialised agencies).

The United Nations Association is an all-party organisation with over 25,000 members organised in Branches and Regions throughout the country. Other UNA central committees which relate to human rights concerns specialise in Economic and Social Affairs, Political Matters, Youth and Overseas Volunteers. The British UNA is affiliated to the World Federation of United Nations Associations (see p. 251), of which its former director, Frank Field, is now Secretary General.

By virtue of the fact that the United Nations is an Inter-Governmental Organisation, WFUNA cannot, for practical reasons, closely associate itself with campaigns against individual governments which systematically violate human rights. Its concern is to strengthen the appropriate UN machinery, and campaign for ratification by member-governments of the United Nations human rights Convenants (on Social and Economic Rights, and on Political and Civil Rights). In March 1976, it decided to participate in Amnesty's international campaign against torture in Uruguay, by requesting UN investigation of the alleged violations as soon as possible. This decision now stands as a precedent for future WFUNA action on specific areas. Similarly, WFUNA made known its concern to the Chilean authorities when these refused a UN mission of enquiry to investigate reported persistent and systematic violations of basic human rights in that country.

WFUNA, like its national committees in 71 countries, also adopts a coordinating role amongst NGOs with a special interest in human rights issues, particularly in relation to lobbying the United Nations and its spcialised agencies. It has on occasion made representations to particular governments to allow national UNAs to promote various UN programmes in their own country (for example, Spain).

Relations with all the UN specialised agencies are good, though more concerted cooperation with the UN High Commission on Refugees appears to be called for.

Finance

The United Nations Association is financed through a basic membership subscription of £3 per annum (£1 associate membership). In addition, it receives a small amount in donations and in *ex gratia* aid from the Foreign Office.

Chapter 2

SCHOLARSHIP AID ORGANISATIONS

For increasing numbers of students throughout the world, the offer of a scholarship is their sole means of escape from an intolerable situation – for a few, it may be the passport which enables them to leave a prison or detention-camp, for others a release from prolonged intimidation and the fear of imminent arrest. Some students may already be refugees at the time of their application, with no alternative means of pursuing their interrupted studies; others may need a period of study to re-qualify, as a means of adapting to standards and conditions in their country of refuge. The scale of the operations undertaken by the voluntary scholarship organisations such as World University Service or the International University Exchange Fund testifies to the extent of these needs.

Groups of student refugees from recognised trouble-spots have over the years been accorded government-funded scholarship programmes, often only after persistent lobbying from the voluntary scholarship organisations. This was the case for the Hungarians and Czechs, for Ugandan Asians, Chileans, Vietnamese, and most recently, Ugandan African students, for whom some 75 scholarships are being awarded by the Overseas Development Ministry through World University Service. Indeed, the Ministry, in line with the voluntary organisations, has come to view aid to student refugees as a long-term investment of future benefit to the development needs of their region of origin. In this respect, they should be treated on a par with other needy overseas students who make use of advanced educational facilities in this country.

But while the problems of certain well-known areas are recognised in this way, more and more it is the steady trickle of individual student refugees from widely dispersed areas of tension and conflict – Kurds, Eritreans, Ethiopians, Namibians, Brazilians, Argentinians, to name but a few – who may be in most desperate need of assistance. And to date, the burden of assisting and supporting these students has fallen almost entirely to voluntary effort.

The scholarship aid organisations are distinguished from the other voluntary aid organisations in several major respects. With the exception of World University Service, they are not constituency-based organisations, which means that they are relatively free of the constraints which public fund-raising on a broad middle-of-the-road basis may impose on them. They have accordingly been able to follow up some of the more controversial implications of overseas development work to a greater extent than the other aid organisations (some of which in fact fund their work).

United Kingdom

This work is defined by a specific area of concern, the provision of scholarship funds to individuals and educational communities which would otherwise be deprived of them for political or economic reasons. Working closely with individual students, refugees and local distributors has led to a far greater degree of identification with their aims and objectives than the major fund-raising organisations could permit themselves. The degree of identification varies from one organisation to another; but whether they adopt a 'political' or a 'humanitarian' approach to their allocation and distribution policies, each organisation is concerned that its money will be spent in the most effective way possible.

To this end, they have been assisted by the Scandinavian, Dutch and Canadian development agencies, and the British Ministry of Overseas Development (ODM), for which they act as channels in sensitive areas, particularly Southern Africa. The governmental aid agencies prefer to channel their money through voluntary agencies, since these have greater flexibility of approach and relative anonymity, and since it means that they — the agencies — are not committed to overt political choice in uncertain circumstances. This is particularly relevant in areas of civil conflict, where relief and development aid are often most urgently required.

This role requires a large degree of freedom of action on the part of the scholarship distribution agencies. They must also realise that, prior to the independence of the communities they assist being achieved, their work is necessarily of a provisional nature. They may continue to supply informal aid for a time following independence, until direct governmental aid is established, and adequate provision for educational opportunities provided by the new government.

The organisations' specific concern with the problems of overseas students has also contributed to the radical political context in which the scholarship aid agencies view their work. While their allocation priorities go first to students at risk in their own country or as refugees, they are equally concerned to provide educational opportunities for those who are deprived of them for racial, social or economic reasons — the most important example of this being the payment of school and university fees for black students in Southern Africa.

A significant proportion of their work is devoted to the placement of and assistance to students in European countries, either because they are refugees, or because the educational facilities are lacking elsewhere. By reason of these activities, they are closely involved with the problems of students in the host countries, and particularly with those who are *de facto* refugees. Where this has not interfered with their charitable status, they have joined with other refugee organisations in pressing for greater governmental recognition of these problems, for increased refugee quotas from areas of high risk, and for improved reception procedures. Wherever possible, however, they seek to localise refugee aid allocation, assisting African refugees in Africa, Latin Americans in Latin countries, and so on.

The scope of the actions undertaken by the scholarship aid organisations thus covers the whole range of development problems from local deprivation, emigration, political harassment and detention, asylum, and refugee resettlement. Because education and political awareness are so closely linked in the rapidly-evolving societies where their efforts are concentrated, the scholarship aid organisations are exceptionally well qualified to contribute to the debate on the definition of human rights questions within the overseas aid programmes, and the strategies and institutions evolved to cope with them.

Africa Educational Trust
38 King Street
London WC2E 8JT
Tel: (01) 836 5075
Director: Mrs. P. Herbert

The Africa Educational Trust was founded in 1958 as a charitable trust concerned with educational and publicity work on Southern Africa. The founder-members, who are still closely involved in the trust's work, reflect the specialist academic and publishing interests behind its inception.

The active interest shown in the Trust's work early on in its career by the Swedish International Development Agency (SIDA) led to an enlargement of its activities to provide scholarship assistance to African students in Britain and overseas. (Sweden prefers to channel its aid direct to Africa, and only sends money to Britain to assist refugee students.)

The great advantage of a small agency like Africa Educational Trust, from the aid agencies' viewpoint, lies in its flexibility and easy adaptability to new circumstances, and its relative anonymity as a pool for channelling scholarship funds. (Inevitably, the extent of the sources and allocation of funds must remain confidential, to ensure their safety and continuity). From the Africa Educational Trust's point of view, there is almost total freedom of action in adopting its own allocation priorities; there are 'almost no strings' attached to the aid monies. As with the other scholarship aid organisations, this working relationship implies a mutual trust concerning the aims and intentions of both donors and distributors, and confidence that both are acting in the best interests of the recipients.

Africa Educational Trust is tough on the allocation of funds it receives and makes sure that they are well spent. This also makes it attractive to the donor agencies. Its priorities are directed towards those students, particularly refugees, who appear most capable of contributing directly to their people's self-reliance rather than on academic criteria alone. To this extent, the scholarship aid allocation priorities are defined by the inescapable political realities of events in Southern Africa. To be most effective, the aid is invested where there is felt to be the greatest potential. It is therefore easily understandable that the educational charities, with their accent on the immediate future, should be more keenly aware of the political options which confront them.

Africa Educational Trust handles about 100 full-time individual scholarships, from secondary school to post-graduate courses, assisting with both fees and maintenance. It is not involved with community projects overseas. In addition, it operates a student counselling service, but only gives advice where it feels capable of backing this up with funds. Co-operation with other human rights organisations tends to be limited by consideration for the security of its scholarship recipients overseas. Publicity actions are also shunned, for similar reasons.

Finance

The Trust does not rely solely on governmental aid, though this constitutes the major part of its budget. Over the years, it has established close co-operation with a handful of charitable trusts devoted to educational aims, and again permitting a highly flexible allocation policy on the part of the Trust. It has found long-term working relationships with the private charitable trusts the only way of obtaining a stable commitment of private funds; few can nowadays respond quickly to emergency demands. The Trust also receives an annual block grant from Christian Aid for student welfare — a scheme much preferred since it attaches no strings.

While funds from private trusts have been in danger of running dry in recent years, those which emanate from the governmental agencies have in contrast been increasing. This reflects the acceleration of the course of events in Southern Africa; with the prospect of black majority rule now no longer on the distant horizon, there is an evident interest in stepping up educational aid in preparation for independence. Direct international aid to black governments may then be taken up without resorting to such expedients as the voluntary educational aid channels, although they may still be required to fulfil an interim bridging role, as for example the British funds for Mozambican students which Africa Educational Trust administers.

International University Exchange Fund
International Development Centre
Parnell House
25 Wilton Road
London SW1V 1JS
Tel: (01) 828 2966/7
Cable: Unifund London
UK Director: Dr Christopher Beer
International Director: Lars-Gunnar Eriksson
P O Box 348
CH-1211 Geneva 11

A non-governmental organisation with an international structure, the International University Exchange Fund (IUEF) operates within a similar framework to African Educational Trust, but on a much larger scale. While this has distinct advantages in, for example, being able to provide support to educational institutions as well as to individual students, the anonymity and flexibility of the smaller-scale organisation tend to be forfeited.

IUEF has 'gone public' about the nature and implications of its work in sensitive political areas — its latest Annual Report is for the first time directed to an external readership — and is quite open about the options it has chosen to take. Both its aims as an educational aid agency and its aid strategy of channeling that aid to areas where it will be most effective lead the IUEF to oppose the white minority regimes in Africa which deny full educational opportunity to the African populations. Allocation policy amongst the African independence movements is, however, neutral, as long as these support the overriding principle of majority rule.

A second area of major concern for the IUEF is now Latin America, where the alarming dimensions of the refugee problem led to the setting up of a scholarship programme in 1975.

Structure
IUEF's head office in Geneva, with a staff of 17, coordinates action, channels funds and handles information. The London office has a considerable degree of autonomy in running its own scholarship programme which, because of traditional British links with Southern and East Africa, has concentrated in the past largely on those areas. Field offices in Costa Rica and Lusaka cope with local applications, maintain contacts throughout the South American and African continents, and initiate their own field research into local educational needs. Owing to a shortage of additional resources, no comparable programmes are envisaged for Asia or the Middle East.

Africa Programme

IUEF's policy is to provide education wherever possible within the student's own continent or region, in keeping with its developmental priorities. Where specialised education is not available elsewhere, or where – as in Britain – the bulk of scholarship applications are made on the spot by *de facto* refugees, funds are made available in Europe. IUEF occasionally feels restricted by government donors who insist that their development aid funds should be used for studies undertaken outside Europe.

IUEF's African programme includes direct funding to the educational programmes of the liberation movements in Southern Africa; these are often in effective control of large areas of territory which official distribution channels could not reach. In the case of Angola and Mozambique, this assistance has carried over into the post-independence period in anticipation of direct external government assistance programmes being set up.

To work effectively, IUEF retains close contact and cooperation with the liberation movements through their representatives in Europe and Africa, and will accept their recommendations when allocating scholarship funds: working in line with the aims and priorities of liberation organisations in direct touch with the local population gives, in IUEF's view, a more meaningful allocation of scarce resources than a blanket response to the country's educational needs could supply. Social aid to liberation movements is a controversial issue, but it is often the only means of reaching areas and people whom the governing authorities cannot, or do not, assist.

Where the Southern African regimes are concerned, IUEF is involved with redressing patterns of racial disadvantage which result from white minority rule. In South Africa, for instance, some 95% of African children do not complete their primary education. IUEF's provision of school and university places is designed specifically to counteract the disadvantages which deny them educational opportunity. IUEF encourages students from minority regimes to take up scholarships in neighbouring independent countries, and this work is complemented by the British scholarship programme, largely inspired by the needs of *de facto* refugees in Britain who could not follow their courses of study elsewhere.

IUEF's actions may also take the form of discreet assistance to students within a country, and this may prove the sole means of support for a student who is denied other sources of income for political reasons (including political detention). Naturally, this work is not viewed favourably by either the South African or the Rhodesian regimes, even though it is of a purely humanitarian nature, and it must necessarily be carried out under a degree of secrecy.

But while attention has inevitably focused on Southern Africa, IUEF has increasingly occupied itself with the wider refugee problem in Africa, which counts over a million refugees. Many of these have fled famine and civil conflict rather than specific forms of persecution. IUEF's approach is clear:

Priority is given to candidates who have had to flee the racist states because of their political action in favour of freedom.

But in addition, a significant number of refugees now come from the independent African countries: refugees from Equatorial Guinea, Ethiopia and Eritrea, the Sudan, Uganda and Burundi have all caused special concern in recent years. Students from independent African countries now constitute roughly one-third of the total of 1,456 African refugee students assisted in their studies during 1975/6.

Only a small proportion of these are studying in Western Europe, where scholarships are usually awarded only to applicants having already secured a university or college place in the country of refuge. The majority of these are Southern Africans. Of a total of 195 students aided in starting or completing their studies in the United Kingdom during 1976/7, all but eleven were from Southern Africa (more than twice that number having applied). Priority in allocating scholarships is accorded to those accepted for courses of a vocational nature, in keeping with developmental priorities of the donor agencies and the liberation movements. Where necessary, IEUF cooperates with the other refugee organisations (see Refugee Section) in steering the incoming student through immigration procedures; a student counsellor is also available to give advice on accommodation and other problems which might arise during the student's stay.

Latin America Programme

This had its beginnings in 1974, following the military coup in Chile, when a scholarship programme for refugees arriving in Europe from that country was launched with a grant from SIDA, the Swedish International Development Authority. In late 1975, a larger programme in Latin America itself was started, also with a first grant from SIDA, and a field office was established, situated first in Buenos Aires and now in Costa Rica.

The unprecedented numbers of political refugees in Latin America, especially those from the 'Southern Cone' countries, confronts the IUEF not only with an immense problem of organisation, but also with a highly delicate political situation because of the hostility shown by many governments in the continent towards political refugees, whom they brand as 'fugitive subversives' of the revolutionary left.

IUEF scholarship policy in Latin American is aimed at guaranteeing minimum conditions of physical and economic security for refugees in countries where they may pursue their studies or training in peace. Priority is given to placement in Latin America, but the programme in Europe continues to be operated as an extension of the IUEF's work in the former continent.

As with the African programme, scholarship assistance in Latin America

United Kingdom

is treated as more than a purely academic concern. The allocation of awards, which emphasises completion of studies, revalidation of qualifications and vocational training, is geared to accord with the refugees' perception of their temporary exile and their future reinsertion in the life of their own countries. In a few instances, Latin American refugees with relevant skills have been seconded to development aid schemes in newly-independent African countries. Together with a number of other agencies and representative refugee groups, IUEF is currently exploring ways of expanding development volunteer programmes for refugees, particularly those who have completed their studies on scholarships provided by the agencies.

The corollary to this action is that IUEF has become more closely involved with the publicising of refugee problems in Latin America, and in the coordination of refugee activities and lobbying procedures with regard to Western Europe. Particular emphasis has been placed on recognition of the needs of *de facto* refugees, and coordination of reception procedures on a European scale, with increasing exchange of information. One step towards this was the commission of a handbook on *Ayslum in Europe*, published jointly by IUEF and the World Student Christian Federation in October 1975.[1]

Finance

The bulk of IUEF funds — roughly four-fifths — come from European and Canadian governmental aid agencies. Their donations during 1975/6 amounted to Sw. francs 5.7 million (£1,322,051), as against Sw. francs 1.7 million (£393,717) from non-government sources.[2] While most of the overseas aid money is channeled directly through Geneva, a substantial proportion is handled by the London office, which also receives monies from voluntary and governmental agencies in this country, notably the Ministry of Overseas Development, Oxfam and War on Want, and from charitable trusts, such as Rowntree. Its overall expenditure (Geneva and London) on grants is in the order of Sw. francs 6.89 million (£1,595,744 — 1975/6 figures).

This represents a substantial increase on funds received in previous years, an indication of international concern with the accelerated pace of events in Southern Africa, and the crisis proportions which the Latin American refugee exodus has reached. Funds have also been received from new non-governmental donors outside the traditional constituency, thereby widening IUEF's support base and consequent freedom of action. As with Africa Educational Trust, the government aid agencies prefer to channel their funds through independent non-governmental organisations when direct educational subsidies would be interpreted as a gesture of

---

[1] Second revised edition due to appear in 1978.
[2] For a rough breakdown of these figures, see IUEF, *Annual Report*, 1975/6.

political support; the corollary to this is that the intermediate aid agencies like IUEF must be allowed their own discretion in apportioning funds. Because of this rule of thumb, IUEF has noted with some concern a recent trend amongst donors to impose conditions on the uses to which this money is put.

Other Scholarship Schemes for Exiled South Africans

The use of other scholarship schemes to help individuals at risk is inhibited by the fact that many of these schemes depend for their effectiveness on the goodwill of governmental or semi-official sponsors in the student's country of origin. They cannot, as a general rule, take the risk of supporting individuals who are *personae non gratae* in their own countries. In addition, the majority of such schemes contain a clause committing the student to return home on completion of his or her studies.

However, some explicit exceptions have been made for exiled Southern Africans wishing to study in the UK or elsewhere.

The **Special Commonwealth Programme for Zimbabweans**, launched in 1966, gives special assistance in the form of study-places, scholarships and employment to suitably qualified Zimbabwean refugees and exiles of at least 'O' level standard. The Programme is coordinated by the Commonwealth Secretariat in London and has so far enabled some 2,800 Zimbabweans to obtain work or study opportunities in 25 Commonwealth developing countries.

The **Commonwealth Zimbabwe Scholarship Trust Fund**, also administered through the Commonwealth Secretariat, was established in 1972 and has provided scholarships for 230 Zimbabwean refugee students in 15 Commonwealth developing countries. Preference is given to applicants who have not previously obtained a technical, vocational or professional qualification and whose proposed area of study corresponds to the anticipated manpower requirements of an independent Zimbabwe. Correspondence courses are also provided for about 100 students within Rhodesia.

The **Commonwealth Fund for Technical Cooperation** (CFTC), under its Education and Training Programme, supports a number of students who are nominated by their governments. It makes an exception for Namibians, who can apply to the CFTC direct. Seventy-six Namibians are currently studying under CFTC scholarships in five Commonwealth developing countries. Arrangements for them are the same as for the Zimbabweans (above), except that there is no minimum required education standard. CFTC's Education and Training Programme also helps to find places for

Namibians at education institutions (the Zimbabweans must as a rule find their own).

The **Commonwealth Scholarship Plan** and the **Commonwealth Educational Fellowship Scheme**, administered through the British Council and the Commonwealth Scholarship Commission, have provided assistance in Rhodesian African students at secondary and post-graduate level in technical, teacher-training and other development-related subjects, the Ministry of Overseas Development acting as their sponsor in lieu of the government. Here the ODM works on the recommendation of voluntary scholarship aid organisations and representatives of the various political movements in London. The majority of students apply from outside the UK; return passages are paid and, through the British Council, some welfare and counselling services are available to students during training. During 1976-7, 1,380 Rhodesian African students were helped in this way, over 1,000 of them at institutions in the United Kingdom (1977-8 figures are somewhat higher, totalling 1,669). It is impossible to tell how many of these may be considered *de facto* refugees.

The **UN Educational and Training Programme for Southern Africans** (UNEPTSA) was set up in 1961 with the express aim of aiding young people living under Southern African minority regimes or as refugees to further their education in the UK or elsewhere. Applicants need not, therefore, apply from their country of origin; they have to show that they have been accepted by a college or university for a course of study.

UNESCO publish a guidebook, *Study Abroad*, which lists a number of scholarships and fellowships for study overseas; available at major reference libraries, or from HMSO.

Oxford Refugee Scholarships (Oxford JCR Scholarships)

A number of colleges and universities maintain their own refugee scholarships and have done so for many years. The Oxford JCR Scholarships Scheme provides a good working example of how local-level initiatives by undergraduate students in conjunction with the college authorities can go a long way to meeting the needs of a wide variety of refugee students from different backgrounds.

The Oxford scheme started some 28 years ago when a committee was set up to persuade Oxford colleges to award scholarship places to student refugees from Southern Africa. After a number of similar initiatives had been launched, the need for more careful coordination of scholarship schemes resulted in the creation of a permanent committee in 1973. Representatives of the 15 or so colleges concerned now meet on a regular basis to exchange notes about their funding programmes, their cooperation with the college authorities, and the progress of their respective refugee scholars.

Some 15 refugee scholars are funded at the Oxford colleges in any one year, and their awards are geared to the level of British undergraduate and postgraduate grants. Funds are raised by a levy on the college dues payable by each student. Since these are in the order of from £1.50 to £3 per head (with the option of opting out), there are occasional fallow years when funds are accumulated in order to pay for the next three-year scholarship. In addition to this voluntary levy, college representatives organise fund-raising events (concerts, discos, sponsored walks) and work to persuade their college authorities to contribute to the scheme in the form of waived fees or other similar concessions. Although contributions may vary considerably, college and academic staff have responded well to these requests. Furthermore, there is an established precedent for the University to waive 60% of fees for all refugee students on a systematic basis.

The scheme is advertised through the offices overseas of voluntary scholarship agencies (Africa Educational Trust, International University Exchange Fund, UK Council for Overseas Student Affairs, World University Service), the British Council and the UN High Commission for Refugees. Local contacts in areas which are refugee centres – for example, the refugee community in Botswana, educational trusts and related institutions elsewhere in Africa, Asia and Latin America – may also distribute application forms to likely candidates. Not all, it should be noted, would necessarily qualify as refugees under international Conventions; one major advantage of the scheme lies in its receptiveness to borderline cases – the refugee who does not qualify for further education in his country of asylum, the student disbarred from further study without being driven from his country, the voluntary exile from situations of intolerable tension and danger. Some of these candidates may themselves contact the colleges quite independently of the advertised network, and these too are eligible for the scheme.

Application forms are sent out in early summer and returned (local censorship and postal services permitting) to World University Service or the separate colleges by December of the year preceding the award. Selection procedures are completed by the following June. Candidates must qualify on academic merit and not simply on the basis of need. While this approach may point to a potential conflict between the criteria involved – academic merit and human need – it is clear that the ability to relate academically as well as socially to fellow-students is an important ingredient in the successful integration of refugee scholars into university life. Furthermore, the fact that a proportion of candidates fail to qualify for this particular scheme points to the need for more generous alternative provision for refugee students in other sectors of the educational community.

31

United Kingdom

From the point of view of the refugee student, the Oxford scholarship scheme has two major advantages, and both derive from its flexibility. First, whereas government-funded scholarship schemes accord a set priority to 'development-related' subjects, which are usually defined in terms of technical or practical training, the Oxford scheme applies to Arts subjects as well, which some might argue were also valid for the tasks of exploring and defining national cultural identity and training future teachers.

The second important advantage lies in the fact that little or no formal distinction is drawn between refugee applicants and other candidates from the Third World — indeed, the scholarships are frequently referred to simply as 'Third World Scholarships'. This open-ended approach is entirely appropriate when large numbers of potential students are 'de facto' or 'disguised' refugees, that is to say, refugees unwilling or unable to declare themselves as such, for fear of jeopardising the safety of family and friends overseas, or their own chances of eventually returning home.

World University Service (UK)
20/21 Compton Terrace
London N1 2VN
Tel: (01) 226 6747
Cable: Interstud London
General Secretary: Alan D.J. Phillips
International Headquarters:
5 chemin des Iris
Cointrin
CH-1216 Geneva

World University Service (WUS) has fifty years' experience of funding overseas students who are prevented for political reasons from following their chosen course of study. As 'an educational charity [which] regards itself as a development agency', it is well placed to tackle human rights questions — in particular, refugee work and scholarship aid — in the context of overseas social, economic and political development problems.

Structure

WUS is an international voluntary aid agency based in Geneva but operating through its international committees in some 36 countries. The Swiss international secretariat with a staff of six or seven is responsible for the coordination of programmes, exchange of information, the development

32

of new national committees, and assessment of overseas projects. But most of the initiative is devolved to the largely autonomous national committees, most of them financially self-sufficient. The United Kingdom branch (WUS/UK) with a staff of 25, works within broad policy outlines laid down by the two-yearly International Council; it sets out its own programme, working in conjunction with those overseas WUS branches which are directly concerned with local projects.

WUS/UK is a constituency organisation, unlike the other scholarship aid organisations in this country. Its 60 or so local groups are all campus based, and set up for the most part by students. Academic staff members provide a degree of continuity and an important element of expertise in the form of advice, contacts and influence on administrative decisions (including the waiving of fees for refugee students). This campus constituency provides WUS with a permanent base, and an outlet for its public education work on overseas development aid; this is particularly useful in that it can harness student enthusiasm, identifying with students overseas and contributing directly to the needs of refugees. Unlike the other constituency-based development aid organisations, WUS is not held back by the inherent conservatism of its constituency; if anything, increased student participation has served to radicalise its approach in recent years on development and human rights questions.

The response elicited by the Chile crisis following the military coup of September 1973 has served to extend this sense of commitment to areas outside the English-speaking world. WUS, especially, helped promote the Academics for Chile campaign whose long-term significance for refugee work is outlined below. This was one of the largest scholarship aid programmes ever initiated in this country. WUS groups throughout the country obtained the guarantee of places for refugee students and the provision of scholarships or waiving of fees. WUS lobbied the government for the provision of vocational training schemes and English-language courses to facilitate adaptation to academic life in this country; it has provided over 500 awards to incoming students and advised them on courses of study and practical problems.

WUS is concerned that adequate facilities for the reception and resettlement of all refugees should be provided by the government in a planned way. In WUS's view, these facilities should include reception at a Reception Centre when the refugees first arrive, English language tuition for all members of families, provision of job retraining and further education. WUS also feels that a structure based on regional refugee committees is necessary, and is proposing that local authorities give responsibility for refugees to one of their officers. Above all, WUS hopes to see a coherent long-term strategy adopted so that emergency situations are met with more than *ad hoc* arrangements.

In its reception and resettlement work, WUS has been active in promoting consideration of the long-term prospects for the Latin American refugees. This new generation of youthful, articulate and politically active refugees has prompted a reconsideration of their role by the refugee agencies; they refuse to accept the idea of permanent exile and view their activities in terms of an eventual return to their own country. In keeping with this perception of their aims, and its own concern with overseas development, WUS is currently examining ways in which post-scholarship refugees can involve themselves in self-help community projects and research schemes in Latin American countries and elsewhere in the developing world.

Refugees

Working closely with refugee students has meant that WUS has responded quickly to new developments in refugee work, in particular to the more active role to be accorded to refugees in relation both to the host community and to the prospect of their eventual return. WUS has pressed for recognition of the rights and needs of the *de facto* refugees, and their continual political activity while in exile. As a development agency, WUS views the refugee problem within the wider context of the political struggles which produce it, and the future options for the country of origin of the refugees. Youthful refugees are no longer seen as a charge on the host community, so much as a valuable resource capable of contributing to that community, and eventually to their own.

The help and understanding which WUS has been able to provide have proved an important factor in the growth of WUS as an international human rights agency, as news of its effectiveness in turn increases the expectations of overseas students and refugees who hear about it.

The Czechoslovak Student Scholarships, which came to an end during 1975-6, provide an example of the 'traditional' response to a particular crises, when funds are raised by appeal to assist incoming refugees. Subsequent crises concerning refugees from Third World countries have demonstrated the need for a more active involvement in local 'rescue' activities, as students directly threatened with imprisonment or house arrest for political reasons were helped into exile.

In 1973, 129 black Rhodesian students were put on trial following campus demonstrations; 109 were imprisoned and subsequently banned from the capital and the campus. WUS provided legal aid and pressed the British government to admit some of the students on scholarships; it secured places for them, and paid their airfares to London. This programme was largely successful and set the pattern for international action by WUS in aid of students at risk.

Overseas Scholarship Aid

While best known in this country for its refugee work, WUS/UK in common with the other scholarship aid organisations adheres to the principle of localising development aid wherever possible. Its international projects include a community literacy project in Nepal, craft cooperatives in Bangladesh (with an outlet through WUS shops and stalls throughout Britain) and local scholarship schemes for West Bank Palestine. WUS's refugee programmes are seen as part of this overall development work — hence their appeal to the Ministry of Overseas Development for funds and the increasing emphasis on vocational as well as academic training.

The most important overseas programme has been the financing since 1973 of some 495 black students to attend courses at the University of Rhodesia which would otherwise be beyond their reach. Most of the funds for this scheme now come from the British Ministry of Overseas Development (ODM) and from the Swedish, Danish and Canadian development agencies; six or seven of the 495 current awards, however, are still paid for entirely out of funds from student unions in Britain. WUS has thus aimed at helping to redress the racial imbalance in higher education by enabling qualified black Rhodesian students to obtain a university education in their own country. All black students who prove academically acceptable to the University of Rhodesia can now be assured of scholarships, and these make up a majority of students at the University. In addition, a majority of black African sixth-formers in Rhodesia now benefit from international WUS grants. WUS is anxious to provide financial assistance to black Rhodesians at all educational levels, and hopes to continue this crucial form of development aid after transition to majority rule.

Human Rights Work

One important aspect of this work has been the direct intervention of WUS on human rights issues. WUS/UK considers the protection of human rights as one of its objectives not only on straightforward humanitarian grounds but also in the longer-term perspective of development work. If a whole generation of the skilled and educated members of a developing society is exiled or eliminated (as has happened in Chile, Uruguay, Uganda) or if they are denied the possibility of specialised training (Southern Africa), the implications for both the development and future independence of the country in question are grave and far-reaching. Human rights considerations are therefore held to be inseparable from WUS's education programmes overseas and from its refugee work. In the context of its long-term development philosophy, WUS's scholarship programme is also a means of direct intervention on human rights issues.

The offer of scholarships has been used consistently to obtain the release of political prisoners in Chile and latterly Argentina, where many had initially sought refuge. Clauses in the emergency laws of those countries allow certain categories of prisoner the option of exile; as of September 1976, none of the 54 detainees awarded WUS scholarships had been refused an exit visa, though serious delays in the screening procedures employed by the British government jeopardised the position of award-holders. WUS has been active in pressing for accelerated admission procedures, as well as persuading colleges and universities to accept temporarily absent incoming students.[1]

Where WUS officers and community development project workers are themselves at risk from repressive governments, WUS will make representations on their behalf by cable, letter or formal delegation. Its college constituency is also encouraged to participate in Amnesty 'Urgent Actions' on behalf of students and academics who have been kidnapped or tortured.

Finance

Over the past six years, WUS/UK has undergone a radical change in its financial structure. Its annual income has leapt from £40,000 in 1973 to over £1 million in 1976, by reason of British and foreign government aid channelled through WUS for specific aid projects. Projects are submitted to government agencies and departments, which are glad to make use of the specialised international voluntary agencies to channel their funds overseas; in this, the Scandinavian donors have proved somewhat more flexible than the British ODM, which has to take into account stricter ministerial budgetary requirements. The government agencies involved approve the projects put to them, or not as the case may be. The administration and development of the programmes are the responsibility of WUS, and this is jealously guarded.

In order to offset this top-heavy financial structure, WUS/UK has sought to strengthen its local campus constituency in this country. This has grown rapidly over the past few years, but the growth has not resulted in a proportionate increase in financial support to the centre. The campus groups are important in raising money locally to provide scholarships. Local groups have raised an estimated £200,000 in the past three years in the form of scholarships, waived fees, and other concessions to foreign students which do not figure on WUS/UK's national accounts. A campaign launched at the start of the 1976/7 academic year asked every student enrolling at British colleges and universities to make an individual contribution to the WUS budget; this scheme, which has expanded far beyond the restricted scope initially envisaged, hopes to double the number of scholarships available from university sources.

At the beginning of the 1977/8 academic year, WUS initiated together with the National Union of Students a Latin American campaign which aimed specifically at raising money towards a Latin American Scholarship Fund for sponsoring individual refugee students.

Income from other sources is derived from student union subscriptions, individual WUS supporters, private trusts and income from investments. 92% of WUS/UK's £1.27 million budget goes on 'international' schemes,

---

[1] *See also* **Academics for Chile** in the section on Chile.

mostly in the provision of assistance and scholarships to refugees in this country. Roughly £¾ million goes overseas. Administrative and placement costs are kept low, amounting to only around 7.5% of the total annual budget. However welcome the addition of government funds, WUS/UK is concerned that it may become over-dependent on central funding and administratively over-centralised. This has added particular significance to the strengthening of the campus constituency base.

Chapter 3

VOLUNTARY OVERSEAS AID ORGANISATIONS

In recent years, the international voluntary aid organisations have involved themselves more directly with human rights issues. This closer involvement has often been the result of human rights cases which implicate their own field-staff, or staff-members of organisations which they have sponsored; it also reflects the wider view of their work over the past few years, the greater attention given both to the political causes of development problems and the social consequences of their own aid programme. This in turn has resulted in new efforts to educate the public at home on the nature and implications of voluntary overseas aid.

The aid organisations, with their roots in relief activities, have traditionally responded to the immediate needs of local communities. In the past, these needs have tended to be articulated by local churches, social workers and aid workers speaking on behalf of the poor; but over the past five years or so, there has been a marked shift away from traditional charitable concerns towards direct support for the deprived and underprivileged themselves — through local community-based projects, peasant movements, minority organisations and so on. This move has corresponded to a desire on the part of the aid organisations to attack the roots of poverty and suffering; it is no longer felt to be enough simply to relieve the symptoms, particularly if by so doing aid schemes foster or perpetuate other forms of dependence.

The priority now accorded to local self-help schemes has demanded a much higher degree of identification by the agencies with the aims and objectives of their local recipients. In many instances, particularly in Latin America, this has entailed a recognition of the political nature of the option, since the groups they choose to assist may well be at risk from repressive governments; in many countries, encouraging the poor to organise and improve their lot is considered politically subversive by those who see their power threatened from below. Development aid workers have become visible targets and risk being branded as foreign agents bent on subverting the structures of society.

Human rights work has thus come to be recognised as an integral part of the agencies' concern with economic and social development. They view the right freely to organise and to put forward individual or collective interests as inseparable from the right to health, home, food, work and family (in some cases, the prerequisite for securing such rights). They may be obliged to defend this view against governments which claim that human rights are a luxury only to be afforded when a sufficient degree of social and economic advancement has been attained. But aid agencies and human rights organisations together consider the one invalid without the other.

Aid organisations have, however, to adopt different working strategies from human rights organisations, since they are frequently obliged to work within, or alongside, existing government aid programmes, and must comply in some measure with the political norms these entail. Their increasing identification with local community projects has often rendered this situation anomalous, since they are concerned to rectify social and economic injustices which may derive from, or be perpetuated by, the governing structure of the country in question. In contrast to the human rights organisations, they have had to strike a balance to ensure the continuation of their aid programmes. They must often adopt a *modus operandi* which precludes overt action on behalf of those deprived of their human rights if their political neutrality is not to be challenged by the government of the day.

This poses a clear dilemma for the aid agencies when members of the local field-staff with whom they are associated are arrested or harassed in the course of their development work: how far are they prepared to go in their defence without jeopardising their long-term aid programmes? The response to this dilemma will depend both on the political context, and on the organisation concerned. Some prefer to maintain their aid and relief priorities, while referring the 'human rights' question to organisations such as Amnesty International. Others are prepared to come to the defence of local representatives in more open defiance of the government which has chosen to view their development activities in political terms. Generally speaking, it is those organisations which are more attuned to the political implications of their work overseas which tend to adopt the second approach. But as the local community workers are increasingly at risk from oppressive governments, the greater frequency with which this dilemma presents itself is an additional spur to recognition by all such organisations of the political context in which they work.

The relationship between the aid organisations in the field and the human rights organisations (which may often rely on them for information on human rights violations) has been the subject of a number of meetings and seminars in recent years. These discussions could usefully be carried further. While the aid organisations are increasingly involved in 'human rights' cases, so the human rights organisations are more aware than ever before of the social and economic pressures which lead insecure or dependent governments to impose measures depriving their citizens of fundamental rights.

United Kingdom

Catholic Institute for International Relations
1 Cambridge Terrace
London NW1 4JL
Tel: (01) 487 4431
Chairman: Colin Edwards
General Secretary: Miss Mildred Nevile

CIIR acts both as a volunteer agency and as a centre for research and public education on major issues of world development and social justice throughout the world. Since its inception in 1941, it has been instrumental in setting up several autonomous non-denominational centres for action, such as the Africa Centre, Christian Concern for Southern Africa, and more recently the Latin American Bureau (in conjunction with Christian Aid and War on Want). It retains close links with the Catholic Commission for Justice and Peace, although unlike this organisation CIIR is not an established body of the Church hierarchy.

CIIR's work is divided between its Volunteer Programme, which sends some 73 volunteers overseas (the majority to Central America); and an Educational and Public Information Programme, which concentrates on Latin America and Southern Africa. The emphasis here is on public education within the UK. CIIR arranges speaking tours for visiting churchmen, human rights workers and experts with first-hand experience of repressive governments. It initiates meetings and seminars amongst journalists, businessmen, politicians and others with a direct interest in current areas of concern. Recent topics have covered political and economic change in Brazil, civil conflict in Angola, Northern Ireland and elsewhere, and the role of the churches in situations where human rights, including those of churchgoers, are systematically violated.

CIIR is concerned to sustain the level of public interest in such areas, and has prepared background *Comments* on a number of countries and topics. More recently, it has published detailed factual studies on *Racial Discrimination and Repression in Southern Rhodesia* (for the International Commission of Jurists) and on *Civil War in Rhodesia* (for the Rhodesian Justice and Peace Commission). It has reprinted Niall MacDermot's address on *The Churches and Human Rights*, which is an invaluable survey of recent church developments and the central role they occupy in human rights work.

Through its many informal contacts in the Third World, particularly South and Central America and Southern Africa, CIIR is well-informed about human rights violations in those areas, though evidently much of this information is confidential and cannot be used publicly without jeopardising CIIR's contacts.

CIIR operates closely with a large number of other committees and voluntary and ecumenical organisations. These include the Chile Committee for Human Rights, Christian Concern for Southern Africa, the Commission for International Justice and Peace, Pax Christi, War on Want, Oxfam (Latin America Committee), and the British Council of Churches (Angola, Mozambique and Guinea-Bissau Committee), on all of which it is represented. It also cooperates with organisations such as **Amnesty** and the **Contemporary Archive on Latin America** (CALA, 1 Cambridge Terrace, London, NW1 4JL, tel: 01 487 5277) at the level of exchange of information. It has published material for the International Commission of Jurists and other bodies.

Finance

Unlike the Commission for Justice and Peace, CIIR is not a body established by the Catholic hierarchy in this country, and while it receives assistance from the National Catholic Fund, it relies largely on subscriptions and donations to maintain the level of its work. Thanks to a special fund-raising appeal in the course of 1976, and an unexpected donation of £10,000, CIIR has been able to consolidate the new initiatives undertaken in recent years. CIIR's working income for 1974/5 (excluding the separate Volunteer Programme budget) was in the order of £30,000, more than doubling that of the previous year.

Christian Aid
240/250 Ferndale Road
P O Box 1
London SW9 8BH
Tel: (01) 733 5500
Cable: Worldaid London SW9 8BH
Telex: 916504 CHRAID
Director: Rev Dr Kenneth Slack

Christian Aid, which came into being out of the earlier 'Inter-Church Aid and Refugee Service', affords a clear illustration of the growing commitment of aid organisations to the human rights content of their work. Beginning as a relief agency under the aegis of the British Council of Churches, and extending its work into a worldwide development programme, it conceives its role in Christian terms as redressing human and social injustices through development aid. With a large public education programme in this country, it is very much aware of the wider political implications of the choices it makes in the allocation of its funds.

Human Rights Activities

Christian Aid's overseas development aid programme is administered in London by its Aid Department, including area projects officers for Latin America and the Caribbean, Francophone and English-speaking Africa, South and South-East Asia, the Middle East, Pacific Region and Europe. The human rights implications of their work and the inevitability of a political component in their aid allocation has been increasingly apparent in Latin America, by reason of the heavily politicised context of the rural development projects there and the stand taken by the local churches on human rights questions. These issues are more clearly defined in Latin America than elsewhere, with the possible exception of Southern Africa.

The Promuri case illustrates Christian Aid's commitment to human rights in Latin America. In 1976, several members of staff of the Urban, Rural and Indigenous Promotion (Promuri) of the Disciples of Christ 'Friendship Mission' in Paraguay were arrested by the Stroessner government for 'subversive activities'. The foreigners among them (one North American, one Chilean) were expelled, and the Paraguayans imprisoned. British, German, Dutch and North American voluntary aid organisations which had sponsored the Promuri programme made representations to the Paraguayan authorities, and in October 1976, acting together with the Councils of Churches in their respective countries, they sent a joint mission of enquiry to the country to seek the release of the Promuri staff. It should be stressed, though, that the form taken by this intervention was determined by the lack of institutional support for human rights coming from within Paraguay. Where possible, Christian Aid prefers to strengthen indigenous human rights organisations. Later in 1976, therefore, Christian Aid made a grant of £12,500 to the newly-founded Churches' Committee for Emergency Assistance in Paraguay, an ecumenical body created to provide legal defence for political prisoners and welfare for their families.

In South Africa, Christian Aid has had to come to terms with the dilemma of open commitment versus the safeguarding of existing programmes. The reserve of former years towards such involvement has now been abandoned, and money goes to black community organisations either directly or through the South African Council of Churches. Where such organisations are in danger of being classified as 'affected organisations' and banned from receiving funds from outside the country, Christian Aid's contribution has in fact been stepped up, in anticipation of any such move.[1]

In Asia, where both developmental and human rights problems exist on a massive scale, Christian Aid has had to exercise care that its human rights activities are not too closely identified with the Western churches. As elsewhere, the scope of their work is largely circumscribed by the position within the country of the National Councils of Churches and other church

---

[1]   The organisations concerned were banned on 19 October 1977.

groups. Thus, in South Korea, where the National Council of Churches has taken a courageous and outspoken stand against human rights violations, community aid projects, such as that outlined above, run the risk of incurring official sanctions. While in a vast country like India, where the Christian churches are a small minority, Christian Aid has had to be careful not to suggest programmes which might place that minority at risk.

Education

Christian Aid's Education Department is aware of the partial contradiction between its educational and fund-raising programmes, not a negligible consideration when some 55% of Christian Aid's annual budget is raised during one week in May. However, there has been no noticeable drop in the rate of Christian Aid's annual budgetary growth since it adopted its more uncompromising approach to the nature of its involvement overseas.

The London-based education staff of twelve are each specialised in approaching a different audience — the schools, universities, training colleges, churches, and so on. In addition, some 45 regional field-staff ensure coordination between local Christian Aid groups and other concerned organisations. The *ad hoc* nature of much of this involvement, especially that mobilised specifically for Christian Aid Week each year (which raises 55% of Christian Aid's annual budget) is an important factor in arousing great interest in the implications of allocation policies. Their work also reflects a concern to move away from the traditional impetus of charitable giving towards a better-informed, and perhaps more responsible, attitude towards overseas aid amongst their constituency. This shift again reflects altered allocation priorities.

Finance

Christian Aid's £4 million-plus budget (financial year ending 30 September 1976) is raised entirely from regular fund-raising, in particular Christian Aid Week in May, and from special emergency appeals. There has been no noticeable drop in the rate of Christian Aid's annual budget growth since it adopted its more uncompromising approach to the nature of its involvement overseas; the overall total has been increasing by roughly 6% a year, though this has not been sufficient to keep pace with inflation. Roughly 22% goes towards fund-raising and administration costs, and over half the total is devoted to development projects, as compared to relief work (18%) and education (4%). Grants to institutions for purposes other than development and relief work are made only from the contributions of those who support this wider range of commitments, which includes human rights activities.

Of the 1975-6 budget of £4,757,910, almost £3.5 million went towards development work. Some £311,629 was expended on refugee work, the bulk of it in Africa. Other projects specifically concerned with human rights include provision for African scholarships, grants to human rights organisations (such as the former Comite pro Paz in Chile), and consultations on human rights questions. Refugees are also assisted through the World Council of Churches, and through voluntary organisations such as the French CIMADE.

Methodist Church, Division of Social Responsibility
1 Central Buildings
Matthew Parker Street
London SW1H 9NH
Tel: (01) 930 2638
General Secretary: Rev John Atkinson
Secretaries: Rev John Hastings, Mr Garth Waite, Mr Brian Callin

---

The Methodist Church, through its Division of Social Responsibility, administers three funds designed to answer human need and remedy social injustice. The Methodist Relief Fund (MRF) deals with immediate calls for assistance, while the World Development Action Fund (WDAF) tries to tackle the underlying causes of injustice and oppression; in addition, a Fund for Human Need answers calls for assistance which may fall outside the usual Methodist or ecumenical channels. In its response to both long-term and short-term demands on these resources, the Methodist Division of Social Responsibility has devoted a considerable part of its programme to human rights activities.

The World Development Action Campaign aims in its programme for administering the Fund to 'attack the roots of poverty and oppression'. Freedom of conscience and freedom from oppression are considered essential human rights along with food, housing, employment, education and the environment as legitimate areas of concern for promoting 'development'. As well as supporting practical development projects overseas, the WDAF provides considerable assistance to organisations involved in public education work within this country. It earmarks just under 20% of its £83,000 annual grants (1975/6) to projects designated under the heading 'Human Rights and Liberation'. In addition to medical and educational aid to Namibia and Zimbabwe, assistance has been channelled through the Methodist churches and their related bodies in Korea, Chile and Indonesia, and to organisations combatting racism in South Africa and the United Kingdom.

Disaster and emergency relief is still the first priority of the Methodist Relief Fund. Founded at the end of the war as a relief agency for refugees, the MRF has since expanded its scope. It can mobilise funds at very short notice, and channels them either directly or through the joint Disaster

Emergency Committee comprising the major voluntary aid organisations. In addition, it funds a number of rural development projects, but is not specifically development-oriented, since this area is covered in the longer term by the WDAF. While the MRF works through Methodist or ecumenical organisations and individuals, the related Fund for Human Need is operated through alternative distribution channels in areas not covered by the MRF network.

Through its overseas church connections, the Methodist Division of Social Responsibility has become directly involved in a number of countries where human rights are threatened or suppresed by the government, in particular, Chile, South Korea and Indonesia. Funds channelled through national church organisations go towards defence costs and relief for prisoners of conscience, rehabilitation for those released, and assistance to those forced out of work for political reasons.

In addition to this financial aid, the Methodist Church frequently intervenes on specific human rights cases, joining in letter-writing campaigns to governments, deputations to embassies and general campaign activities. As well as the three countries mentioned above, the Division of Social Responsibility has been particularly involved with events in Southern Africa, and provides secretarial support for the recently-created Task Force for Cooperative Action on Southern Africa (see under 'Committees'). However unhesitating in committing its name to such actions, the Methodist Church has always to ensure that the safety and continued work of its representatives in the field are not jeopardised. To this end, it cooperates with human rights and church organisations in ensuring that adequate publicity is given where appropriate, including areas – such as Haiti – which receive little attention outside informed circles. The South Korean situation was initially one of low publicity coverage and high risk before the local churches spoke out on behalf of human rights; support from internationally-based churches can here provide a degree of protection for those who have chosen to take such risks.

The Methodists can draw on an impressive network of church contacts, as is demonstrated both by their funding and by the extent of their international contacts. They recognise the relative lack of public concern about human rights issues in this country, and are making use of the potential at their disposal for a more concerted effort to raise the level of public awareness about the interdependence of development programmes and human rights issues.

Finance

Income for the Funds derives from covenants, donations, church collections and occasional legacies; administrative costs are kept low and funded entirely from interest on the Funds, which enables the Methodist Church to assure donors that every penny of their money goes towards relief, development and other humanitarian work at home and abroad. Because it relies on the Methodist network of regular donors, widespread publicity is not felt necessary, even for the emergency appeals, since the response is readily forthcoming. The 1976 income for the Methodist Relief Fund, for instance, stood at £120,000 (with an additional £20,544 balance from the previous year).

Third World First
232 Cowley Road
Oxford OX4 1UH
Tel: (0865) 45678
Coordinator: Rev Dr Brian Wren

Third World First (3W1) began as a public education programme on overseas development issues aimed at students and young people. In advance of the growing awareness amongst aid workers of the political implications of aid policies, it has chosen to concentrate on the political issues behind world poverty, though its approach remains non-partisan.

In 1977-8, 3W1 is campaigning for human and democratic rights in the ASEAN (Association of South-East Asian Nations) countries, Zimbabwe, the Sahara and Uganda, and is publishing information and campaign material on these themes.

3W1 is aware of the close connection between human rights questions in the Third World with political opposition movements and the related political options inherent in Western aid policies. As part of its education work, it has chosen to publicise a wide range of crucial issues in conjunction with support groups, *ad hoc* committees and human rights organisations.

— It issues a regular *Campaigns Bulletin* to members throughout the country giving details of current actions and campaign work initiated by the groups and committees, and suggesting ways in which 3W1 members can participate. Material from the committees is circulated to members along with the *Bulletin*. 3W1 is also preparings an *Activists Handbook*, with advice on campaigning methods and techniques.

— 3W1 has set up a *Reactive Network* of individuals willing to intervene by telephone, letter or cable on specific issues and cases where there is a need for quick action. These may involve: internal cases, especially those of overseas students threatened with deportation (and who may be *de facto* refugees), or external cases, such as the release of political prisoners or torture victims. The Network may also initiate concerted lobbying on wider issues, such as arms deals and trade with repressive governments (individual cases are referred to 3W1 by organisations such as the Joint Council for the Welfare of Immigrants, National Union of Students, Anti-Apartheid and Amnesty International's Urgent Action Network).

— 3W1 publications include briefings on questions related to development issues, particularly as they affect the home population. One recent example is a short booklet on *Racism in Schools.*

— The Third World First Education Trust has in the past provided finance for a number of educational and public information projects in the United Kingdom, amongst them the Contemporary Archive on Latin America (CALA), the Chile Committee for Human Rights and the *New Internationalist* magazine.

Finance

The organisation is financed by the Third World First Educational Trust, a registered charity, by membership fees and local fund-raising, and through sales of publications, education kits and posters. Some 50 college and university groups throughout the United Kingdom are encouraged to campaign for human rights and development issues and raise funds for development work overseas and public education in Britain.

War on Want
467 Caledonian Road
London N7 9BE
Tel: (01) 609 0211
General Secretary: Mary Dines

War on Want is striving to create a greater awareness of the causes of under-development and to help Third World communities in their efforts to change the social economic and political factors that contribute to their own poverty and powerlessness. In Britain War on Want seeks to inform both the public and its decision-makers of the needs of the deprived world.

For War on Want (founded in 1951), the shift in emphasis towards direct aid to the organised poor was a deliberate move undertaken in 1974. This resulted directly from War on Want's own experience, when it became evident that the poor themselves were best able to define their own needs. War on Want recognised that the trust of the recipients is a determining factor in the success of local aid projects. It is sceptical of the benefits of aid programmes which disregard the social and political implications of

United Kingdom

re-allocating scarce local resources.

In its aid allocation policies, War on Want fully accepts the inevitability of such choices, and identifies itself with the groups it funds, whether or not it agrees entirely with their strategies towards developing their own self-reliance. 'Working with the poor and submitting our views and funds to their judgment does not mean we can absolve ourselves from responsibilities and the consequence of their actions.'

This work involves support in cases where the fundamental rights of the recipients are at stake. The determining factor is that the recipients are themselves prepared to take risks. War on Want feels that the effects of this kind of assistance are incalculable, and possibly of greater immediate importance in their morale-boosting effect than some of the long-term benefits of economic aid.

War on Want is reluctant to compromise its commitment to the redress of social injustice. The decision to support the community programmes of the liberation movements in Southern Africa, for instance, and the withdrawal (after much heart-searching) of support for relief and welfare work within the South African Bantustans has given rise to adverse reactions from a few former donors. On the other hand, it has reinforced the public education efforts of the organisation on this controversial issue. In comparison with the other British voluntary aid organisations, War on Want devotes a slightly larger proportion — roughly 7-8% — of its budget to information and publicity work.

Finance

The proportion of War on Want's £674,000 overseas aid budget[1] which is devoted to specific human rights cases by the local recipients is impossible to compute. As with the other aid organisations, such expenditures are not earmarked, and in keeping with the devolution of responsibility to local project organisers, there is no central accountability for such costs. Specific monies do go, however, to refugee projects, such as the Zambian farms for SWAPO refugees from Namibia.

---

[1] *See* 1976 Annual Report.

Chapter 4

CHURCHES AND RELIGIOUS ORGANISATIONS

It is often said that the Christian churches have been in the human rights business longer than any other institution. They occupy a unique position in being able to protect and defend the inviolability of the individual person, which is at the very core of their mission in the world. Since the war, however, two new elements in particular have brough about profound changes in church attitudes. The present in areas of acute civil conflict of missionaries, church-workers, and in some instances the church hierarchy has led to a closer identification of the church with the defence of individuals and communities deprived of social justice or political freedom. The ecumenical movement has, through contact, example and exchange of ideas, helped consolidate the resulting re-definition by the churches of their pastoral responsibilities, both centrally and more important, amongst local church bodies.

The turning-point may be seen as the joint statement issued by the WCC and the Pontifical Justice and Peace Commission on the 25th Anniversary of the Universal Declaration of Human Rights in 1973, which appealed

> to local churches, and particularly to Christian leaders and educators, to initiate or intensify programmes of instruction and sensitisation on human rights and corresponding duties so that every person, regardless of race, religion, class or nationality, may be aware of the equalities of human life to which he is entitled.

This statement recognised both the existing key function that churches can and do play in on-the-spot human rights work and also the need to complement this action by increasing public information (and the consequent pressure of informed international public opinion). As a further step in this direction, the WCC at its 5th Assembly at Nairobi in 1975 identified six specific areas which were to be regarded as priorities:

- the right to basic guarantees of life
- the rights to self-determination and to cultural identity and the rights of minorities
- the right to participate in decision-making within the community
- the right to dissent
- the right to personal dignity
- the right to religious freedom

Significantly, the right to basic guarantees of life – to work, food, health, housing and education – is the base from which the other rights emanate. This reflects the churches' conception of their own pastoral mission. The emphasis on the other rights listed marks the churches' increasing identification – often by force of circumstances under repressive regimes – with the demands and aspirations of the peoples amongst whom they work. Human rights violations are not therefore viewed as isolated aberrations, but as the symptoms of wider social and economic injustices and deprivations. This was stated explicitly at Nairobi.

Following the Nairobi recommendations, and in the light of the Helsinki Conference on European security, the WCC held a colloquium at Montreux in July 1976 on the implications of Helsinki for the churches' activities in East and West Europe. In attempting to define freedom of religion at Nairobi, the WCC Assembly had included in its understanding of this term 'the right and duty of religious institutions to criticise the authorities where necessary, on the basis of their religious convictions'. The Montreux colloquium urged WCC member-churches to set aside the necessary human and financial resources to implement the human rights recommendations of the 5th Assembly at Nairobi.

To a large extent, the churches in their secular work share the internal conflicts and ambiguities of the major development aid agencies, caught between a relatively comfortable home-base and the inherently radical position of many of their field-workers. Even more than the aid agencies, locally recruited church workers and those working for church-related bodies may find themselves at risk from repressive governments by reason of their work amongst the poor and the deprived. This has happened, for example, with the Urban Industrial Mission in the Far East, with the Christian Institute in South Africa, and with the Chilean Comite pro Paz working with the families of political prisoners. In each of these instances, local churches were working together in an ecumenical spirit; there has been little dissension within the churches at this level in understanding their role.

In other cases, the simple fact of worship may be treated by governments as an act of defiance or of unacceptable dissension. This may be because the churches provide a safe refuge and focus for unofficial opposition, as has happened in South Korea or formerly in Vietnam. Or, as may be the case with the Baptists and other Christian groups in the Soviet Union, because the churches represent an alternative set of values and, when they depart from a purely passive role, a potential rival source of authority or national identity.

By reason of their local-level presence and universal vocation, the churches are in a privileged position, in comparison with other non-governmental bodies, when it comes to assisting not only their own priests and congregations, but those at risk in the population at large. Church structures act as channels for relief and material assistance to victims of oppression, and also provide a primary source of information about human rights violations in many countries. As Niall MacDermot has put it in his invaluable outline in *The Churches and Human Rights*:[1]

> The Churches . . . make a unique and vital contribution to the promotion of human rights. They have access to reliable factual information about what is happening; their word is generally credible in these matters in a way that that of interested political organisations is not; they usually enjoy a certain immunity from repression at least in professedly Christian countries, and finally they have channels of communication to interested persons and organisations outside their countries who are ready to help them.

He goes on to outline the different ways in which the churches can contribute to the promotion of human rights work, both through their own congregations and in cooperation with non-religious organisations. The corollary to the churches' existing role in collecting and disseminating information about human rights violations[2] is the lead they can give in public education on human rights by restating the universal values underlying all such work, whether church-based or not. Their moral authority can be brought to bear on governments and government officials who may otherwise prove indifferent to public appeals for leniency in their treatment of political opponents; and in encouraging others already committed to humanitarian values to pursue their human rights work further. Lastly, while many churches already serve to channel relief aid and legal aid to victims of repression and their families, they are well placed to raise further funds for this cause through their church congregations and related church activities.

Jewish Organisations

Next to support for the continued existence of the state of Israel, the numerous Jewish organisations in this country have concerned themselves very closely with the situation of Jewish communities overseas. This very strong sense of solidarity is expressed both in large-scale relief aid and in public and private activities aimed at securing recognition for the rights of those communities at both national and international level.

Of particular concern to all the organisations has been the difficult circumstances of Jews in the Soviet Union, particularly those who have expressed a wish to emigrate to Israel. Many have been subjected to harassment, whether directed at their families or their work, and some have been imprisoned as a result. Without claiming any special privileges

---

[1]   CIIR/ICJ, 1976.

[2]   One source worth particular mention is IDOC-International (International Documentation on the Contemporary Church), Via S. Maria dell'Anima 30,00186 Rome. This Catholic-based organisation acts as a clearing-house for information on churches of all denominations throughout the Third World and Eastern Europe. Its monthly *Bulletin* is an invaluable source for human rights workers.

for Soviet Jews apart from those formally guaranteed to all religious and national minorities by the Soviet Constitution, representative Jewish bodies in this country and elsewhere have been particularly active campaigners for the full respect of those rights.

Elsewhere, they have provided support, both moral and financial, to Jewish communities at risk in situations of heightened civil tension. Longstanding concern for Jews in North Africa, the Middle East and Eastern Europe has now been extended to the vulnerable position of those living in Ethiopia and the Argentine.

More than most interested groups, the Jewish organisations are motivated by a powerful sense of solidarity, backed up by well-developed national and international support structures.

Aid to the Church in Need
3-5 North Street
Chichester
West Sussex PO19 1LB
Tel: (0243) 87325
Director (UK): Philip Vickers

Aid to the Church in Need (ACN) was founded in 1947 to provide relief for refugees and displaced persons in Europe after the war. It has since expanded its work to the support of Church activities throughout the world, with special emphasis on Christian activities in Communist countries. It does so on a large scale: subsidies in 1976 totalled over US $ 18 million. An emergency relief fund of over US $ 250,000 is also maintained. Aid to the Church in Need is approved by the Vatican and recognised by the Catholic Church hierarchy. It is the only international Catholic relief agency to be working directly in communist countries.

Aid to the Church in Need is planning an international information service, to be launched in 1978. This aims to provide information on: the situation of the Churches in Eastern Europe, the failing Churches in Western Europe, refugees, third world activities, Eurocommunism and the activities of Aid to the Church in Need worldwide.

ACN publishes a bi-monthly news bulletin, *The Mirror*, which is available free to benefactors, as well as a detailed Annual Report.

Finance

Income derives from donations, gifts in kind, legacies and bequests, church collections and sale of old material. The money is apportioned to three groups of recipients: 'refugees' (roughly 10%), 'the Persecuted Church'

(31%), and 'the Menaced Church'(18% to Africa, 7% to Asia, 29% to Latin America, 36% to Western Europe). This includes relief aid to families of political prisoners and subsistence and study-grants to priests and seminarists; the bulk of the funds are spent on religious materials, church repairs and new buildings, cars and lorries, clothing, medicines and food, as well as for religious books, publications and radio broadcasts.

Anglo-Jewish Association — Woburn House (5th floor), Upper Woburn Place London WC1H 0EP Tel: (01) 387 5937/8. *Secretary:* David M. Jacobs

The Anglo-Jewish Association (AJA) has made its primary concern interventions on behalf of Jews in difficulty because of their religion throughout the world. It is a member of the **Human Rights Network**, and one of three constituent organisations forming the Consultative Council of Jewish Organisations, which has a consultative status with the UN.

Baptist Union of Great Britain and Ireland — Church House, 4 Southampton Row, London WC1B 4AB Tel: (01) 405 2727

The Baptist Union has taken up a number of cases with the appropriate embassies in London, in conjunction with the British Council of Churches and Amnesty International. It has undertaken publicity and campaign work on human rights issues through the Baptist churches. Its special interest is in the plight of Baptist prisoners of conscience in the USSR.

Board of Deputies of British Jews — Woburn House, Upper Woburn Place, London WC1H 0EP Tel: (01) 387 3952. *President:* Lord Fisher of Camden

The Board of Deputies of British Jews is the representative body for the whole of Anglo-Jewry and as such maintains a high level of interest and information on the situation of Jewish communities in other parts of the world. Two committees in particular, the Committee on Foreign Affairs and the Committee on Jews in Arab Lands, maintain a watching brief on the problems of Jewish communities at risk; two recent areas of concern involve the rights of Jews in Argentina, and the position of the Falashi Jews in Ethiopa.

The Board of Deputies is a member of the **Human Rights Network**.

United Kingdom

British Council of Churches
2 Eaton Gate
London SW1W 9BL
Tel: (01) 730 9611
Associate Secretary (Division of International Affairs):
Rev Brian Duckworth

The British Council of Churches is an umbrella organisation for the churches in England, Scotland, Ireland and Wales, including, amongst others, the Lutherans and the Greek Orthodox Church. The Society of Friends and the Unitarians are Associate Members; the Roman Catholic Church is a Consultant Observer. The BCC functions as a central secretariat and clearing-house for member churches, liaising with other religious bodies, the World Council of Churches, and government departments; it raises matters of current concern amongst member churches and through its four Divisions: Community Affairs, Ecumenical Affairs, International Affairs and Christian Aid. The associated Conference of British Missionary Societies is to become a full Division of the BCC, as the Council for World Mission, in 1978.

The British Council of Churches is an autonomous body responsible for its own finances, which derive from its member churches. It is an Associated Council of the World Council of Churches (see below) and acts as a channel of communication for programme initiatives from Geneva concerning, for instance, human rights questions for discussion and action by its member churches, many of which are also, separately, members of the World Council. The BCC is currently considering ways in which the British churches can involve themselves in the work of the WCC's Advisory Group on Human Rights which will seek cooperation from its member churches and denominational bodies in investigating and, where appropriate, taking action on human rights cases and issues. This may mean, eventually, seeking further resources to focus attention on the human rights aspect of BCC's work. However, it should be stressed that this only represents a new emphasis: human rights work has always played an integral part in the churches' overseas relief and development mission. (*See* **Christian Aid**.)

The BCC is also a member of the Conference of European Churches, based in Geneva, which in 1977 in conjunction with its fellow Canadian and US Councils of Churches, established a Working Committee to supervise the programme of the Churches in the 'Helsinki Area' in relation to the proposals of the Conference on Security and Cooperation in Europe ('Helsinki Conference').

Catholic Institute for International Relations, *see* p. 40.

Central British Fund for Jewish Relief and Rehabilitation
Woburn House
Upper Woburn Place
London WC1H 0EP
Tel: (01) 387 3925
Joint Secretaries: Miss Joan Stiebel and Mr Sidney H. Somper

Founded in 1933, to assist German and Austrian victims of Nazi oppression, the Central British Fund has expanded its activities to many areas of relief to Jewish communities around the world. Through its case-work body, the Jewish Refugee Committee, it provides assistance to Jewish refugees arriving in this country.

The arrival of some 1,800 Jewish refugees from Hungary in 1956 and a comparable number of Egyptian Jews following the Suez crisis gave a new impetus to the Fund's work. It was decided that henceforth assistance should be extended to refugees and persecuted and underprivileged groups in other countries as well as the UK. For the past twenty years, an annual appeal has raised new funds to meet the demands of new areas of work. These now cover emigration and resettlement grants to émigrés, aid to the sick and elderly who have remained behind, rehabilitation programmes in countries of refuge, bridging loans and transit grants to refugees, as well as a few small-scale welfare programmes in Israel.

Of the £190,000 spent on relief and refugee work (1975-6 figures), some £73,000 went as a matter of priority to aiding Jews in Eastern Europe and Jewish emigrants from the Soviet Union. Similarly, funds were allocated directly to Jewish welfare organisations in Ethiopia (£2,000), India (£3,500), and Syria (£10,000) and to resettlement work for refugees in Morocco, Tunisia and France (£13,000). The CBF also works closely with the American Joint Distribution Committee Overseas and also with HIAS (the Hebrew Immigrant Aid Society).

See also: **Jewish Refugees Committee**, pp. 181-2.

Christian Concern for Southern Africa – 1 Cambridge Terrace, London NW1 4JL Tel: (01) 935 5260. *Chairman:* Trevor B. Jepson *Secretary:* Tim Sheehy

This group does research and supplies information on the economic relationships between Britain and Africa. It is financed by the British Churches who are advised on the issues involved, particularly with regard to their investments. It also seeks to educate the general public and bring pressure to bear on the government and the business community.

Church of England, Board of Social Responsibility
Church House
Dean's Yard
London SW1
Tel: (01) 222 9011
Secretary: Giles Ecclestone

Under the impulsion of the World Council of Churches' Nairobi recommendations and moves within its own structures, the Church of England has in recent years devoted more of its time to the interpretation of its social responsibilities in terms of the relatively new concept of 'human rights' work. Following the General Synod's debate on Religious Conditions in Eastern Europe which took place in February 1975 (before Nairobi), the Board of Social Responsibility was asked to prepare a report for further debate. This was published in February 1977 as 'Human Rights: Our Understanding and Our Responsibilities'. This report explores the tensions which exist between the universally-accepted and therefore 'established' rights and the relativist concept which tends to view 'rights' as demands made by persecuted individuals and oppressed minorities; it concludes that the Christian understanding of man 'places a responsibility upon the Church to support action to recognise and safeguard human rights'. It asked the Board of Social Responsibility to report from time to time to the Synod on the specific human rights activities in which it is engaged.

This was not a change of approach — the Church of England has always involved itself in what is now known as human rights work — but marks a shift of emphasis towards public action on specific cases and issues of the type pioneered by Amnesty International.

The Board of Social Responsibility is one of several such advisory bodies which assist the General Synod, the supreme governing body of the Church of England, but which also take on some executive functions. Since the structure of the Church at diocesan level is largely autonomous, with no tight central control, central policy on human rights largely confirms the general orientation already undertaken by many local churches, some of whom had 'adopted' prisoners of conscience or taken up campaign work of their own accord.

The central structure is funded by the parishes and dioceses, but disposes of no special relief or emergency funds. Local churches may, however, undertake fund-raising for specific cases they have concerned themselves with, and indeed they provide an ideal platform within the community for publicising and enlisting support for individual casework.

The Board of Social Responsibility does occasionally take up individual cases, but on a very *ad hoc* basis as they are referred to it by external organisations (in particular Amnesty groups seeking church interventions by prominent churchmen). One recent example was the case of the Anglo-Chilean prisoner Guillermo Beausire Alonso, brought to the Board's attention by AI and taken up by the Church of England with the Foreign Office. There are no specific provisions for refugees arriving in this country, though here again local churches have provided a focus for reception arrangements.

Resolutions passed in recent months by the General Synod have included one on Chile expressing support for church work amongst the oppressed and poor, and one expressing deep disquiet at the persecution and imprisonment of Namibians who promote peaceful change.

One further important element in the Church's stance on human rights has been its understanding of its responsibilities as a major shareholder. The Church Commissioners handle some £500 million annually in landed income and industrial stock holdings. Their policy has been not to invest knowingly in any company operating wholly or mainly in South Africa (though it has not always proved possible to know this in advance). The Church has made it its concern to ensure that the policies of the companies in which it invests do not depart from its principles of social justice. In this, it prefers in general a discreet approach to open public shareholder action.

See also: **Christian Concern for Southern Africa.**

Commission for Justice and Peace
44 Gray's Inn Road
London WC1X 8LR
Tel: (01) 405 0925
President: Bishop Mahon
Secretary: Robert Beresford

Following the recommendation of the Second Vatican Council that an agency of the Roman Catholic Church be set up 'to stimulate the Catholic community to foster progress in needy regions, and social justice on the international scene', a Pontifical Commission for Justice and Peace ('Iustitia et Pax') was created in Rome in 1967, to be followed by national Justice and Peace commissions in over 60 countries. At the same time, special funds were set up by the Catholic hierarchies to finance the new commissions, in both their public education activities and their work on overseas development.

The Commission for Justice and Peace is an appointed body of the Catholic hierarchy in this country. It acts as an advisory body to the Catholic bishops, and works through Diocesan Justice and Peace groups and the Catholic community at large to promote reflection and action on major issues of social justice. Its wide brief and its cooperation with the **Catholic Fund for Overseas Development** (CAFOD, 21a Soho Square, London 21V 6NR, tel: (01) 734 4158, (01) 439 7938) means that it is concerned with world development, social justice and human rights as closely inter-related issues of direct concern to the Catholic Church.

The Commission itself through its twice-yearly meetings establishes general policy guidelines and follows up the work of a number of advisory Working Parties, through which most of the research and educational work of the Commission is carried out. The Commission has taken part in actions over a wide range of countries, often in conjunction with other non-governmental organisations, such as Amnesty International, Chile Committee for Human Rights, International Commission of Jurists, the Minority Rights Group and the National Council for Civil Liberties. Over the past year (1976-7), the Commission's President Bishop Mahon has expressed the Commission's concern for disappeared Chileans, for those imprisoned for religious reasons in the USSR, for clergy and religious harassed by officials in the Philippines and for the imprisoned Korean poet Kim Chi-ha, who is a Christian convert. Cases in other areas have also been followed up as appropriate.

Finance

The Commission's small permanent staff in London works on a £15,000 annual budget (1976-7), funded through the National Catholic Fund, which draws on annual collections from the 19 Catholic Dioceses in England and Wales. The Secretariat services the Working Parties, maintains contact with local and national voluntary organisations, liaises with other national Justice and Peace Commissions, and publishes study materials and pamphlets, in cooperation with the Catholic Information Office for England and Wales.

(See *Justice and Peace: the work of the Commission*, London, June 1974).

Committee for the Release of Soviet Jewish Prisoners
Tel Hai House
71 Compayne Gardens
London NW6 3RS
Tel: (01) 458 2653
Chairwoman: Barbara Oberman

The Committee works on behalf of Jews in the Soviet Union who are detained, harassed or otherwise prevented from emigrating to Israel. It circulates case-histories and coordinates letter-writing campaigns amongst its 200 plus membership. The Committee holds peaceful demonstrations to draw attention to the plight of Jewish prisoners of conscience held in the Soviet Union. It keeps a close watch on events in the Soviet Union and campaigns on behalf of those who are under surveillance or in danger of wrongful arrest and imprisonment.

For **Medical and Scientific Committee for Soviet Jewry**, see pp. 112-13.

Friends Service Council
Friends House
Euston Road
London NW1 2BJ
Tel: (01) 387 3601
General Secretary: Walter Martin

Friends Peace and International Relations Committee
Tel: (01) 455 3198
Secretary: Cecil Evans

The Society of Friends (Quakers) has a long history of relief and development work overseas, with an impact far in excess of their relatively small numbers. The Quaker approach has always emphasised the importance of the individual dimension to such seemingly insuperable problems as poverty, hunger, illiteracy, the largescale displacement or disruption of communities, and war. This means that individual human rights, including the right to conscientious objection, have always occupied a special place in Quaker concerns. The Quakers stress that they are not a professional relief agency; their extensive community and development work is, however, a direct expression of their social commitment as a religious community.

In the course of their work at home and overseas, Quakers frequently concern themselves with human rights cases (in the sense employed in this survey). These may involve only a few individuals or an entire community (the work of the American Friends Service Committee in Vietnam for example was well-known and widely appreciated). There is no set machinery for dealing with casework, but these will be handled informally by those directly concerned, whether at the centre or the local level. Such work — counselling, relief, emergency aid and so on — is continuous, but the Friends Service Committee and the Peace and International Relations Committee do not give it wide publicity. However, it is widely known

United Kingdom

amongst other non-governmental organisations throughout the world, and there is a constant exchange of information with these.

Through the Friends World Committee for Consultation, the Quakers maintain a permanent presence, in conjunction with other NGOs, in Geneva and New York.[1]

Friends Peace and International Relations Committee, which is a committee of the Friends Service Council, arranges conferences and seminars on themes connected with peace and human rights issues. During 1976, it launched an 'Action Programme to Help Abolish Torture', which encouraged local public education initiatives, letter-writing campaigns and petitions on behalf of torture victims.

Finance

Friends Service Council finances its operations on an annual budget of £279,000 (1975 figures). This is derived from subscriptions, donations and legacies, and grants, including support from Christian Aid. In addition, there is an Overseas Development Fund totalling around £45,000 (1975).

International Council of Jews from Czechoslovakia
Suite 68
12-13 Henrietta Street
London WC2E 8LH
Chairman: K. Baum

The International Council of Jews from Czechoslovakia was formed in 1968 to help Jews coming from Czechoslovakia to the West and to Israel in establishing themselves again. However, the principal concerns of the ICJC are aid to Jews and the Jewish community within Czechoslovakia; their defence against manifestations of anti-Semitism, frequently surfacing in the guise of anti-Zionism and enmity towards Israel; the reunion of families and friends; advice to victims of Nazi persecution on claims and legal issues; and research into the history, culture and social structure of Czechoslovak Jewry.

The ICJC publishes a quarterly newsletter containing extensive material on the situation of Jews in Czechoslovakia, and a periodic *Report on Czechoslovak Jewry*.

---

[1]   Quaker House, 13 avenue du Mervelet, 1209 Geneva; Quaker UN Office, 345 East 46th Street, New York NY 10018, USA.

Keston College (Centre for the Study of Religion and Communism)
Heathfield Road
Keston
Kent BR2 6BA
Tel: (0689) 50116
Director: Rev Michael Bordeaux

Keston College (the Centre for the Study of Religion and Communism) acts as a research centre, collecting information, often at first-hand, about religious liberty. It deals not only with deprivation of religious liberty and with active persecution for religious views or allegiances, but with all aspects of religious life in the countries studied. It is a non-political organisation, but confines its attention to the position of the churches and religious life in the Soviet Union, Eastern Europe, China and other communist countries. It is non-denominational, and does not limit its researches to the Christian religion; Islam, Buddhism and the Jewish faith are also covered.

The Centre was set up by its present Director in 1970. Its Council of Management comprises academic specialists in Eastern European and Soviet studies, and churchmen. A small research staff studies, translates and disseminates the material received. This also forms the basis for an archive which is intended for use by scholars throughout the world. Contacts are maintained and information circulated to other non-governmental organisations, churches, universities, trusts and foundations in the UK and overseas.

The Centre is a registered charity, and derives its income from donations and covenants. Major fund-raising initiatives have secured it an annual budget of around £60,000 per annum.

Methodist Church, Division of Social Responsibility, *see* Chapter 3, Voluntary Overseas Aid Organisations, p. 44.

National Council for Soviet Jewry of the United Kingdom and Ireland
183-189 Finchley Road
London NW3 6LD
Tel: (01) 624 0181/2
President: Lord Fisher of Camden, President of the Board of Deputies of British Jews
Chairwoman: Mrs June Jacobs
Executive Director: Alan Gold

The National Council for Soviet Jewry (NCSJ) is the umbrella organisation for the official bodies working to ameliorate the conditions of Jews in the USSR. It aims to mobilise Anglo-Jewry to this end through public meetings and informal discussions. It publishes a bi-monthly *Newsletter* and circulates current information on the situation of Jews in the Soviet Union;[1] it liaises with other national organisations in planning joint activities; it engages in representations to government, parliamentarians and other public bodies in all relevant matters concerned with the welfare of Soviet Jewry.

The National Council was set up early in 1976, and works in conjunction with a number of associated Working Groups, which include:

— an *Interdenominational Working Group* which liaises with church bodies in matters connected with Soviet Jewry, and helped organise a joint conference on Soviet Jewry in April 1977;

— a *Telecommunications Working Group* which advises members telephoning or writing to the USSR, and maintains a National Register of refusenik adoptions; a report of its monitoring activities was submitted in connection with the Belgrade Conference;

— a *Travel and Tourism Working Group* monitors the results of visits by members to the USSR;

— a *Prisoners of Conscience Working Group* organises and coordinates an adoption scheme for Soviet Jewish political prisoners;

— a *Book Committee* has initiated programme for sending books of relevant interest to the USSR;

— an *Academic Committee*, only recently created, will campaign specifically on behalf of non-scientific Soviet Jewish academics;[2]

— a *Finance Working Group* concentrates on fund-raising.

In addition to these, there is a *National Youth Council for Soviet Jewry* (address: as for National Council, above) which focuses on information and fund-raising work amongst young people.

The NCSJ's funds are derived from affiliation fees paid by member organisations, from individual donations and from fund-raising events.

---

[1] The weekly *Jews in the USSR* is published under its auspices from: 31 Percy Street, London W1P 9FG, tel: (01) 580 0681.

[2] *See also* **Medical and Scientific Committee for Soviet Jewry**, pp. 112-13. As with virtually all the organisations concerned with Soviet Jewry, this committee is affiliated to the National Council.

Pax Christi
Pax Christi Centre
St Dominic's Priory
Blackfriars Hall
Southampton Road
London NW5 4LB
Tel: (01) 485 7977
Secretary: Ms Valerie Flessati
President: Bishop Victor Guazzelli

Founded in 1945 in a spirit of postwar reconciliation, Pax Christi is an international movement working for peace and disarmament though pacifism is not a condition of membership. It is centred, though not exclusively, in the Catholic church, and counts a number of prominent churchmen amongst its animators: Cardinal Alfrink is the International President.

One of Pax Christi's major preoccupations is with the spread of the international arms trade. Its particular human rights concern is with the problems of conscientious objection, and the British Pax Christi centre has been closely involved in the recent creation of a Conscientious Objectors' Advisory Team (COAT, q.v.).

Pax Christi is not a fund-raising or relief organisation. It undertakes campaign work from its London office and through its 600-odd membership throughout the United Kingdom. Members participate in letter-writing actions, discussion groups, talks, lectures and public education work largely through the local churches. Pax Christi works closely with CIIR, the Justice and Peace Commission, and a number of pacifist organisations, solidarity committees and support groups, and helps to distribute their literature. It acts as the London base for the Northern Ireland Peace Movement, and provides premises and support for the Conscientious Objectors Advisory Team.

Pax Christi centres exist throughout Western Europe and North America. The Dutch, German and Austrian sections are perhaps the most active on human rights questions. Each has developed a particular area of concern: the Austrians with East-West relations, the Dutch with Conscientious Objection, and so on. The national centres are largely autonomous, raising their own funds, and coming together in an annual International Council. The interim Executive Committee is based in The Hague, as is the Secretariat (Celebesstraat 60, Den Haag 2040, Holland), from where an international *Bulletin* is produced.

The British Pax Christi centre functions on a shoestring budget of around £5,000, which finances two full-time workers, pays the expenses of a number of volunteers, and funds a range of campaign work and related activities. Income is derived from donations, subscriptions, summer youth hostels and an annual grant of around £1,000 from the Catholic bishops. It is not, however, an appointed body of the Church hierarchy, but an autonomous membership organisation responsible for its own funding.

United Reformed Church
86 Tavistock Place
London WC1H 9RT
Tel: (01) 837 7661
Secretary, Church and Society Department: Rev John Reardon

The United Reformed Church has joined in occasional protest action to governments and embassies, with the British Council of Churches and Amnesty International. By reason of its overseas links, the United Reform Church has been particularly concerned and active on human rights questions relating to South Korea, Taiwan and Southern Africa. Limited financial resources mean that more sustained campaign work is not possible.

Women's Campaign for Soviet Jewry ('35s')
148 Granville Road
London NW2 2LO
Tel: (01) 458 7147
Officers: Rita Ekar, Linda Isaacs and Margaret Pyle

The Women's Campaign for Soviet Jewry seeks to call attention to the treatment accorded to Jews in the Soviet Union who are imprisoned or persecuted for having sought leave to emigrate to Israel, the 'refuseniks'. Its first public action in May 1971 involved 35 women who were the exact contemporaries of a 35-year-old woman refusenik — hence the name '35s'. Membership — now approximately 2,000 throughout the UK — is voluntary, and open to all, regardless of age or faith.

The 35s have focused on public protest demonstrations as an immediate response to refusenik and political prisoner cases, often employing considerable ingenuity in attracting press and media coverage. This is backed up by information work amongst churches, trade unions, schools, universities and youth groups. Support is canvassed amongst Parliamentarians and prominent public figures. Guidance is provided on letter-writing campaigns for groups and individuals who decide to 'adopt' a Soviet Jewish prisoner or refusenik.

Since 1974, members have been involved in studying the progress of the Conference on European Security and Cooperation, which resulted in the Helsinki Agreement; this was the occasion for a further public demonstration by 35s from several countries in Western Europe and North America, who by now had set up an International Women's Committee for Soviet Jewry. From February 1976, 100 Helsinki Watchdog Committees for Soviet Jews have collected evidence for submission to the British government delegation to the Belgrade follow-up Conference; refusenik cases are examined by a panel comprising a lawyer, an MP, a trade unionist, a church leader and a member of the refusenik's own occupational group.

World Jewish Congress

55 New Cavendish Street	1 rue de Varembé
London W1M 8BT	Case postale 191
Tel: (01) 935 0335	1211 Geneva 20
Telex: 21633	Tel: 34 13 25
Cable: Worldgress London	Telex: 289 876
	Cable: Worldgress Geneva

The World Jewish Congress (WJC) is a representative body of Jewish communities and organisations in 64 countries (excluding the USSR). The British participant is the Board of Deputies of British Jews. Founded in 1936, the WJC's history reflects the dramatic events of the last 40 years. In working to foster and develop the Jewish religious, cultural and social heritage, the WJC seeks to 'secure the rights, status and interests of Jews and Jewish communities and to defend them wherever they are denied, violated or imperilled'.

These statutory aims involve representations of the interests of WJC participating communities before governments, inter-governmental and international non-governmental organisations. As the diplomatic arm of its constituent communities, the WJC has thus been particularly active in establishing a dialogue with the Soviet authorities on the position of the Jews in the Soviet Union. The WJC has initiated proposals at international conferences on Soviet Jewry, designed to protect the minority rights of Soviet Jews. It has on several occasions made public appeals to the relevant authorities in this connection. (It does not, however, undertake individual case-work.)

The WJC maintains close contact with Jewish communities in Eastern Europe. It numbers representative bodies from Rumania and Yugoslavia.

The WJC has also been preoccupied with the position of Jews in Arab lands and has interceded on behalf of Jews subjected to arbitrary arrest and harassment, and pressed for the right to emigrate. It adopts both public and private approaches on these questions as appropriate, and cooperates closely with other international NGOs.

Within the appropriate UN bodies the WJC has consistently supported the right of Jewish communities as well as of other minorities, to religious and cultural self-expression. Further, the WJC has opposed all attempts within UN bodies to identify Zionism with racism.

It has submitted evidence on human rights violations to the relevant UN committees, and made suggestions on procedures for handling complaints at intergovernmental level. It takes an active part in international human rights initiatives by the NGOs, and has backed moves for the abolition of capital punishment, the condemnation of torture and the implementation of human rights safeguards at national level. It has been particularly involved in supporting measures designed to eliminate racial discrimination.

The Institute of Jewish Affairs (IJA)[1] is a distinct body which works in close association with the World Jewish Congress, providing comment and analysis on current questions of interest to the Jewish community. Since the 1960s, the emphasis has been on social and cultural problems, as well as on the political and legal context in which they are situated. The IJA represents an invaluable source of published and periodic material on Jewish affairs throughout the world since 1941. In addition to its regular publications, *Patterns of Prejudice* (bi-monthly), *Christian Attitudes on Jews and Judaism* (bi-monthly), and *Soviet Jewish Affairs* (6-monthly), the Institute issues topical Research Reports and occasional background studies. It has also published a number of *samizdat* materials circulated clandestinely by Jews in the Soviet Union, and is engaged on a number of related research projects.

[1] Institute of Jewish Affairs, IJA, 13-16 Jacob's Well Mews, George Street, London W1H 5PD, tel: (01) 935 1436, cable Ijastudies London. *Director:* Dr Stephen J. Roth, *Assistant Director:* Dr Elizabeth E. Eppler.

Chapter 5

COMMITTEES AND SUPPORT GROUPS

The multitude of support movements, ad hoc groups and committees are too numerous to list in their entirety. Given their changeable character and sometimes ephemeral existence, any comprehensive record would soon be obsolete. And yet their role in undertaking and stimulating human rights work is often important: they provide a focus for exile activity, they provide the necessary political dimension to such work, and they enter into the work, more often than not, with a single-mindedness of purpose which leaves other, more cautious, organisations standing. Each of these three advantages may also be seen as a disadvantage: their detractors tend to view them as generating more heat than light, as sacrificing broad humanitarian interests for narrow political advantage, and as jeopardising the diplomatic approach of the broader-based human rights organisations. Ultimately, this difference between critics and supporters of the committes is based on an acceptance or rejection of the political objectives which may determine the direction and scope of their human rights activities, in particular on the question of violence as a legitimate means of political opposition.

We have included below those long-standing organisations without which any survey of human rights activities would be incomplete. We have also listed some of the more recent support groups and ad hoc committees, and apologise to those which, through oversight, we may have omitted. In most instances, the wording of the descriptions was suggested by the organisations themselves.

Academics for Chile – see under 'Chile' below page 74.

Ad Hoc Group for Democracy in Thailand – c/o 103 Gower Street, (Basement), London WC1E 6AH

The group campaigns for the release of Thai workers, student leaders and other political prisoners held since the 6 October 1976 massacre and take-over by military junta. They do research and produce publications on Thailand. The organisation is a member of COBRA (below).

United Kingdom

Africa Release Campaign – c/o 103 Gower Street, (Basement), London EC1E 6AH

This organisation is a grouping of organisations working together for the release of political prisoners in Africa.

Anti-Apartheid Movement
89 Charlotte Street
London W1P 2DQ
Tel: (01) 580 5311
Chairman: Robert Hughes MP
Executive Secretary: Mike Terry
Honorary Secretary: Abdul Minty

The Anti-Apartheid Movement is a membership organisation which campaigns for freedom in Southern Africa, employing a variety of approaches to raise the level of public awareness and educate public opinion on the nature of racism and apartheid. It seeks the total isolation of the racist regimes and supports the liberation movements in Southern Africa. It is closely associated with two related organisations (both at the above address): SART (Stop All Racist Tours), which campaigns against British sporting links with South Africa, and SATIS (Southern Africa – The Imprisoned Society), a British campaign for the release of South African political prisoners.

Anti-Apartheid's campaigning activities cover all aspects of South African racial policy and its external links through investment, trade and tourism, with particular emphasis on South African military and intelligence activities abroad. Anti-Apartheid campaigns at national and local level by means of public meetings, rallies, pickets, distribution of literature and lobbying of MPs. These activities are backed up by publications providing analysis of topics of current concern, such as the South African government's Bantustan policy or agreements on arms sales and nuclear know-how.

Anti-Apartheid also maintains a close watch on South African activities in the UK and elsewhere, including its intelligence-gathering. In addition to endorsing a cultural and sporting boycott of South Africa, it has, for example, initiated proceedings against South African advertising in this country under the Race Relations Act, and lodged a similar complaint with the Independent Broadcasting Authority.

On Rhodesia/Zimbabwe, Anti-Apartheid has given wide circulation to its own publications and those of other organisations (IDAF, ICJ, AI) through to its 500 local AA groups. It has approached trade unions, student unions, community relations bodies and local political parties amongst others, analysing recent developments and urging support for anti-apartheid policies.

Work on behalf of political prisoners and detainees is organised by SATIS (Southern Africa — The Imprisoned Society) which comprises a number of related British organisations. SATIS administers an adoption scheme through local AA groups, student bodies, church groups, trades councils and others, and issues an annual listing of political prisoners, those detained without trial, and those under house arrest or banning orders. Further activities have included a nationwide petition, representations on particular cases and show-trials, attempts to gain wider national publicity on detention, hangings, torture and police brutality in South Africa.

Structure

Anti-Apartheid's individual membership is now over 3,000, and its 300 affiliated organisations cover colleges, universities, union branches, trades councils and local political groups. Policy is decided by a national committee, of whom 30 are elected by the Annual General Meeting, and 20 drawn from affiliated national organisations; in addition, up to 10 members may be co-opted, and observers are invited from liberation movements and others who share Anti-Apartheid's aims. An Executive Committee including the Movement's five officers, together with eight elected members, advises the National Committee and ensures the implementation of policy and the overall work of the movement.

Anti-Apartheid has consultative status with the UN as a Non-Governmental Organisation, and works closely with both the UN Committee against Apartheid, and the UN Commission on Human Rights. It is a member of the UK Task Force on Southern Africa (see below).

Finance

AA is funded by donations, and has received grants during 1975-6 from the World Council of Churches and the Rowntree Social Services Trust. It is currently engaged in new fund-raising activities. Its 1976-7 working budget was in the region of £40,000.

Argentine Support Movement — 1 Cambridge Terrace, London NW1P 2DQ Tel: (01) 580 5311

The group does campaign work and publicity on behalf of victims of political persecution in Argentina.

United Kingdom

Bertrand Russell Peace Foundation
Bertrand Russell House
Gamble Street
Nottingham NG7 4ET
Tel: (0602) 74504
Cable: Russfound Nottingham
Directors: Ken Coates, Chris Farley

The Bertrand Russell Peace Foundation was launched in September 1963 to perpetuate Bertrand Russell's work for peace, social justice and human rights throughout the world. Run by a small staff, the Foundation enjoys a considerable reputation, particularly in non-aligned countries. Appeals and approaches to governments have been made on behalf of political prisoners, dissenting individuals and persecuted minorities in over 40 countries, and the Foundation claims some success in obtaining prisoner releases, better conditions and commutation of death sentences.

The International War Crimes Tribunal on Vietnam attracted world-wide attention in 1966 for its exposure of atrocities against civilians. This approach, based on public indictment, was repeated in 1974 and 1976 with the hearings of the Russell Tribunal II on human rights violations and social injustice in Latin America. Smaller-scale conferences and seminars seek to focus international opinion on other important areas of concern (nuclear power, threats to the environment).

Finance

The Foundation's work is financed by donations, by subscriptions to its regular journal, *The Spokesman*, and sales of its books and pamphlets.

British Campaign for an Independent East Timor – 40 Concanon Road, London SW2. Tel: (01) 274 9308/5945 *Secretary:* John Taylor

Solidarity with Fretilin struggle against the Indonesian takeover of East Timor (former Portuguese colony) is the aim of this group. Sponsors include Liberation, Bertrand Russell Peace Foundation, Student Christian Movement, MPs and trade unionists. It is a member of COBRA (below).

British-Kurdish Friendship Society
C/o Millbank
London SW1
Chairman: Kenneth Lee
Secretary: Steven Lukes

Information on the situation of the Kurds in Iraq, Iran, Turkey and Syria and intervention through the proper channels to relieve Kurdish oppression is the aim of this group. It helps with placing Kurdish students in education in this country and raising funds for their courses; representations on behalf of Kurdish refugees. Cooperation with non-governmental organisations, refugee organisations and some human rights organisations, as well as Kurdish friendship societies in other countries have been established with the purpose of helping the Kurdish people.

Campaign Human Rights '78
158 North Gower Street
London NW1 2ND
International Coordinator: Rita Maran

This is a year-long action campaign for the establishment of a UN High Commissioner for Human Rights and a Special Session of the UN General Assembly devoted solely to human rights questions. It is a broad-based European-wide campaign aimed at bringing together NGOs, humanitarian organisations, trade unions, church groups and others to share their experiences and work together to these ends. Sponsored in the UK by the Fellowship of Reconciliation, Women's International League for Peace and Freedom (British Section), War Resisters' International, and other concerned organisations and individuals, the group has national coordinating committees in eight Western European countries.

CHILE

The voluntary response to the Chile crisis following the September 1973 coup has created many valuable new precedents and broken down former inhibitions about the nature and limitations of voluntary work. The new demands and dimensions of the crisis, in particular the enormous number of refugees seeking asylum in Europe and North America, prompted the creation of new institutions and new approaches to their work.

The emergency reception of refugees from Chile on a continual basis following the September 1973 military coup has posed an exceptional

71

challenge to refugee organisations in the United Kingdom and other European countries. The Chileans, who in previous years would have sought refuge in neighbouring Latin American countries, have been forced to flee to Europe in substantial numbers owing to the widespread repression in Latin America today. In this climate, the plight of refugees and nationals in Uruguay and Argentina has become desperate. The refugee problem in the 'southern cone' countries has reached such dimensions that more refugees will undoubtedly be forced to flee into Europe.

Refugees from Chile have been arriving in the United Kingdom since June 1974 following a decision by the Home Secretary in March 1974 to admit refugees from Chile, subject to prior security clearance. This also applies to refugees who initially sought asylum in Argentina, and who were subsequently forced to seek further refuge following the military coup in 1976. After an urgent appeal by the UN High Commissioner for Refugees, an initial quota for 75 urgent cases from Argentina was granted by the British Government in July 1976. Further approaches are likely to be made for a more comprehensive intake of Latin Americans in acute danger in their own countries.

The 2,000 refugees from Chile who have arrived in the UK since 1974 have placed particular demands on refugee work in this country. Many suffer from the physical and psychological effects of flight, exile, imprisonment and torture; those arriving from Argentina have experienced terrible stress resulting from the daily fear of kidnappings, killings and disappearances. Whole families, including children, have been deeply affected by the emotional shock of these circumstances. Prolonged exile in difficult conditions may further entrench their feelings of bitterness and despair.

It is estimated by the International Commission of Jurists that 150,000 people had left Chile as refugees by October 1974. More recent estimates have doubled this figure. The Inter-Governmental Committee for European Migration (ICEM) has helped to move over 22,350 Chilean refugees to various countries throughout the world by the end of May 1977. Between July 1974 and December 1975, the Joint Working Group (below) resettled 1,297 refugees in the United Kingdom.

The boundaries between government responsibilities and the burden shouldered by the voluntary sector have never been well defined. More than any other country, Britain has the habit, ennobled into an unspoken tradition, of offloading most of this burden onto voluntary organisations; and many of them have accepted this load, some even bravely defending the independence of the voluntary effort. With the influx of large numbers of Chilean refugees, however, it was clear that the refugee organisations could not accept the additional burden without considerable outside assistance. Moreover, a significant body of opinion within the voluntary sector thought the government ought to increase the number of refugees it was prepared to admit. Lobbying by the voluntary organisations for increased government action at the international level and more direct governmental involvement was more intensive, public — and necessary — than perhaps it had ever been before.

Above all, the demands of the Chileans required a political understanding of the events which had produced, and are still producing, the refugees. Voluntary organisations in Britain could no longer take refuge in a scrupulously non-committal form of charity. The arrival of Latin American refugees contributed to an understanding among some of the agencies of a need for a new approach to refugee work. Among other things they found it necessary to question the manner of their reception, the degree of integration, the numbers accepted, and the nature of continuing aid and relief programmes in Chile. Thus charity extended to solidarity. It no longer simply began at home, but was recognised to have repercussions overseas.

The setting up of an independent Joint Working Group for the resettlement of refugees from Chile in Great Britain was a measure of this need. The Joint Working Group was able to provide an active lobby on refugee intake as well as effective liaison with the Human Rights Committee and the Solidarity Campaign, and, with the help of these two bodies, a degree of local-level reception which existing refugee organisations could not have hoped to mobilise in time.

The Chilean resettlement programme is exceptional not only in the extent of its decentralisation and local liaison, but by its recognition of the central importance of the political dimension to the refugees' lives. This is largely due to the close interlacing of resettlement activities with the Human Rights Committee and Solidarity Campaign, whose local groups often form the nucleus for the Refugee Reception Committees. In addition to assuring the necessary link with local authorities and other voluntary organisations, and helping to organise work, accommodation and language courses, they have provided a sympathetic outlet for the refugees to make known their situation, and that of their compatriots who have remained behind.

The Solidarity Campaign provides a focus for the political aspirations of many of the refugees, and for those in Britain who had watched the Popular Front experiment of the Allende government up to its overthrow by the military. This sense of solidarity was thus very real. It did not stop short at assistance to the refugees but worked with them on behalf of their colleagues who were being persecuted by the new regime in Chile.

In contrast to the Solidarity Campaign's straightforwardly political approach, the Human Rights Committee aimed at mobilising a wider spectrum of opinion through its broad 'human rights' approach. Although 'political' in terms of its support for the victims of the Junta, it was 'nonpolitical' in terms of internal British politics, basing its approach solely on pressure for observance of international commitments and human rights law. Its programme of prisoner adoptions, like the local refugee reception committees, proved an excellent means for concerned individuals to identify with the Chileans, to learn about their problems, and to take up some form of humanitarian action on their behalf.

This system has the additional advantage of reinforcing the commitment of those who had involved themselves in the support movement by direct identification with the needs and problems of individual Chileans. Thanks to this two-way process, the Chilean problem became known to the public at large not just as a refugee 'problem', but in the wider context of international politics.

Academics for Chile
C/o WUS
9 Bruce Grove
London N17
Tel: (01) 801 5003
Secretary: Alan Angell

Academics for Chile was set up by a group of Latin-Americanist academics and researchers one month after the September 1973 coup d'état, which hit the Chilean academic community particularly hard. Several universities had been closed, thousands expelled from their courses of study and large numbers of students and teachers — Brazilians, Uruguayans, Bolivians and others as well as Chileans — had sought refuge in foreign embassies or fled abroad.

The aim of this informal group was to coordinate the response of the British academic community to this emergency, and to act as a clearing-house for information on incoming refugees and what could be done for them by universities and other educational institutions. With the help of WUS/UK, whose President launched the programme publicly in a letter to *The Times* in December 1973 and an appeal to Vice-Chancellors and Principals in January 1974, banking and administrative facilities were provided for a major fund-raising effort at local university and national levels.

Within four months of this appeal, universities had raised well over £8,000 between them and provided some 40 scholarships and fellowships;[1] Christian Aid had given £10,000, the Ford Foundation £7,000, the Swedish International Development Fund £1,141 (through International WUS), official university sources and other charitable trusts £5,000.

From the start, WUS had acted as a clearing-house, collating the offer

---

[1] Some universities have endowments specifically for refugees, see *Oxford Refugee Scholarships*, p. 30.

of university places with demand from refugees in Latin America (through CLACSO office in Buenos Aires) and those already in Britain. Refugees seeking places registered with WUS, which kept track, through official and informal channels, of the universities' response and referred the Chileans to the most appropriate openings for their field of study and eventual prospects. WUS in turn cooperated with the wide spectrum of voluntary bodies who had offered their own specialised assistance — these included the Chile Committee for Human Rights (information), the Chile Solidarity Campaign (political lobbying), Amnesty International (information on prisoners and campaign work worldwide), the Association of University Teachers, ATTI and ASTMS, etc.

Academics for Chile was never intended, however, as a centralised agency. Local Academics for Chile groups on campus used their own contacts and professional standing to apply for scholarships and press for waiving of fees, invitations from senior academics and other immediate forms of assistance from the governing bodies of universities. Over the three years in which the programme had been in existence (i.e. up to the start of 1977) an estimated £200,000 has been raised by university bodies (this estimate includes waived fees and other forms of material aid).[1]

Following the infusion of government funds from the Overseas Development Ministry (via WUS/UK), there was a shift of emphasis from funding refugee scholars to finding suitable positions in universities for those receiving the WUS/ODM grants. While local committees still played a considerable part in exploring the possibilities for posts and additional funds on campus, sub-committees were set up by WUS to deal with allocation of government funds, and coordination of present and future activities. Members of the WUS secretariat attended Academics for Chile discussions and AFC officers were co-opted onto WUS award committees. WUS also serves to maintain contact with some 30 national and international bodies associated with the programme.

The Academics for Chile programme was not without precedents for immediate action on refugees by the academic world. Response amongst the academic community to successive crises from the interwar refugee influx from Nazi Germany, to the Hungarians, Czechs, and Ugandan Asians has been spontaneous and generous. It may be that the decentralised structure of university funding and policy-making, coupled with the greater awareness of the international needs of their professional colleagues overseas means that the academic community is geared to respond to such crises in a way that the doctors or teachers, for example, were not.

It had been hoped that other professional bodies, amongst them

---

[1]   An important concomitant of local funding and placement was that the exiled scholars should not be seen as occupying places which would otherwise go to non-refugee students and teachers by the usual processes of allocation.

doctors, architects, teachers, etc., would establish similar structures for their exiled Chilean counterparts; this did not happen. The Academics for Chile campaign was better coordinated and on a far larger scale than previous emergency arrangements, and will serve as an invaluable precedent for possible future actions of this nature.

Chile Committee for Human Rights
1 Cambridge Terrace
London NW1 4JL
Tel: (01) 935 5953
President: Joan Jara
Executive Secretary: Wendy Tyndale

CCHR and its associated Chile Relief Fund were set up in January 1974 as a fund-raising, research and campaign centre to increase public awareness in Britain of the situation in Chile and its consequences in human terms. It liaised with the church-based Comite pro Paz in Chile, which before its suppression channeled material aid to political prisoners and their families and defended their interests as far as was possible; in Britain, CCHR by its broad and 'non-political' appeal to humanitarian sentiments, was able to complement the mobilisation of political support carried out by the Chile Solidarity Campaign (q.v.). A registered charity, the Fund has shifted its emphasis from purely relief work to aid projects: a programme for children's canteens and a handicrafts outlet, with all profits from the latter returning to the detainees who make the craftwork for sale in Britain.

CCHR was instrumental, with BCAR, in setting up the Joint Working Group to handle the administration of Chilean refugee reception in this country. One of the advantages of the spread of organisations dealing with Chile has been the recognition in institutional terms that overseas human rights work and refugee work are integrally related, the refugee being only one end product (and by no means the most tragic) of civil and international conflict.

CCHR still works closely with JWG's support activities, since together with CSC, it provides a programme for action against the continuing violation of human rights in Chile as well as a clearing-house for information from and about political prisoners remaining in Chile.

CCHR with advice from Amnesty International have carried out an adoption scheme which has led to the sponsorship of over 500 Chilean political prisoners largely by trade union branches. Quite apart from any beneficial effects for the prisoners themselves, this scheme has proved successful in educating the public at large about events in Chile by providing the degree of identification with individuals which appears to be the essential prerequisite for lasting commitment. In some cases, the adopted prisoners are able to opt for exile, and the groups may then find themselves acting as Refugee Reception Committees (see JWG, above).

CCHR also has eighteen local groups which can approach local unionists, students, churchmen, women's groups and other sectors of society with a plea for action (whether in the form of letter-writing campaigns, petitions, fund-raising, sale of handicrafts, etc.) which in turn provides a good focus for local public interest.

Given the often delicate strategic nature of campaigning at this level, there is always a need to ensure that guidelines for action are observed and follow-up information provided. Such work inevitably places a large burden of work on the staff, which means sacrificing other initiatives. This is a serious drawback, but it has so far always been thought that on the whole the scheme justifies this level of effort.

Information about events in Chile is circulated in a *Newsletter,*[1] which appears every six weeks, as well as through occasional reports and publications, and a long list of speaking engagements.

Finance
The CCHR operates on a shoestring budget of £8,000, which includes the salaries of two full-time workers, drawn largely from church and development aid sources: Christian Aid, War on Want, the Methodists and the Church of England.

Chile Solidarity Campaign
129 Seven Sisters Road
London N7
Tel: (01) 272 4298
Chairmen: Brian Nicholson (T&GWU), George Anthony (AUEW)
Secretaries: Mike Gatehouse, Colin Henfrey

Chile Solidarity Campaign has been the focus for uniting political opposition to the Chilean Junta, and has been instrumental in rallying the British Labour Movement behind a very effective Parliamentary lobby. Launched by the anti-colonial movement Liberation, it approaches the human rights issues involved from a strictly political standpoint − torture, arbitrary detention, disappearances and other grave abuses of human rights in Chile are being considered the unhealthy symptoms of the political malaise. On this broad anti-fascist base, the Campaign enjoys the active support of

---

[1] This now covers Argentina and Uruguay as well.

the Labour Party, the British Communist Party and Young Communists, the International Marxist Group and the International Socialists.

This approach has the advantage of attracting support from political and labour bodies which had hitherto appeared to be rather lukewarm in their protests about human rights violations in other areas — such as Uruguay — where the political issues are not perhaps so clear-cut. On the other hand, the political approach may tend to alienate other potential supporters (including some Chilean exiles) whose common cause with the Chilean Left does not extend to the internal politics and strategies of the Solidarity Campaign. On the whole, however, as the issues are clear-cut, so is the Solidarity Campaign remarkably coherent and determined in its efforts.

From the start, the Chile Solidarity Campaign has had the advantage of good advice and excellent contacts with a number of priminent politicians. It can count on the active support of a significant number of Labour and Liberal MPs, eight affiliated political organisations, and 28 national affiliated unions. But even more important is the local basis of this support, which exists through some 66 Chile Solidarity Committees, 45 trades councils, 85 constituency labour parties, 126 trade union branches, shop stewards committees, district and regional committees and 50 student unions up and down the country. This amounts to a formidable network of support.

While the impetus for campaign work is provided from the central office in London, initiatives for action are largely decentralised. The starting-point for rallying the support of the unions (266 of which were represented at the Campaign's October 1975 conference) was the ruthless suppression of their counterparts in Chile, the imprisonment and torture of leading unionists, and the severe economic hardships which the Chilean workers now have to endure. Longstanding contacts with CUT, the Chilean TUC, have brought home the enormity of these events and strengthened the commitment of the British unions to the Chilean case.

Union actions have included: blacking Chilean government contracts, boycotting Chilean goods, mass demonstrations, relief fund-raising, resettlement of refugees and adoption of political prisoners. Prisoner adoptions are organised through the Chile Committee for Human Rights; to date, an estimated 400 plus separate trade union organisations have been involved in this scheme, which has been concerned with the fate of some 600 imprisoned trade unionists. Refugee work is coordinated by the Joint Working Group; union involvement has proved highly valuable for the refugees' integration into British society, their search for work, and their need to publicise the continuing crisis in Chile. All these activities are carried out at local level, in conjunction with national initiatives from the centre.

Chile Solidarity Campaign has also made a significant contribution to the current moves to link government policy on economic aid to human rights considerations. It took the lead in this approach in its February 1975 campaign which succeeded in obtaining the government's refusal to renegotiate Chile's foreign debt to the UK on human rights grounds.

The Solidarity Campaign thus complements the human rights and refugee work of the Joint Working Group and Human Rights Committee by providing the political impetus necessary to sustain an overall nationwide campaign. JWG and CCHR are independent bodies with a non-political stance; their function meshes closely with that of Chile Solidarity, which can supply this additional dimension.

Joint Working Group for Refugees from Chile in Britain
21 Star Street
London W2 1QB
Tel: (01) 262 4926/5274
Coordinators: Ann Browne, Gordon Hutchinson

The Joint Working Group was set up in July 1974 and is composed of representatives of the British Council for Aid to Refugees, Chile Committee for Human Rights, Christian Aid, Chile Solidarity Campaign (co-opted in November 1974), World University Service, Ockenden Venture, and the Standing Conference on Refugees, which has observer status.

The exceptional dimensions – political as well as numerical – of the refugee inflow from Chile provided a new experience for Britain and the organisations, both voluntary and governmental, which have been involved in refugee work. The JWG believes that the structure evolved, based on a reception centre and local committees, provides the best possibility of integration for the refugees and has the flexibility which such work requires.

The structure and approach which the JWG has adopted has set a practical example which is likely to alter the character of future large-scale refugee work should similar demands be placed on the voluntary network. This in spite of the fact that the JWG has had to carry on its work in conditions of great uncertainty, both as regards numbers of incoming refugees and its own future financial resources.

The JWG is funded by a grant from the Voluntary Services Unit of the Home Office, renewable every six months. Christian Aid and BCAR also contribute to it funds. The estimated average cost of resettling the first 1,300 refugees between July 1974 and December 1975 was put at a mere £65 per person.

United Kingdom

Resettlement

Given the heavy influx of refugees from Chile and the consequent high level of demand on the reception centres (at Southampton University initially, London and Birmingham subsequently), the JWG was forced to adopt a policy of rapid dispersal of the refugees into the host community. This was carried out through the local committees of the Chile Committee for Human Rights and the Chile Solidarity Campaign up and down the country, which, on the basis of voluntary effort, were able to establish the necessary links with local housing authorities, social security offices, language classes, trade unions, schools, universities and local education authorities, doctors and dentists, and other local groups. This has enabled the programme to provide essential moral support and political sympathy for the refugees as well as contributing towards their integration into the community.

Reception

Upon their arrival in the UK, the refugees are taken to a reception centre where arrangements are made for them to receive living and clothing grants from the Department of Health and Social Security. The refugees are granted visas which entitle them to work, thus making them eligible to claim supplementary benefit. Other immediate needs such as urgent medical and dental problems are attended to. The refugees generally stay in the reception centre from three to eight weeks until accommodation has been found. Some English classes are given in the reception centre, although more important at this stage is adjustment to the realities of their new prospects and the identification of particular problems prior to their resettlement.

Although this interim reception period has proved necessary, the lack of advance warning and information about new arrivals and the inadequate facilities in the reception centre has resulted in a hastier resettlement of newly arrived refugees than the JWG staff would have wished, as well as producing further strains and tensions in the refugees themselves. Since 1975, the JWG has been pressing for the provision of better reception facilities, a plea which has been taken up by the Standing Conference (see above) on behalf of all voluntary organisations.

Lobbying

As a new, flexible and largely voluntary effort, the JWG is aware of its own shortcomings in dealing with the emergency intake of refugees from Chile. From the start, lobbying has been integral to its reception and resettlement work, since it pressed for official support, whether in the form of more solid advance information about incoming refugees, greater financial security, or assistance with permanent reception facilities. These are still the three main areas of concern.

Pressure to speed-up the processing of refugees at risk in Argentina was a central problem at the end of 1976. As this flow began to increase at the beginning of 1977, the inadequacies of existing reception facilities became more pressing. Uncertainty about finance has always made it difficult for the JWG to plan ahead with much confidence. The JWG has joined with other refugee organisations in pressing, through the Standing Conference, for government assistance with the establishment of a permanent joint reception centre which would combine services and facilities for all incoming refugees.

The JWG is increasingly confronted with longer-term problems as the refugees' prospects of an immediate return diminish. The JWG has always chosen to tackle these problems by encouraging self-help amongst the refugees themselves. Proposals are currently under way for a Latin American cultural centre, to encourage interaction between the refugees, exiles and the native British population; recreation and welfare services combined with exhibitions, meetings, seminars, concerts and the sale of books and handicrafts are intended to help create a wider public awareness of the refugees' problems, and the situation they have left behind in Latin America.

Latin American Centre

Proposals initiated by the JWG for a Latin American Centre in London (and which are now rapidly approaching realisation) aim to cater for the various needs of the Latin American exile community under one roof. The Centre will seek to provide a central meeting place for refugees, exiles and other interested individuals which, in addition to encouraging exchange and contacts in a relaxed atmosphere, will also provide service — a bookshop, cafe, workshop, meeting rooms, and some small-scale employment for the refugees. Most of all it seeks to provide a public focus and identity for the Latin American community in this country.

This project has brought together some 17 organisations involved in refugee and support work in Latin America.[1] Premises were obtained from a church order; support and backing were also canvassed amongst local community organisations in the Borough of Hackney, where the Centre is now situated. The address is 17 Hoxton Square, London N1. Telephone 739 2910. The director is Duncan McIntosh.

Chile Committee for Human Rights — see above, page 76.

Chile Solidarity Campaign — see above, page 77.

---

[1]   Including: JWG, IUEF, Christian Aid, CCHR, UNA, WoW, CALA, Liberation Brazil Committee, ASM, WUS, CSC Cultural Committee, CHRU, Society of Friends, Oxfam, Latin America Bureau.

COBRA (Conference for Basic Human and Democratic Rights in the ASEAN Alliance Countries) — 6 Endsleigh Street, London WC1

Standing Conference to act as lobby on political repression in Thailand, Malaysia, Singapore, Indonesia, Philippines. Member organisations include: TAPOL, FUEMSSO (Malaysian and Singapore students in Britain), Ad Hoc Group for Democracy in Thailand, Europe-Third World Research Centre, British Campaign for an Independent East Timor, Labour South-East Asia Group, 3W1.

Committee Against Repression in Iran — Box 4, Rising Free, 182 Upper Street, London N1

This is a group of student unions and political groups working against repression in Iran and SAVAK (Iranian secret police) activities on campus. It campaigns for the release of Iranian political prisoners. The group produces publications and the *CARI Bulletin*.

Committee for the Defence of Ukrainian Political Prisoners in the USSR — 49 Linden Gardens, London W2 4HG. Tel: (01) 229 8392 *Joint Secretaries:* Dr S. M. Fostun, Mr I. Dmytriw

This is a permanent committee comprising some 15 Ukrainian exile groups, set up in March 1974, to receive and disseminate information about conditions of Ukrainians in the USSR, and to organise support in Britain for those Ukrainians persecuted or imprisoned in the USSR for political reasons.

Committee for Human Rights in Argentina — 1 Cambridge Terrace, London NW1 4JL *Acting Secretary:* Val Roche

A human rights committee launched in summer of 1977, this group works for the restoration of the rule of law in Argentina. It campaigns to inform public opinion about tortures, summary executions and disappearances in Argentina, and tries to obtain visas from the British government for Argentine political prisoners opting for exile.

Committee in Defence of Soviet Political Prisoners — c/o 67 Grangewood Street, London E6 1HB

The committee has been set up as a broad-based committee to defend Soviet political prisoners, regardless of what their views might be, and to defend the democratic right of all people in the Soviet Union to freely express their views. It aims to inform public opinion in Britain and internationally on the question of Soviet political prisoners. The group works 'only with democratic groups and individuals who do not support political repression elsewhere'.

Committee to Defend Czech Socialists – c/o International Confederation for Disarmament and Peace, 6 Endsleigh Street, London WC1

The group organises support for signatories of Charter 77 amongst British Labour movement and sympathisers. Sponsors include: Labour Party National Executive Committee, Bertrand Russell Peace Foundation, trade unions.

Ethiopian Human Rights Committee in Europe
34 Bayston Road
London N16 7LT
Tel: (01) 249 0739

The Ethiopian Human Rights Committee exists to make public the persistent violation of human rights in Ethiopia, to solicit financial and material aid for Ethiopian refugees in Europe, Africa and the Middle East, and to develop contacts between Ethiopian exiles and concerned NGOs, religious and human rights bodies. The Committee is non-partisan and makes no discrimination amongst the refugees it assists. Its headquarters are in London, with offices throughout Europe, and special representatives in Geneva and Stockholm.

Fellowship of Reconciliation
9 Coombe Road
New Malden
Surrey KT3 4QA
Tel: (01) 942 6521
General Secretary: Rev Hamish Walker

An interdenominational movement opposed to war and all forms of violence, the origins of the Fellowship of Reconciliation (FOR) go back to 1914. Through the International Fellowship of Reconciliation,[1] it is in contact with 28 national branches throughout the world, the largest being in the United States. FOR's 7,000 members in the UK (under the aegis of

---

[1]   Veerstraat 1, Alkmaar, Netherlands.

six regional councils) take part in a wide range of activities — lobbying, meetings, non-violent protest action — often cooperating with other initiatives against war, violence, environmental pollution, and forms of physical and social oppression.

FOR supports work for 'human rights in their totality, including economic as well as politcal rights . . . [and] the right to free expression'. Its traditional special interest has been in the right to conscientious objection. Recent initiatives have served to focus attention on the question of religious freedoms in Vietnam, and on human rights violations in Argentina. FOR co-operates in Campaign Human Rights '78 (above), and publishes *Reconciliation Quarterly* and a newsletter *Newspeace*.

Finance

FOR is financed almost entirely through its membership subscriptions and donations. It contributes to the annual budget of IFOR, which is projected at £42,000 for 1977-8.

International Confederation for Disarmament and Peace — 6 Endsleigh Street, London WC1. Tel: (01) 387 5754 Cables: Nonaligned London *General Secretary:* Peggy Duff

The confederation of peace and anti-war movements in Europe, North America, Asia and Australasia works for human and democratic rights, disarmament and the liberation of peoples within the context of a just sharing of the world's resources. Special emphasis is placed on the Middle East, Africa, ASEAN and South Korea, NIEO, aid and multinationals, arms sales and détente. It publishes *Peace Press* and *Vietnam — SE Asia International*. The group maintains an extensive library of books, pamphlets, documents and press cuttings on all the above issues.

International Defence and Aid Fund for Southern Africa
104-5 Newgate Street
London EC1A 7AP
Tel: (01) 606 6123/5
President: Canon John Collins
Deputy Director: Rev David Mason
General Secretary: Phyllis Altman
Publications: 2 Amen Court, London EC4M 7BX

The International Defence and Aid Fund (IDAF) was set up in 1964, and under the leadership of Canon John Collins has established a worldwide reputation for its work in aiding the victims of political discrimination in

Southern Africa and in publicising their cause. The scale of this work is impressive. IDAF receives at least £1,000,000 annually, which is used to aid, defend and rehabilitate the victims of unjust legislation and oppression, to support their families and dependants, and to make known their plight through publicity, documentation and public education. Until 1966, IDAF worked openly in Southern Africa, but was subsequently decreed a banned organisation. It remains operational, despite attempts by the South African government and its supporters to inhibit its work. While this work is strictly humanitarian, IDAF does not pretend to ignore the political implications; under systems based on racial supremacy, humane action on behalf of subject races is seen, and acknowledged, as inherently political action.

IDAF's actions fall under three headings, defined by its major objectives: legal defence costs, relief, research and publications. The first two have traditionally been given priority, though the third is now given increasing prominence (publication sales were up by £10,000 in 1976, and there is greater emphasis on well-substantiated documentation and visual publicity — photographic exhibitions and films — as a means of reaching international public opinion).

Allocation of funds to Southern Africa is determined in response to requests which are carefully checked by the Head Office in London. Most of these requests are of an emergency nature, and the response is guided by humanitarian concern, irrespective of the political persuasion of the applicant. IDAF does not support violence or supply money which might be spent on arms. It is concerned that all political detainees should receive a fair trial, regardless of whether they have been charged on counts involving violence: under an unjust legislation, defendants who have supported liberation movements in whatever way may find themselves arrested for complicity in acts of violence or intended sabotage.

IDAF's field of action now covers English-speaking Southern Africa. It cooperates with a number of other non-governmental organisations, in particular with the Anti-Apartheid Movement, Amnesty International and the International University Exchange Fund. IDAF's recent publications have covered such topics as: South Africa's Bantustans, Education under Apartheid, Political Prisoners in Rhodesia, and Fact Papers on the Black Theatre in South Africa, the Windhoek Talks, and the security legislation currently enforced in Rhodesia.

IDAF provides funds directly to individual refugees. In this way it helps former political prisoners with rehabilitation grants, gives assistance in case of emergencies, and, on occasion, tides over refugees who have scholarships from other organisations. It also gives assistance to the liberation organisations for the welfare needs of their members abroad. IDAF has not in the past operated large-scale refugee programmes in Africa; but since the Soweto uprising in June 1976, its obligations in this field have been considerably increased and continue to grow. All refugee work is done within the terms of reference of the Fund.

Finance

IDAF's income for relief and defence costs is without strings and allocated strictly within the terms of reference of the Fund. About 25% of this £1 million budget is raised by affiliated committees and private donations. The remainder, which covers most of the overseas aid budget, comes from the United Nations Trust Fund and some 25 governments (mostly Western European, but with a small but significant number of Third World governments).

Joint Working Group for Refugees from Chile in Britain — see above, page 79.

Latin America Bureau
P O Box 134
London NW1 4JY
Tel: (01) 486 1730
Executive Secretary: Jan Karmali

Established in March 1977 with the help of voluntary development agencies and church organisations, the Latin America Bureau aims, through research and documentation, to raise public awareness of the causes of social injustice in Latin America, provide back-up for organisations and individuals in Central and South America, and in cooperation with Latin America support groups in this country, enlists the involvement of churches, trade unions and other groups with an active interest in Latin American affairs. There is particular reference to Central America and the Andean countries.

Liberation
313/5 Caledonian Road
London N1
Tel: (01) 607 0465
President: Lord Brockway
Chairman: Stan Newens, MP
Secretary: Tony Gilbert

Liberation, which adopted its present name in the late 1960s, was established in 1954 as the Movement for Colonial Freedom primarily to champion the cause of national independence for the colonies of Britain and other colonial powers. Its main constituent organisation was the Congress of Peoples Against Imperialism, founded in 1948; but it may be regarded as the heir of the pre-war League Against Imperialism of which Fenner Brockway was chairman, as long ago as the 1920s.

As a result of its efforts in the past, Liberation can lay claim to good relations with many Afro-Asian countries. It has since extended its activities to support for the liberation movements, especially in Southern Africa, and for initiatives to establish a New International Economic Order. While its association with the liberations struggles of the Third World have led to unpopularity in some circles (particularly on the question of the use of violence), Liberation claims that its reputation amongst the Afro-Asian countries gives it greater leverage for action than does the 'non-political' approach of the strictly human rights organisations (although of course this will depend on the nature of the regime in question).

The objectives promoted by Liberation are briefly: the abolition of imperialism and neo-colonialism and the right of all peoples to full political and economic independence; the principle of mutual and un-exploitative aid at all levels between countries; the abolition of all forms of discrimination amongst peoples and the application of the Universal Declaration of Human Rights.

It is within this context that Liberation views its actions on human rights questions, and as such this approach is straight-forwardly political. Freedom of expression, opinion and association are considered in relation to social and economic priorities – a political evaluation which might, for instance, preclude unqualified support for the release of certain political prisoners if these were held to be hindering the advancement of society's wider interests.

Liberation concentrates its attention on Third World issues, but includes in its brief the repercussions on British policy, whether in combatting racism at home, fighting the deportation of immigrant workers, or campaigning for a New International Economic Order (in conjunction with the World Development Movement and War on Want). It does not usually undertake formal work on Eastern Europe, although unofficially its sympathies lie with the position of the Labour Left on the question of the expression of dissident views.

Liberation was instrumental in setting up committees on South Africa, Vietnam and Chile, which in time became the Anti-Apartheid Movement, the British Campaign for Peace in Vietnam, and the Chile Solidarity Movement, and it continues to work closely with these. It has played an important part in promoting the active involvement of the British Labour Movement in these and other issues, such as the case of Desmond Trotter in Dominica (where capital punishment is still applicable under the ultimate sanction of the British legal system), or the issue of torture and ill-treatment of Iranian political prisoners. Liberation has supported TAPOL's work on Indonesia, and the work of some of the Latin American support groups. It extends informal assistance in individual cases which are brought to the attention of the office in London.

Structure

Liberation is a membership organisation based on the Labour Movement. It can call on 100 sponsoring MPs (and some members of the House of Lords), and was able to mobilise the entire National Executive Committee of the Labour Party on the Desmond Trotter case. Its 15 affiliated national unions (including the Musicians Union and ACTT), 30 member organisations and support groups[1] and 200 local labour parties, trades councils, union branches and cooperative organisations represent a formidable force for spreading information and campaigning. While conscious of the importance of public education, Liberation does not always have the financial resources to make full use of its information potential, since it depends entirely on affiliation and membership fees and donations.

Finance

Liberation is funded through its membership and affiliation fees, donations and the sale of literature. It operates on a shoestring budget of around £4,500 a year. It has no standing funds for campaign work, but consideration is given to funding particular campaigns from the General Fund.

Namibia Support Committee — 21-25 Tabernacle Street, London EC2A 4DE. Tel: (01) 588 4342 *Secretary:* Dave Simmonds

The group provides political and financial support for SWAPO (same address), and publicity and education on Namibia. Its main campaign is concerned with the raising of funds for medical aid, both for casualities in the fighting and for use by SWAPO field doctors amongst the rural population. Bishop Colin Winter runs a centre for Namibian exiles, Ya Toivo House, 20 Cephas Avenue, London E1.

---

[1] Including the Iraqi students, Kurdish students, General Union of Arab Students, Arab Ba'ath Socialist Party (UK), Bangladesh National Action Committee, Union of Turkish Progressives, Union of Cypriots in Britain, MAPAM Socialist Zionist Party, Mauritius United Society, TAPOL, Committee for Puerto Rican Independence, Peoples' Progressive Party of Guyana (UK), and Caribbean Labour Solidarity.

Oxford Committee for Human Rights in South Asia — c/o 30 Marlborough Road, Oxford *Chairman:* Chris Morris *Secretary:* Simon Collings

The group undertakes lobbying, protest action and produces occasional publications on human rights issues in South Asia. It is currently campaigning for the release of all political prisoners in Bangladesh, and against the sale of British equipment to the Bangladesh police.

Parliamentary Committee for Aid to Indochinese Refugees — c/o Philip Goodhart MP, House of Commons, Westminster, London SW1A 0AA

This all-party Committee seeks to call attention to the plight of Cambodian, Laotian and Vietnamese refugees from the Communist regimes in Indochina, and attempts to increase the amount of assistance given to them by voluntary and Governmental agencies.

TAPOL (British Campaign for the Release of Indonesian Political Prisoners) — 103 Tilehurst Road, Wandsworth Common, London SW18. Tel: (01) 373 8442/874 9684 *Chairman:* Roger Hibbitt

TAPOL conducts campaign work and publicity on political prisoners in Indonesia and on human rights violations perpetrated by occupying Indonesian troops in East Timor; and lobbies on British aid to Indonesia (the largest overseas aid recipient outside the Commonwealth). TAPOL-USA (PO Box 609, Montclair, N.J. 07042) is also active and groups are in preparation in other countries. It is a COBRA (above) member.

Task Force for Cooperative Action on Southern Africa — c/o Rev John Hastings, Methodist Division of Social Responsibility, Central Buildings, Matthew Parker Street, London SW1H 9NH. Tel: (01) 930 2638

This is an informal network of over 40 organisations working on Southern Africa (and the result of a Human Rights Network initiative). The organisations involved have pooled their resources for publicity, lobbying, campaign work.

Uganda Freedom Committee — 90 Fawe Park Road, London SW15 2EA

The committee acts as a lobby for official British policy against General Amin (including the severance of trade links), and for more responsible press coverage of the repression in Uganda. Its membership is drawn from sympathetic individuals, organisations and Ugandan exiles.

United Kingdom

Uruguay Human Rights Committee – 1 Cambridge Terrace, London NW1 4JL

Publicity and lobbying on the current situation in Uruguay, particularly the plight of individuals arrested or persecuted by government authorities and those seeking visas from Britain is the committee's work. It gives informal assistance (not financial) to Uruguayan exiles in the United Kingdom. See especially *Uruguayan Refugees*, January 1977.

II Professional Organisations

Chapter 6

ACADEMICS

The success of a scholar's work depends as much on the freedom of others to study and research as it does on his own.

Scholarly Freedom and Human Rights, 1977

Academic communities are prime targets for repressive regimes. Their function is essentially critical, and this is something few insecure regimes can tolerate for long. Intolerance is compounded by fear of intellectuals and their power to influence – or 'corrupt' – the young. It is an odd recognition of the power of ideas that their exponents are often so ruthlessly persecuted, and ironic that this recognition is accorded most promptly and forcefully by those who affect to despise them.

Large-scale purges of university ranks, such as took place in Chile and Czechoslovakia, attracted wide publicity and a positive response, particularly in the provision of academic posts, amongst university staff in Britain and the other Western countries. Other major crises – Uruguay and Argentina are the latest – have not, to date, generated the same degree of action. Yet in both these countries, it is fair to say that many areas of academic life have been mutilated.

This is not to say that concerted action on particular cases has not been taken. In many instances, the speed and generosity of the response has been outstanding. But, as in many other areas of human rights action, the effectiveness of such measures is more often than not the work of a few strategically-placed individuals capable of mobilising economic and moral support at short notice.

More than any other professional category or institution, the academic community transcends national boundaries. Each scholarly discipline and research specialisation conducts its affairs, plans its research programmes, publishes findings and meets to exchange notes within a wide multinational context defined only by a common enthusiasm for the advancement of their work. A special sort of freemasonry thus develops within each specialisation, often sustained by rivalry but conscious of the interdependence of its international members for its progress, and ultimately its validity.

Any encroachment on this confraternity of interest, whether in the form of infringements on freedom of movement and ideas or of official interference with teachers and research projects, is immediately felt by the community as a whole, since the entire scholarly enterprise may be jeopardised by external pressures. If these pressures take the form of direct sanctions against the scholar for political or other related reasons – if, for example, he is prevented from working or publishing or meeting his colleagues — morale will also suffer. But it takes an extra push for professional colleagues to come together and express their common concern as a body. Until now, the machinery for such joint actions and expressions of solidarity has not existed, or if it has existed, has not been used. The signs are that academic specialists have become less inhibited about taking a public stand on humanitarian issues affecting their profession, although there is still a considerable body of opinion which views such actions as political, and thus professionally taboo (it will always be argued in reply that non-intervention is equally political — by default).

The remarkable actions of the mathematicians on behalf of their imprisoned colleague Leonid Plyushch (and latterly for the Uruguayan Academician Luis Massera) testifies to the effectiveness and appropriateness of such actions: precisely because they are professional colleagues, the action is non-political, and seen as such: their motivation draws not only on humanitarian concern, but on an awareness of the indivisibility of their common work. And however much political interest should or should not play a part in these actions, the non-political concern of professional colleagues stands a better chance of success with the authorities.

Mention should be made here of the privileged position of the Northern hemisphere (East as well as West) in relation to the academic communities of South America, Africa, Asia and to some extent, Australasia. While there exists a well-developed Atlantic circuit for visiting academics, this tends to neglect colleagues from the Southern hemisphere, often for economic as much as academic reasons. Greater accessbility of the latter to the former could be of crucial importance when an invitation to an overseas lecture-tour, visiting fellowship or learned conference might serve to extricate a lecturer or research scientist from a dangerous situation.

As in every other area, the degree of initiative and the effectiveness of human rights interventions are largely dependent on the commitment of a few hard-working individuals. By reason of the decentralised nature of the academic community, its consequent heavy dependence on personal contact and recommendation, and perhaps because of the lack of any established coordinating body for academic initiatives,[1] academic action on behalf of persecuted colleagues overseas has usually been of an *ad hoc* nature, no less effective for being carried out quietly behind the scenes. Indeed, there is a strong tradition of what might be termed humanitarian self-help amongst academics, which relies on the international grapevine and the resources on which university departments can draw. This system is a tried and tested one, and has proved especially useful in the reception and settlement of academic exiles.

However, the growth of public concern about the number of seemingly intractable cases of imprisoned and persecuted scholars has placed greater

---

[1]   Cf. **Academics for Chile**, pp. 74-6.

demands on the academic community to make some form of public response. These demands have found the academic community at odds with itself as to whether to abandon is habitual low profile and commit itself to statements, actions and interventions which may well be interpreted as being of a political nature.

Association of University Teachers
United House
1 Pembridge Road
London W11
Tel: (01) 221 4370
General Secretary: L.J. Sapper

Following a lengthy debate on Academic Freedom at its 1975 Council Meeting, the AUT, which is the main body representing university teaching staff in the UK, has passed a number of resolutions expressing its concern about the situation of academics at risk, under pressure or in some way restricted in their work. Recent examples have included the position of teaching staff in Uganda, and the official vetting of academic candidates for their political sympathies in West Germany. The AUT occasionally intervenes in particular cases, with letters to embassies and governments.

Early in 1977, the AUT Executive set up an *Overseas Academic Trust Fund*, which provides contingency grants of around £50 for 'the relief in the UK of refugees in necessitous circumstances and being academic or related staff previously employed by universities or equivalent institutions in countries other than the UK and their immediate dependents'. While these awards apply largely to British academics in difficulties overseas, they are not in fact solely applicable to British nationals. Assistance with assessing overseas cases is given by a member of WUS/UK's Executive Board.

Policy resolutions passed by the AUT Council have included defence of the right of university staffs to adhere freely to any religious, political or philosophical views, and their right to publish freely, subject only to academic criteria imposed by editors. AUT's overall policy on academic freedom and its relation to the purposes of Higher Education is expressed in a document adopted by Council in May 1975.

United Kingdom

British Sociological Association
13 Endsleigh Street
London WC1H 0DJ
Tel: (01) 387 3627
President: Keith Kelsall
Hon General Secretary: Alan Watson

The British Sociological Association has taken up with the appropriate embassy or government cases involving sociologists overseas who have been imprisoned or persecuted for their political beliefs or professional activities. Cases are referred to them by academics, or through the World University Service. The BSA has cooperated in the Academics for Chile programme (a high proportion of Chilean refugees being social scientists), urging members to look out for vacant posts in sociology and related subjects, and to encourage appointments boards to view Chilean applications with sympathy in the light of their difficult situation.

Council for Academic Freedom and Democracy
C/o National Council for Civil Liberties
186 Kings Cross Road
London WC1X 9DE
Tel: (01) 278 4575
Cable: Civlib London WC1X 9DE
Honorary Secretary: Professor John Griffith

The Council for Academic Freedom and Democracy, an offshoot of the NCCL, is primarily concerned with issues of academic freedom in the United Kingdom. It is also concerned to campaign for the more democratic operation and structure of institutions of higher education. In addition to contributing to the debate on academic freedom, it is involved with case-work on behalf of university teachers and staff who may be subject to dicrimination or denial of educational rights. A small proportion of these cases concern British nationals teaching overseas.

International Association of University Professors and Lecturers
Rutland Hall, University Park
Nottingham N97 2Q2
Tel: (0602) 56101
Hon Treasurer: Donald Varley
Secretary: Professor A. Hacquaert, Rozier 6, Ghent, Belgium

The IAUPL is a small international confederation of 25 affiliate national unions with a wide range of international contacts. Its constitution permits the possibility of mutual support on request from affiliates if cases are brought to its attention. To be of direct concern to the IAUPL, these cases would have to involve infringements of the rights of university teachers and professors in the pursuit of their professional objectives. No standing funds are available, but the Association may make representations through affiliates or related professional associations. It does not itself directly intervene with governments or inter-governmental organisations on particular cases (although it may give advice on such contacts to member organisations), but it does take up questions of principle with them. Its forthcoming Central Council meeting has been asked to examine the implication for universities of the Helsinki agreements.

National Association of Teachers in Further and Higher Education
Hamilton House
Mabledon Place
London WC1H 9BH
Tel: (01) 387 6806
General Secretary: Stan Broadbridge

NATFHE has taken a number of initiatives in connection with the protection of teachers. It has informed its branches about procedures for adopting Chilean prisoners and refugees, has contacted a number of international organisations drawing attention to the *Berufsverbot* legislation affecting teachers in West Germany, and is currently lodging a protest with the Argentinian government about the imprisonment of academics. It is affiliated to the Anti-Apartheid Movement, and may shortly be soliciting materials and funds from its membership for South African refugees.

National Union of Teachers
Hamilton House
Mabledon Place
London WC1H 9BD
Tel: (01) 387 2442; 387 9191/3
Cables: Curriculum London WC1H 9BD
General Secretary: Fred Jarvis
Organising Secretary: N.L. Jones

The NUT through its local teachers associations, and through its affiliations to the TUC, Amnesty International and the international teachers organisations, occasionally learns of cases where human rights violations directly involve teachers or educational issues. In these cases, its Executive is empowered to decide on the appropriate action to take.

Recent instances have included: a request for information from the Soviet Embassy in London about a teacher imprisoned in the Soviet Union; a representation to the Chilean Embassy about the large-scale detention of teachers; a request to the World Confederation of Organisations of the Teaching Profession to investigate the disappearance of a Dominican student; and public protest about the events in Soweto.

The NUT has no standing funds, but may circulate its local associations with details on specific cases for voluntary contributions.

Society for the Protection of Science and Learning
3 Buckland Crescent
London NW3 5DH
Tel: (01) 722 2095
Chairman: Lord Ashby
Secretary: Miss Esther Simpson, OBE

The Society for the Protection of Science and Learning (SPSL) has over 40 years' experience in placing academic refugees at universities in Britain and the United States. Its main function is to arrange placements at colleges and universities. It disposes of a small fund for interim resettlement grants, but these are largely dependent on securing a permanent position for the applicant at a university.

The Society has its origins in the reception of academic refugees from pre-war Nazi Germany, many of whom have now attained positions of eminence in the academic world. It is proud of its record of 'backing winners' when awarding research grants, and retains its strict criteria of academic excellence in assisting refugee scholars, maintaining that this is a realistic approach in the refugees' own best interest; to raise the expectations of those less well placed to find permanent posts will, they claim, only postpone eventual disappointment. These will instead be advised on possibilities in teaching, industry and the professions generally, and on occasion provided with contacts which may lead to employment. Many of these have also proved remarkably successful in their chosen careers.

Unlike WUS, the only other pre-war refugee organisation to have survived to the present day, the Society has neither the academic resources nor the funds to expand its catchment area beyond the university circles with which it deals. Indeed, but for the Hungarian crisis in 1956, the drop in refugee work might have led it to close down altogether. Subsequent emergencies — Czechoslovakia and Chile in particular — have been handled almost exclusively by WUS, who have assimilated junior academic refugees into their own post-graduate scholarship placement programme. The SPSL cooperated closely with WUS, particularly where the junior university teachers were concerned. In addition to the Chileans mentioned above, the Society is currently assisting exiled Argentinians.

Procedures

The Society has been a success in spite of its small permanent staff and relatively low funds. This is largely due to the emphasis placed on the personal contact, professional encouragement and moral support afforded by the academic environment.

Applicants are asked to supply the names of referees who are expected to act to some extent as their sponsors. These are approached by the Society, on the understanding that any facilities extended to the applicant should be accompanied by a hospitable reception and some assurance of their belief that the relevant university department will be of help to the recipient in finding eventual employment in the United Kingdom.

Once there appears to be a strong possibility of obtaining a permanent position through the Society's university contacts, the Allocation Committee will decided on the possibilities for interim funding of the applicant.

Finance

A small standing fund is available for interim subsistence grants, but these are limited and largely dependent on the applicant being found a more permanent post through the Society's academic network of informal contacts. Interim arrangements may also be made through the provision of lecture tours, particularly on the American lecture circuit (which frequently results in permanent posts being secured). These, like the scholarship provisions in this country, are set up informally through university and college contacts, and funded (or fees waived) by the university in question. Such arrangements are designed to avoid competition for existing places with non-refugee candidates, which, it is felt, might provoke resentment and bad feeling.

United Kingdom

The standing fund results from the original appeal made in 1933 which, by judicious investment and supplementary donations, has been maintained to the present day. The donations and trust funds on which this fund have relied are now drying up, and no future appeals are planned to sustain the fund, unless a further emergency involving considerable numbers of academics prompts a new appeal.

Chapter 7

STUDENTS

Twenty-two Sudanese students studying in the UK on Sudanese government scholarships, most of them at post-graduate level, have had their scholarships abruptly terminated by their Embassy and have been requested to return to the Sudan immediately. The reason for this is political and the students would be gravely at risk if they did return.

UKCOSA News, Summer/Autumn 1976

Mrs Judith Hart, Minister for Overseas Development, is to be asked to intervene to finance 40 Ugandan students stranded in Britain on degree courses because of the murder or disappearance of their relatives under the Amin regime . . . A meeting of representatives from World University Service, the National Union of Students, the Uganda Freedom Committee, and the Africa Educational Trust decided yesterday to ask Mrs Hart to intervene before the next university term.

Guardian, 11 August 1977

Because of their traditions of political radicalism and intransigence in the face of disapproving authority, students throughout the world have proved a more ready target for persecution, imprisonment and exile than most other sectors of society. The recent example of the Thai students is a case in point: over 3,000 students were reported arrested following the disturbances which accompanied the military seizure of power in 1976, and several hundred students held in detention without trial or transferred to 're-education centres'.

Unlike many other social categories, however, students tend to be mobile, and many choose to escape persecution by fleeing to other countries, either as refugees, or more frequently, as *bona fide* students. Many such students who are *de facto* refugees will only reveal their political reasons for leaving when the possibility arises that they may be obliged to return home on completion of their course of study or on the imminent expiry or non-renewal of their entry permits in their chosen country of refuge. Others on scholarships provided by their home governments (and this is sometimes used by governments as a convenient way of disposing of troublesome students) may find these cut off due to events at home or because of political activities undertaken while abroad.[1] They too may then choose to appeal on political or compassionate grounds for an exten-

---

[1] Private students in a similar position may find foreign exchange cut off or their parents no longer in a position to send money because of political changes.

sion of their stay in the receiving country.

Under British Immigration Regulations, students may enter the United Kingdom on a 12-month renewable permit if they can furnish evidence that they are *bona fide* students, i.e. have been accepted for a full-time course of study at a university or college in this country, and that they are able to meet the full cost of their subsistence for the duration of their stay; they are expected to return home on completion of their studies.

A number of factors have contributed to the increased numbers of *de facto* student refugees who 'surface' during their stay here. The increased fees for overseas students have in many cases placed the course of study which they were pursuing beyond their financial reach. They can then no longer support themselves for the duration of their stay, even with part-time work which *bona fide* students are allowed to undertake under the terms of the Immigration Regulations. It has become increasingly difficult for students to obtain part-time work (a) because of lack of jobs and (b) because Department of Employment approval may be withheld even when an employer is willing to take a student on. (The number of potential student refugees who have been deterred from coming to Britain for these reasons may never be computed.)

Those who are unable to support themselves adequately now run the risk of deportation without appeal if they fail to apply for renewal of their permission to stay before it expires (see section on Refugees); and they stand a low chance of converting their student status to work-permit status since one of the conditions of entry as a student is their eventual return; attempts to alter their status tend to be viewed with suspicion by immigration officials as a possible back-door for immigration. If they put forward political reasons for wishing to stay, these too may be greeted with distrust: why, it will be asked, did they not make this claim on arrival?

The private educational trusts which have traditionally provided emergency help for students in financial straits can no longer be counted on. They are inundated with applications for grants from students of all kinds, at a time when their often limited resources are being depleted by the effects of inflation. Most are fully committed, none provide loans any more. We have accordingly refrained from listing educational trusts and grant-making agencies, great and small. These may be found in *Educational Charities* (35p, NUS, 3 Endsleigh Street, London WC1H 0DU). In addition, a section on Education is included in the *Directory of Grant-Making Charitable Trusts*, published by the Charities Aid Foundation, and available for consultation in most local reference libraries; also a comprehensive register of educational trusts for England and Wales is maintained by the DES (Legal Branch), Elizabeth House, London SE1.

The Educational Grants Advisory Service, 26 Bedford Square, London WC1B 3HU, provides liaison and coordination for students seeking educational grants from charitable trusts and other organisations, on an individual basis. Many such grant-making trusts and organisations are, however, tightly circumscribed in their allocations, and the average grant thus obtained is in the region of £75.

Many scholarship foundations and trusts are obliged, by reason of their charitable status and their professional standing, to base their allocation priorities on criteria of academic merit alone; some are in addition afraid of jeopardising their relations with educational bodies by taking other considerations into account. Therefore, the student advisory bodies outlined above provide an invaluable service in the form of sympathetic advice to students in political as well as financial difficulties, although it is difficult when it comes to reconciling the students humanitarian demands with their academic needs. The advisory bodies steer threatened students in the right direction, apply for funds on their behalf, or avert disappointment by advising them on alternative courses of action.

Churches Commission on Overseas Students
60 Westbourne Grove
London W2 5FG
Tel: (01) 229 9268/9
Executive Secretary: Ms Jill Hutchinson
Chairman: Rev Douglas A. Brown

The CCOS was set up at the initiative of the British Council of Churches in October 1975, in response to a number of issues concerning overseas students, including the fees increase and the plight of Rhodesian students in Britain. Its *raison d'être* is to increase awareness of the academic, material, social and spiritual needs and potential of overseas students at national and local level. The Commission represents eighteen denominations, missionary societies and other Christian organisations. Since September 1976, it has had a permanent staff, with a part-time Executive Secretary (also employed by UKOSA and located at their offices) and a £6,000 budget (roughly half of which comes from the Overseas Student Trust, and half from five of its member churches).

CCOS supports the churches in their existing work among overseas students through local churches, international hostels, specially appointed chaplains or other fieldworkers and chaplains in colleges, polytechnics, universities and teaching hospitals. It aims to keep them informed of current developments on overseas student issues, to liaise between the churches and secular organisations involved in this field and to further a common approach amongst the churches. Its April 1976 Conference of fieldworkers, after examining the question of increased tuition fees, urged members of churches to make representations to the relevant government ministries.

United Kingdom

National Union of Students
3 Endsleigh Street
London WC1H 0DU
Tel: (01) 387 1277
International Student Officer (1977-8): J.B. Provost
Scottish Office: 12 Dublin Street. Edinburgh EH1 3PP
Tel: (031) 556 6598

Some ten or so cases concerning overseas students are referred to NUS each week. In the light of the British government's cut-backs in expenditure, tuition fees for overseas students have increased steeply, often prohibitively. Consequently, financial and immigration difficulties for overseas students have intensified. Students who are *de facto* refugees are also affected in other ways — some may have their grants from home cut off because of political events (for example, the Sudanese), others may be reluctant to return home in the light of their political activities while abroad (Ethiopians), yet others may fear the activities of intelligence agents from their country on campus (Iranians).

NUS attempts to provide advice on these problems, and in many instances refers the students to other organisations which give help. On immigration questions, NUS works closely with the Joint Council for the Welfare of Immigrants (JCWI), which will represent students on immigration matters. The NUS itself has no standing funds available for emergency use, but may appeal to voluntary organisations or to government departments for help in such cases.

In view of the complexity of the immigration legislation governing the entry and stay of overseas students in the UK, the NUS has issued detailed proposals to college authorities and student unions throughout the country. These include reminders to overseas students to renew their student visas before they expire. For those students who are refused renewal of visas, NUS makes further representations on their behalf or refers them to JCWI. In addition, NUS urges student unions to press for the following:

— restoration of the right of appeal for those students who have applied for their visas to be renewed or extended after the expiry date and who face deportation
— the cessation of the Home Office tendency to assume that a student seeking extension of his or her visa has no incentive to return home on completion of studies
— pressing the Home Office to allow visitors to this country to change their status to that of student (the Home Office as a rule refuses to grant student visas to visitors who have secured a place at a recognised course of study in this country).

As the representative of the student movement in the UK, NUS has actively campaigned against the current increase in tuition fees. A particular feature of this campaign has been the discriminatory level of fees charged to overseas students. *De facto* refugee students who are not funded by any agency and who are unable to pay the increase in fees are also affected, and of course may then face immigration difficulties.

Another feature of the NUS campaign on overseas students has been to oppose the government's proposals to institute a quota system for the overseas student intake into the UK.

The NUS continues to advise student unions in colleges and universities to give special consideration to the problems of groups of students, such as Iranians, Zimbabweans and South Africans, whose security in this country may be placed in jeopardy by the current measures. NUS liaises with the overseas students unions in this country which represent such groups of students.

For information on possible sources of funding available to postgraduate students, see NUS publication *Educational Charities* (NUS, price 35p). For details on immigration, see *Students and Immigration Controls* (NUS, 2/77).

Student Christian Movement
Wick Court
Wick, Bristol
Tel: (027) 582 3377
Student President: B. O'Neill
Publications: 168 Rathgar Road, Rathmines, Dublin, Ireland

Although SCM has no funds available for human rights work, through its magazine *Movement*, which goes out to SCM campus groups throughout the UK, and through occasional conferences, SCM gives occasional publicity to human rights cases and issues. Past examples have included the campaign to free Leonid Plyushch, and a detailed pamphlet on *Repression and Christian Resistance in South Korea* (1975), using material from the WCC, AI, missionary organisations and churchmen and church workers in South Korea.

SCM is an affiliate of the World Student Christian Federation (37 quai Wilson, 1201 Geneva), which coordinates the activities of its largely autonomous national affiliates.

United Kingdom Council for Overseas Student Affairs
60 Westbourne Grove
London W2 5FG
Tel: (01) 229 9268
Chairman: Lord Gladwyn
Executive Secretary: William Beale
Student Counsellor: Rosamund Henriques

UKCOSA was set up following the increase in overseas students' fees in 1968. Its membership includes some 100 local and national organisations concerned with student welfare, and it also has the support of a large number of affiliated educational institutions throughout the United Kingdom, for whom it provides information, representation and the impetus for new initiatives on behalf of overseas students. UKCOSA's £37,000 annual budget (1976) is drawn from affiliate subscriptions, trust funds and donations, and various grants from the Dulverton Trust, the Gulbenkian Foundation, and the British Council. The administrative costs are supported by the Overseas Student Trust and the Fund for International Student Cooperation. It does not dispense funds to individual students, but may assist in obtaining money for students in need from a number of trusts and foundations by means of a referral service.

UKCOSA's work is carried out at three levels: lobbying and campaign work at national level; initiatives amongst its affiliated educational establishments; and individual student counselling.

UKCOSA applies pressure on overseas student issues through a well-organised lobby comprising its member organisations (including professional and academic bodies, teaching unions and student bodies), affiliated institutions and a number of sympathetic MPs and peers. It takes care to present the case for overseas students within the context of the education debate as a whole, so as not to appear to be championing a distinct and isolated interest. It believes in the efficacy of close cooperation with government departments in obtaining benefits for foreign students, and hopes to involve a number of government departments in these decisions, in particular the Department of Education and Science, the Foreign Office, the Home Office, the Department of Health and Social Security and the Ministry of Overseas Development.

UKCOSA has negotiated 'package deals' with government departments on behalf of particular groups of students who are *de facto* refugees. Biafrans, Bangladeshis, Cypriots and Ugandan Asians have all been helped in this way through UKCOSA, in some cases by special arrangements with the Supplementary Benefits Commission. In this work, it cooperates closely with other organisations, such as Africa Educational Trust, International University Exchange Fund, and World University Service.

The Rhodesian Students Working Party[1] has kept a watching brief on the situation of Zimbabwean students who are in the UK trying to continue their education. Dialogue with the Ministry of Overseas Development and continuing pressure has resulted in a significant expansion of the Ministry's normal programme. The Working Party also successfully negotiated a special additional programme of 100 new awards in the 1977-8 academic year.

UKCOSA has joined with UKIAS, JCWI and NUS in pressing for official guidelines for students on the Immigration Act, and for a more comprehensive official implementation of the Immigration Regulations where students (including refugee students) are concerned. However, the increases in tuition fees, against which UKCOSA is still fighting nine years on,[2] are likely to be a far stronger deterrent on overseas students seeking to continue their studies.

Amongst its affiliate colleges and training establishments, UKCOSA seeks to promote a greater sense of responsibility for the reception and welfare of foreign students; it tries to ensure that prospective students are fully informed of potential difficulties of life in Britain both before they come, and through introductory courses on arrival. UKCOSA has prepared a series of leaflets in conjunction with this campaign, with advice on practical details, such as immigration regulations.

UKCOSA also provides an individual counselling service for overseas students, usually referred to the Secretariat by welfare staff in affiliated institutions. About 100-150 students seek advice each month, though these figures may increase during crises affecting particular groups of students, such as the Cypriot students during the Cyprus emergency. Many of the problems facing overseas students concern immigration difficulties — for example, students who are refused extension of stay or who are threatened with deportation for contravention of the immigration regulations. A proportion of these are 'hidden' refugees: UKCOSA will normally refer their cases to UKIAS or to JCWI for advice — it is not qualified to steer them through the complex legal procedures involved. The student counsellor may help with channeling emergency applications for funds to a limited number of private trusts, but UKCOSA does not

---

[1] *The Rhodesian Students Working Party* comprises representatives of the British Council, Africa Educational Trust, IUEF, Christian Aid, Royal African Society, Zimbabwe Students Union, NUS, Community and Race Relations Unit of the British Council of Churches, Campaign for the Relief of Zimbabwean Political Prisoners, Commonwealth Fund for Technical Cooperation, Commonwealth Secretariat, National Union of Zimbabwean Students, Friends International Centre, Rhodesian Student Trust, WUS, African National Council, ZAPU, SCOR, Overseas Students Trust, Budirio Trust, Patriotic Front ZANU, African National Council ZANU, British Council of Churches, and JCWI.

[2] See *Overseas Students — the case against higher tuition fees*, UKCOSA, 1976, and *Overseas Students — the reaction to higher fees 1977-78*, UKCOSA, 1977.

dispose of funds of its own for such purposes.

UKCOSA's 109 member organisations comprise specialist societies, church and other religious groups, professional institutes and associations, teachers' and students' unions, welfare councils and reception centres, international exchange and award schemes, and some nine educational trusts. Amongst its student union members are representative bodies for Ghanaian, Ugandan, Nigerian, Malawi, Israeli, Iranian and Zimbabwean students. Details of these organisations and a listing of the further 200 affiliated university, polytechnic, college and local bodies, are to be found in UKCOSA's Annual Report.

World Union of Jewish Students – 247 Gray's Inn Road, London WC1X 8QL *Secretary:* Irving Wallace

An umbrella organisation for 34 national unions, the WUJS cooperates with non-Jewish student organisations on educational and political matters, including human rights issues.

Chapter 8

SCIENTISTS

Scientists tend to be very divided over how to react to political pressure on scientists in other countries. Some feel they have no right to meddle in the internal affairs of foreign states. Some feel that if there is to be protest it is better conveyed privately than publicly. Some argue with great conviction against pushing protest to the point where contacts with other countries are broken, or international bodies split. Some withhold judgement on the grounds that there is no way of determining objectively the point at which political policies should be regarded as intolerable, so that scientists should stick to science and leave politics to the politicians.[1]

Because of their frequent contacts with fellow scientists overseas, and particularly in Eastern Europe and the Soviet Union, the scientific community is perhaps more keenly aware than most of the dilemma between 'dialogue' and 'protest' on human rights issues and individual cases. These two approaches are not, however, as mutually exclusive as they are sometimes made to appear; pressure, whether public or private, on individual cases does not necessarily constitute a threat to continuity of contacts and flow of information if it is handled with care, since the need to sustain this flow is ultimately a more pressing concern for both sides. There is little evidence to indicate that moves by scientists in the West on behalf of professional colleagues elsewhere has seriously inhibited scientific exchange in the long term.

At the level of the scientific academies and professional bodies, this dilemma is more keenly felt. As they are directly involved in securing cooperation with fellow-specialists at an institutional level, they are more liable to feel that overt corporate action on their part may jeopardise these good relations and with them any hope of bringing influence to bear on the behaviour of the scientific establishment in other countries. However, where such 'good offices' have manifestly failed to obtain results, such an approach is always open to criticism from proponents of a more forceful public stand on crucial cases and issues.

By way of comparison, the American scientific community has become, over the past few years, far more outspoken than its British counterpart. (This does not necessarily mean, of course, that it has achieved any more concrete results.)

However, a recent booklet, *Scholarly Freedom and Human Rights* (Barry Rose Ltd, 1977), may prove a first step in increasing and coordinat-

---

[1]   *The Times*, 18 February 1977.

ing the human rights work of the scientific community in Britain. Published on the initiative of the Council for Science and Society, it attempts to spell out the responsibilities of the scientific community towards those of its members who are deprived of basic rights, including the free pursuit of their researches and dissemination of their findings to colleagues in other countries. The report identifies the right of protest as one key area of responsibility, rejecting an overscrupulous attitude of non-involvement. Drawing on the corpus of international human rights instruments, it recommends that

— scientists should keep a watching brief on freedom of enquiry, research and communication and use all legitimate means to defend it;
— a clearing-house should be set up to collect and evaluate information about the infringement and suppression of those rights;
— scientists should acquaint themselves with international human rights legislation and publicly pledge their support for provisions relating to academic freedom.

The report thus seeks to instil a more active sense of corporate responsibility into the scientific community. It states that 'where human rights are wrongfully denied by or in one state, it is in our view not only the right but the duty of those living in states which do not deny freedom of expression to protest . . .' While some might quibble at the implicit distinction between 'free' and 'unfree' states, the appeal to existing sentiments of professional solidarity is aimed to reinforce and coalesce attitudes of mutual support which many individual scientists have felt, but which up until now they have not been able to express through established procedures or machinery.

British Scientists' Committee for the Defence of Sergei Kovalyov
87 Meadway
Barnet
Herts EN5 5JZ
Tel: (01) 440 1681
Secretary: Daniel Servini

The *ad hoc* committee provides one example of the sort of small-scale initiative which may result from appeals on individual cases. Sergei Kovalyov is a distinguished biologist who was sentenced in 1975 to seven years' hard labour and three years' internal exile for the circulation of allegedly false statements about the Soviet state — charges resulting from his involvement in human rights activities in Moscow and in the publication of the clandestine *Chronicle of Current Events*.

The committee was set up on the initiative of British Amnesty. It resulted from a plea by the wife of Academician Sakharov, and a complaint from another prominent human rights spokesman, Valanetin Turchin, that the international scientific community had betrayed Kovalyov by not speaking out sooner on his behalf. The committee's founders approached individual scientists throughout Britain for support, by writing letters and articles, and organising a petition. They encountered mixed reactions: only half of those contacted replied and their private expressions of sympathy did not always extend to open public commitment. Prominent patrons were found, and contact established with sympathetic publications and the major American scientific associations.

The scientists' committee is in close contact with British Amnesty and has drawn up its own statutes within the guidelines of Amnesty's work, thereby ensuring access to AI's information on the case, as well as its own credentials for impartiality.

United Kingdom

Council for Science and Society
3/4 St Andrews Hill
London EC4 5BY
Tel: (01) 236 0032
Chairman: Professor John Ziman, FRS
Vice-Chairman: Paul Sieghart
Acting Secretary: John Hillier

The CSS was set up in 1973, with the aim of stimulating public debate about the effects of new developments in science and technology on society, and the scientists' resultant responsibilities. It aims to discuss these eventualities before, rather than after, they occur, and to this end brings together scientific specialists with lawyers, philosophers and related experts in a series of conferences, seminars and working groups.

One result of this initiative was the publication in 1977 of a booklet *Scholarly Freedom and Human Rights* (see introduction), produced in conjunction with the British Institute for Human Rights (q.v.). The Council is currently evaluating the response to this publication amongst the scientific community.

The primary aim of this booklet was to bring to the attention of the scientific community the ways in which they could help their persecuted or imprisoned colleagues within the provisions of international human rights law. Recognising that such activities 'are unevenly distributed among the various cases that arise, and are seldom coordinated' and that 'there is not even a reliable clearing-house for information about problems, actions taken, and results',[1] the report hopes to serve as a stimulus to concerted action within the scientific community, by drawing attention to the possibilities for action, information and coordination.

Medical and Scientific Committee for Soviet Jewry
2 Frognal Rise
London NW3
Tel: (01) 794 3324
Coordinator: Mrs Joan Dale
Chairman: Dr Gary Low-Beer

The Medical and Scientific Committee for Soviet Jewry is specifically

---

[1] This is open to challenge in the light of Amnesty International's extensive files on individual prisoners, though it certainly holds true for the scientific community as such, and for cases of harassment and persecution which do not involve imprisonment.

concerned with the rights of Jewish scientists, technicians and medical personnel refused permission to leave the Soviet Union. Many of these have been penalised following their request to emigrate; sanctions include: banning of published work and elimination of all mention of their work from learned journals, loss of research posts and even subsequent charges of 'parasitism' for having no job.

The Committee, in company with its counterparts in the US and Western Europe, has built up an active and vocal lobby in Parliament and amongst the scientific and medical communities in support of the 'refuseniks'. They maintain contact by letters, by personal visits, and by exchange of specialist materials, and they keep up a constant pressure in the press, in Parliament and through public meetings and actions on their behalf. The American, British, Dutch, Swedish and French committees pool their information through an International Coordinator based in Paris (Jacques Shoshan, Bibliothèque Juive Contemporaine, 23 rue de Cléry, 75002 Paris).

The British Committee has about 400 supporters in the United Kingdom, over half of them active campaigners. Groups of academics in nine university towns maintain contact with some 200 Soviet scientists and doctors, and a further 400 engineers. When individual adoptees run into particular difficulties, the Committee as a whole can initiate publicity and protest action. In a few outstanding cases, it can bring full pressure to bear in a nationwide campaign; the campaign for the release of Dr Shtern, carried out at an international level, is considered the most successful recent example.

The Committee has informal links with the National Council for Soviet Jewry, and cooperates with the '35s' group of the British Women's Campaign for Soviet Jewry. Apart from its academic contacts, it does not work closely with professional bodies or human rights groups, perhaps because its field of concern is so specialised. Finance is through donations alone.

The Committee has built up a strong Parliamentary lobby in both Lords and Commons, through extensive personal contacts established over the years, and through grass-roots pressure on local MPs. A House of Lords Committee under Baroness Seear has been formed to sponsor a learned conference on the 60th birthday of Professor Levich, the only Soviet Academician to have applied for (and been refused) permission to emigrate.[1]

The Committee has found the scientific community responsive to their appeals for support, the more so as eminent scientists have added their support. In their relations with the press, Committee members have learned from experience the key importance of establishing their

---

[1] The Conference, to which 300 Russian scientists were invited (though none have accepted), is sponsored by 19 Nobel Laureates and several national academics, including the American National Academy of Sciences.

respectability in attracting high-level support. The publication of a petition from prominent doctors or scientists, or an article in *The Times* may be the deciding factor in bringing home their case. This approach has its drawbacks: the Committee has not been able to attract much support amongst youth and student bodies, who identify it too readily with anti-Soviet motivation – an interpretation which the Committee rejects, maintaining that its commitment is to universal principles of freedom of movement and non-discrimination on political or religious grounds.

'Nature' Magazine
C/o Macmillan Journals Ltd
Little Essex Street
London WC2E 3LF
Tel: (01) 836 6633
Editor: Dr David Davies

Nature, a weekly magazine with wide circulation within the scientific community, has proved particularly vigilant in its coverage of the rights of scientists. One recent example was the publication of a letter from Italian scientists in support of some 550 Argentinian colleagues sacked from their jobs ('released from duty' in the official jargon) without explanation, some after 20 years' specialisation. *Nature*'s editorial on the subject backed up the letter's plea for continued contact and support, and appealed to scientists to look beyond the interests of the well-established European-North American circuit to the wider community in less secure areas of the world.

It goes without saying that constructive advice of this sort reaches far beyond the immediate readership of the journal, and may prove vital in mobilising concerned action amongst professional colleagues. The case of the Argentinian scientists prompted an immediate response; *Nature* advised enquirers to contact Amnesty International, to maintain contact with the scientists, and to consider future provision of academic places in anticipation of a large-scale scientific exodus.

Coverage of Eastern European rights questions is extensive, and the problems of dissident scientists are regularly discussed.

Royal Society
6 Carlton House Terrace
London SW1
Tel: (01) 839 5561
President: Lord Todd
Secretary: John Deverill

The Royal Society is the oldest scientific academy in the world with a continuous history. It is not a representative body of scientists in quite the same way as other professional organisations, but a learned society which exists to 'promote natural knowledge for the benefit of mankind'. As such, worldwide scientific interchange of both information and people is a central concern.

The Royal Society has to date refrained from making public interventions on specific human rights cases and issues concerning scientists, preferring direct approaches to their overseas counterparts, or referral to the Special Committee of the International Council of Scientific Unions (below), to which it is the national adhering body in this country. At the same time, Fellows of the Royal Society are encouraged to undertake individual initiatives on human rights.

The Royal Society's position was made plain in the annual address given in November 1976 by its President, Lord Todd, who, while approving individual protest action against violations of basic rights, added that

> It is entirely right and proper that individuals should express their indignation about such cases by declarations or in any way they wish, but it is hard to see in what way the Royal Society can occupy a special position in the matter of human rights in general.

Recalling the Society's long tradition of upholding freedom of scientific enquiry, its cooperation in this regard with the International Council of Scientific Unions, and its representations to the Soviet Academy of Sciences and other learned bodies, Lord Todd added,

> It is my firm belief that the Society as such can achieve much more in this way than it can by subscribing to or issuing public declarations. For it must be recognised that a scientist, as such, is in the same position as any other citizen of his country, subject to the same laws and having the same obligations to the society in which he lives. His profession does not entitle him to special privileges; nor should it deny to him those privileges which are the right of every man.[1]

This position was reiterated following an exchange letters in *The Times* on the publication of *Scholarly Freedom and Human Rights*, when the Society's Foreign Secretary wrote:

---

[1]   The Royal Society, Address of the President, Lord Todd, at the Anniversary Meeting, 30 November 1976.

115

> A scientist should . . . protest not *qua* scientist, but rather as a citizen . . . The Royal Society, as such, has no special position or qualification in the human rights issue, but this will not prevent fellows, including officers, from taking action as individuals.

A number of scientists would claim that the Royal Society is uniquely well qualified to take a more open corporate stance on occasions when private representations by learned colleagues have proved fruitless. However, it would appear that the majority of the Society's 850 Fellows agree with its present less public policy on human rights.

World Federation of Scientific Workers
40 Goodge Street
London W1P 1FH
Tel: (01) 580 8688
Cable: Mondscifed London
President: Professor E.H.S. Burhop (University College London)
Secretary General: Professor M. Legay (Lyon)

The WFSW was set up in July 1946 with the aims of promoting scientific and technological development to peaceful ends through international cooperation and exchange; increasing public and professional awareness of the relations between science and society; and protecting and improving the status of scientific workers (i.e. those employed in all branches of the natural and social sciences, engineering and applied technology).

The 30th Anniversary Meeting of WFSW was, like its founding Conference, held in London, and was attended by representatives of 22 national affiliates, members from nine other national organisations and some seven international organisations.[1] The WFSW is well represented in the communist and socialist countries, including the countries of Eastern Europe and Vietnam, as well as in Western Europe and Japan; its membership is less in evidence in Third World countries (other than India), where the scientific community is nascent (or expatriate), or – in the case of Chile and Uruguay – has been systematically suppressed by the governmental authorities.

Activities

The WFSW frequently hears, through its members and affiliates, of cases of alleged victimisation of scientific workers throughout the world. Its

---

[1] A protest resolution was passed by the Conference at visa delays which prevented many participants from arriving in time for the opening of the Conference. One Russian academician was inexplicably denied an entry visa altogether.

policy has been to consult with the affiliate organisation or corresponding members in the country concerned, to give certain cases wide publicity — which can act as an external 'insurance policy' against further maltreatment or harassment — and to intervene with the government concerned, either alone or in conjunction with other professional or human rights bodies.

However, it is clear that the WFSW is inhibited in this context by the policy of only acting with the agreement of its member organisations. Like many other international professional organisations confronted with this difficulty, it has refrained from committing itself on areas of debate considered sensitive by member organisations. The misuse of psychiatry for political purposes, for example, has never been raised.

The most pressing area of concern for WFSW at present is the situation in the 'southern cone' of Latin America. Its affiliate organisation in Chile has been suppressed by the Junta; prominent members, including university professors and academicians, subjected to arbitrary imprisonment and torture in Uruguay; scientists and academics risk kidnapping, torture and summary execution in Argentina, or join the ever-growing diaspora of academic talent seeking refuge overseas.

The right to freedom of movement is another issue of particular concern to scientists. On this question, the WFSW adopts a qualified view, maintaining that the permanent emigration of scientists may constitute a 'brain drain' with deleterious effects on the country of origin. WFSW is committed by its charter to the right to free movement of men and ideas. However, it considers that 'some of the current campaigns in support of the rights of scientists are politically motivated'.

The Final Act of the Helsinki Conference has had a major impact on the WFSW, both as regards disarmament and in the clauses relating to the increased flow of information and personnel between countries. While condemning what it terms 'the systematic campaign of denigration of Helsinki that has been waged in many Western countries', the Federation has asked member organisations to maintain their vigilance to ensure that the Helsinki undertakings are being observed.

WFSW has instituted a Sub-Committee on the implementation of the UNESCO instrument on the Status of Scientific Research Workers (1974).[1] This committee will also serve as an advisory committee for cases of alleged victimisation which are referred to the President or to the Secretary General.

Close in spirit to the UNESCO instrument, and in some respects its

---

[1]   The November 1974 UNESCO Instrument states *inter alia* that 'Member states should actively promote the interplay of ideas and information among scientific researchers throughout the world . . . and to this end should take all measures necessary to ensure that scientific researchers are enabled, throughout their careers, to participate in international scientific and technological gatherings and to travel abroad.'

precursor, is the *Declaration on the Rights of Scientific Workers*, adopted by the WFSW's 1969 Conference. This recognises — in addition to the social and economic rights of scientific workers — that

> Scientific workers, regardless of their sex, race, nationality, creed, and political conviction, should have all civil rights defined in the General (i.e. the Universal) Declaration of Human Rights . . .

as well as the

> right to free exchange of views and experiences on scientific work and its economic and social consequences, on both a national and an international scale

and the entitlement for scientific workers to defend those rights. Governments are enjoined to

> refrain from interference with the freedom to express scientific views or to publish the results of scientific research and should take steps to prevent other interference with this freedom.

A full analysis of the implications of this and other texts is to be found in *Scholarly Freedom and Human Rights.*

Chapter 9

MEDICINE

The medical profession is one area where pressure for action on human rights issues has come from within its own ranks. This is because doctors and medical personnel run a stronger risk than most other professionals of being caught between two rival allegiances — the doctor's duties to society's interests, as vested in the state, and his obligations, laid down in the Hippocratic oath, towards the individual patient. Traditionally, the relationship between doctor and patient has been the basis for all decisions regarding ethical conduct within the profession: the doctor is committed to respecting the patient's wishes, and must exercise his or her individual judgement regarding treatment in this light.[1] Where the doctor's primary obligation towards the patient is threatened or encroached upon by the state or other external sources of authority, this moral commitment may, and in many countries does, find itself without formal protection under the law, or from security forces and police who may themselves be accomplices or initiators of repression and violence. By maintaining the obligation towards his patient while under pressure, the doctor or nurse concerned may place himself at risk.

Certain aspects of this dilemma have received particular attention in recent years. In many of the countries where torture is systematically practised as a means of interrogation, intimidation or revenge by state functionaries, doctors and medical auxiliaries may be required to attend. In some cases, they may be directly involved — in reviving torture victims for further sessions, or making them 'presentable' prior to release; in other instances, doctors may be forced to withhold treatment from sick prisoners who are deliberately denied attention by the authorities as further punishment. Whether active or passive, the role of medical personnel in countries where human rights are open to flagrant violation could no longer, it was felt, be passed over in silence: the individual conscience of the doctors and medical personnel involved, and with it the integrity of the profession as a whole, was seen to be in need of formal protection from external abuse for political ends. Where the state could no longer afford this protection, it was up to the professional bodies to reassert the code of ethics governing medical practice in such circumstances.

At the 1974 Assembly of the World Medical Association in Stockholm,

---

[1] The WMA's 1946 Declaration of Geneva states: 'I will maintain the utmost respect for human life from the time of conception; even under threat I will not use my medical knowledge contrary to the laws of humanity.'

the Irish and British Medical Associations volunteered to study these questions, through a special Working Party. This resulted in a text put forward to the World Medical Association at its 1975 Tokyo Conference. The *Guidelines for Medical Doctors*, adopted by the Conference and later known as the 'Tokyo Declaration', spelled out the duties and obligations of medical personnel towards prisoners, torture victims and hunger-strikers. Basing its precepts on the primacy of respect for the patient, the World Medical Association reaffirmed the individual doctor's right to refuse cooperation in particular circumstances on moral grounds:

1) The doctor shall not countenance, condone or participate in the practice of torture or other forms of cruel, inhuman or degrading procedures, whatever the offence of which the victim of such procedures is suspected, accused or guilty, and whatever the victim's beliefs or motives, and in all situations, including armed conflict and civil strife.

2) The doctor shall not provide any premises, instruments, substances or knowledge to facilitate the practice of torture or other forms of cruel, in-human or degrading treatment or to diminish the ability of the victim to resist such treatment.

3) The doctor shall not be present during any procedure during which torture or other forms of cruel, inhuman or degrading treatment is used or threatened.

While it is one thing to proclaim these principles, it has proved quite another to attempt to enforce them. The World Medical Association, as a non-governmental organisation without Russian or American membership, does not have the strength to do so. Moves are now under way amongst non-governmental organisations, including those of the medical profession, to press for the United Nations to initiate some form of implementing machinery for a similarly-worded code of ethics, and for the setting-up of a Medical Reference Committee which would receive allegations of medical abuse and report on these to the General Assembly.

Apart from this initiative, support for human rights questions amongst the medical profession has come from individual doctors. Except for psychiatrists (q.v.), there has been no organised response in the United Kingdom. This is the usual pattern for doctors, whose profession is by tradition individualist, and who are much concerned, at the local level of hospitals and research units, with questions of medical ethics in their day-to-day application.

When the Medical and Scientific Committee for Soviet Jewry (see under Scientists) launched its medical petition on behalf of Dr Shtern, since allowed to emigrate from the Soviet Union. 1,000 eminent doctors were approached *individually* by the organisers. This was an extraordinary effort, and because it was direct it elicited an excellent response. Yet although individual doctors are aware of such issues, and willing to express their concern in this way, there is no permanent coordinating body capable of mobilising medical opinion in such a way, unless one counts the British Medical Association Council, which also appealed to the Soviet

Government on behalf of Dr Shtern.

British Medical Association
Tavistock Square
London WC1H 9JP
Tel: (01) 387 4499
Cables: Medisecra London WC1H 9JP
Secretary: Dr E. Grey-Turner

The British Medical Association (BMA) has from the start concerned itself with ethical questions as an integral part of the doctor's individual responsibility to his patients and his profession. Since 1947, its Central Ethical Committee has taken the initiative in considering questions arising within the profession.

During the early 1970s, the British Medical Association was urged by certain doctors, particularly medical officers in the armed services, to provide guidelines on how they were to act in circumstances surrounding the interrogation of persons detained under the Prevention of Terrorism Act. The BMA responded by stating categorically that 'No doctor should take part, directly or indirectly, in interrogation procedures'.[1]

A further issue which preoccupied the Central Ethical Committee was the forcible feeding of hunger-strikers in British prisons. The dilemma for attendant medical personnel in these circumstances was acute, since their presence might serve to prevent suffering while being viewed as complicity with what was considered unethical or undesirable actions. The basis for resolving this dilemma has always been sought in the primacy of the doctor-patient relationship, which is no different within prison from what it would be outside: in respecting the patient's wishes, the doctor must exercise his individual judgement regardless of external pressures, and may accordingly withhold treatment where the patient so wishes. This principle was reaffirmed by the January 1975 meeting of the BMA Council, which stated that a doctor should be able to exercise his or her own judgement free from pressure, to decide on the prescribing relationship between himself and the patient.

In addition to its stand on these essential ethical questions, and its pursuit of their endorsement by the World Medical Association, the BMA is able to assist doctors arriving in this country through its Commonwealth and International Advisory Bureaux. These will advise newly-arrived doctors on the procedures for re-qualification prior to registration

---

[1]   Chairman's statement, BMA Central Ethical Committee, 24 August 1972.

United Kingdom

with the General Medical Council (Commonwealth doctors benefit from reciprocal recognition), and on how best to look for work here. In 1957, the BMA was actively involved in helping many Hungarian doctors arriving in the United Kingdom; in 1968, it helped doctors from Czechoslovakia, and more recently Asians from Uganda and other, individual, cases, including émigré medical personnel from the Soviet Union. The BMA has no funds of its own available for interim loans for exiled or refugee doctors, but may help to obtain grants from other sources.

Chapter 10

PSYCHIATRY

The position of psychiatrists has been central to the mobilisation of the medical profession as a whole on human rights issues. Here again, the pivot for psychiatrists' involvement has been the question of their corporate responsibility for safeguarding professional ethics. The debate arose over repeated allegations of the abuse of psychiatric institutions and techniques for political ends of control and punishment. Such allegations have emanated from a number of countries, but to date only in the Soviet Union has the practice of forcible psychiatric internment of dissenters been extensively documented.[1] Such well-publicised cases as those of Major Pyotr Grigorenko, Leonid Plushch and Vladimir Bukovsky have brought home these issues, often in graphic detail, to the public at large. And quite apart from any humanitarian involvement, they raised questions about areas of psychiatric ethics which were of direct concern to all members of the profession: the independence of psychiatrists from external authority, the social expediency of diagnosis, the potential abuse of dangerous drugs and isolation techniques, and the understanding of what constitutes 'treatment' in politically-charged circumstances.

Recognition of the professional issues at stake amongst the international psychiatric community came only slowly. Corporate disapproval of such practices was sometimes opposed on the grounds that it would constitute 'a Cold-War action', and some scrupulous professionals felt that outright condemnation would be 'meddling in politics'. The World Psychiatric Association, which unlike the WMA has both American and Soviet representation, gave the impression that it was determined to suppress any discussion of the matter for fear that the Soviet Union might walk out.

By acquiescing in Soviet arguments that such cases were internal affairs of state as a pretext for inaction, the WPA laid itself open to the charge that it was neglecting its primary function of safeguarding professional standards for the sake of maintaining an outward appearance of unity. The issue at stake was, after all, not whether the WPA was according any implicit support to Soviet dissidents, but whether the integrity of the psychiatric profession throughout the world was being discredited by its

---

[1] Isolated allegations have come from Brazil, Czechoslovakia, East Germany, South Africa, Argentina, Chile, Yugoslavia and recently Romania and China, but with, the exception of Romania, there is little firm evidence to hand. The Soviet cases are documented in Amnesty International's *Prisoners of Conscience in the Soviet Union*, 1975, and in Sidney Bloch and Peter Reddaway, *Russia's Political Hospitals: the Abuse of Psychiatry in the Soviet Union*, Gollancz, 1977.

misapplication in one member country.[1]

Alternative initiatives on psychiatric abuse had meanwhile to come from outside the established channels of corporate interest. Following the arrival in the West of a solid dossier of hard evidence about individual cases of forcible internment of dissenters in Soviet psychiatric and prison hospitals, a small but highly effective lobby in Britain was formed around the Working Group on the Internment of Dissenters in Mental Hospitals (see below). Working largely within the psychiatric profession, it was able to lay a solid basis for future action in terms of well-presented evidence and clarification of the issues at stake. A Symposium on Medical Ethics and Abuses of Psychiatry, convened by Amnesty International in Geneva in April 1975, resulted in a call by 60 eminent psychiatrists and jurists to medical associations throughout the world.

> no longer to hesitate, despite threats of withdrawal by member countries, expressly to condemn those abuses of psychiatry wherever they occur, and to boycott the doctors involved and the organisations which refuse the necessary investigations.

The Symposium set up an Initiating Committee Against Abuses of Psychiatry for Political Purposes, and sections of the Committee came into being shortly afterwards in Britain and Austria (see below, CAPA). Similar groups appeared in France, Germany and the USA. CAPA's actions, aimed at publicising the issue of psychiatric abuse to a wider public, complemented the groundwork accomplished within professional circles by the Working Group. The issue of psychiatric abuse came to occupy something of a privileged position amongst human rights activities in Britain. This was largely due to good publicity and intensive lobbying, partly to the release from psychiatric internment of a number of eminently sane critics of the Soviet system as a result, apparently, of such external pressure.

As in a number of other areas, a rough division of labour has sprung up amongst the organisations concerned with the question of psychiatric abuse. The different approaches of CAPA and the Working Group (see below) answer the need for a dual strategy, one arm working mainly within the psychiatric profession, the other, more publicly, from without. This specialisation also serves to lighten the load of each: the Working Group is freer to conduct a low-key, 'scholarly' campaign, while CAPA, which occupies more of the limelight, can cope with the time-consuming press and publicity side of this work. The two organisations cooperate closely, and indeed have many members in common.

At the international level, the national professional bodies and action groups encountered strong resistance to their attempts to have free debate

---

[1] For detailed discussion of the WPA's position, see Malcolm Lader, *Psychiatry on Trial* (Penguin), 1977, chapter 10; and Bloch/Reddaway, *Russia's Political Hospitals*, chapters 4 and 10.

and discussion of abuses of psychiatry within the World Psychiatric Association. Initiatives centred on the WPA's Sixth World Congress of Psychiatry, held in Honolulu in August-September 1977. A strongly worded resolution proposed by the British Royal College of Psychiatrists, condemning the abuse of psychiatry for political purposes and specifically naming the Soviet Union as the major offender, was informally debated in a special open session, called at the request – under implied threat of withdrawal – of the 23,000 strong American Psychiatric Association. An Australasian amendment to this resolution, of similar content, was then passed by 90 votes to 88 by the WPA's governing body, and an American resolution to set up a WPA committee which would monitor political abuse in any country and recommend counter-measures was passed by 121 to 66. In contrast to this, the WPA's Secretary General, British psychiatrist Dr Denis Leigh, and the WPA's Ethics Committee had proposed a declaration of the General Principles underlying the Ethical Practice of Psychiatry, which each national affiliate would have the option of incorporating – or not – into a national code of practice. 'Thus,' commented Dr Leigh, 'we avoid problems connected with religion, national policies, forms of political belief and so forth, and can concentrate on the principles.' This initiative was seen by the action groups as a deliberate attempt to throw out the humanitarian baby with the political bathwater; they saw it as a compromise measure aimed at defusing a potentially explosive situation, but which lacked any machinery to ensure observance of its terms. However, as the above-mentioned resolutions had been passed, the declaration of ethical principles was also approved without much debate. Uncertainty remained, however, as to how quickly the WPA would set up the monitoring committee, and how vigorously it would then function.

The British Psychological Society
St Andrews House
48 Princess Road East
Leicester LE1 7DR
Tel: (0533) 549568
Scientific and Professional Secretary: Dr Ralph Hetherington

The British Psychological Society, which is the chartered body representing professional psychologists in the United Kingdom, set up in 1976 a Working Party to study abuses of psychology for political purposes, with special reference to the USSR and Northern Ireland. This group reported in February 1978 and recommended that the Society should endorse and implement the 'Resolution Concerning Professional Ethics of Psychology' which was unanimously approved by the International Union of Psychological Science in 1976. This declared the IUPS's active opposition to the misuse of psychology to infringe 'the inviolable rights of human beings'.

Campaign Against Psychiatric Abuse
Napsbury Hospital
St Albans, Herts
Tel: (056) 612 3333
Secretary: Dr Lawrence Ratna

CAPA was launched in September 1975 as a publicity and action campaign directed against psychiatric abuse wherever it occurs, but particularly in the Soviet Union. Unlike the Working Group, it aims at a large membership and concerns itself with well-publicised activities and public campaign work. CAPA came into being as a result of the 1975 Geneva Symposium (see above) and remains the British branch of the Initiating Committee which resulted from it. Two of its founder-members, the former internee Viktor Fainberg and British actor David Markham, had been led to this initiative by their frustration at the slowness of the psychiatric profession to commit itself to an issue of such urgent humanitarian and professional concern.

CAPA's aims are to examine, investigate and publicise abuses of psychiatric practice for political ends wherever these occur (its concentration on the Soviet case is a result of the large quantity of hard evidence to hand). CAPA is extremely active on the publicity front, with well-attended rallies and frequent eye-catching public action with the support of prominent figures from the world of theatre, music and the arts. The presence of a growing number of exiled Soviet dissidents has contributed greatly to the amount of press coverage they have received. Behind the intensive lobbying and campaigning, CAPA's work is based on a sound knowledge of the situation of the interned dissenters through frequent contact with their friends and associates in the Soviet Union.

CAPA publishes an occasional newsletter, *Straitjacket*.

Royal College of Psychiatrists
17 Belgrave Square
London SW1X 8PG
Tel: (01) 235 2351
President: Professor Desmond Pond

The Royal College of Psychiatrists, an autonomous professional body which received its Royal Charter in 1971, has passed a number of strongly-worded resolutions on the abuse of psychiatry in every country but especially in the Soviet Union. In January 1973, as the debate on psychiatric abuse began to get under way in Britain, the Royal College declared itself 'firmly opposed' to 'the use of psychiatric facilities for the detention of persons solely on the basis of their political dissent no matter where it occurs'. In November of the same year, following a visit by psychiatrists to the Soviet Union, it issued a less guarded resolution which 'deplores the current use of psychiatry in the Soviet Union for the purpose of political repression and condemns the activities of doctors who lend themselves to this work'.[1] By July 1975, after the arrival in Britain of first-hand witnesses from the USSR, the President of the College protested to leading Soviet psychiatrists about what 'appears a perversion of psychiatric practice and denial of natural justice'. The protest referred to three cases soon to become well-known: those of Gluzman, Bukovsky, and Plyushch.

In November 1975, the Royal College of Psychiatrists took the then unprecedented step of expressing its readiness to despatch a commission of enquiry conjointly with the Bar Council to report on alleged abuses of psychiatry in the Soviet Union. This offer was refused by the Soviet authorities. An additional resolution of 1976 reiterated the Royal College's refusal to tolerate the abuse of the skills of their profession for political ends. Like the earlier resolution, this was passed by a large majority of those present.

In June 1978 the College protested about the arrest of Alexander Podiabinek, and set up a monitoring committee on political abuses of psychiatry.

[1] Cited in Bloch and Reddaway, *Russia's Political Hospitals*, p. 295 ff.

Working Group on the Internment of Dissenters in Mental Hospitals
13 Armitage Road
Golders Green
London NW11 8QT
Honorary Secretary: Helena Abram

The Working Group was set up in 1971 in response to a dossier of detailed evidence of psychiatric abuse in the Soviet Union which had been sent to the West by Vladimir Bukovsky, and for which he was subsequently arrested. The material he collected was translated by the group and disseminated to professional colleagues and humanitarian organisations in Britain and overseas, and this work has continued on the basis of the information which filters through to the West.

One immediate result of the initial material was a letter to *The Times*, signed by 44 psychiatrists who affirmed that they could find no medical basis for the forcible internment of the subjects listed in Bukovsky's dossier, and concluded that this practice accordingly represented a grave violation of professional ethics on the part of Soviet psychiatry.

The philosophy of the Working Group remains true to this approach. Its aim is to bring home to the psychiatric profession the issues at stake in the misuse of psychiatric institutions to political ends, particularly, but not exclusively, in the Soviet Union — it also monitors abuses in other countries, and its first *News Bulletin in Psychiatric Abuse* (June 1977) mentioned abuses in Romania, East Germany, Argentina, Chile and South Africa — and to attempt to mobilise psychiatrists in the United Kingdom in defence of the ethical standards of their profession. It does this on a shoestring budget supported by voluntary contributions. Its active membership remains small, and comprises a mixture of psychiatrists, psychologists and human rights workers, with a wider international mailing list of several hundred; it enjoys a wide range of contacts with analogous groups throughout North America and Western Europe.

The Working Group does not proceed by widespread publicity, but its persistent and painstaking lobbying within the medical and psychiatric world has been largely responsible for the high level of professional awareness of the issues. A book by two of the Group's members, Peter Reddaway and Dr Sidney Bloch, entitled *Russia's Political Hospitals: The Abuse of Psychiatry in the Soviet Union*, was published in the United Kingdom and simultaneously in the United States under the title *Psychiatric Terror: How Soviet Psychiatry is Used to Suppress Dissent*, in time for the WPA's Honolulu Congress. Its appendix documents 210 cases of individuals incarcerated in psychiatric institutions and prison hospitals for protest action, whether on grounds of religious, nationality or human rights activities, or the wish to emigrate; each case is summarised, with details of the source and quantity of information available outside the

Soviet Union.

In addition to organising mailings, articles, lectures, meetings and press coverage to disseminate this information, the Working Group maintains close contact with human rights activists within the Soviet Union, and has been greatly encouraged by the release of some of the remarkable individuals on whose behalf it has worked, amongst them its own 'prime mover', Vladimir Bukovsky.

For further information *see also The Political Abuse of Psychiatry in the Soviet Union*, Working Group, London, 1977.

Chapter 11

WRITERS

Creative writers and artists frequently appear to occupy a privileged place amongst dissidents. The public nature of their work may give voice to the private dissent of a far wider number of individuals; they are thus accorded a representative role far beyond their purely artistic function, both by their supporters and, tacitly, by the government authorities who harass them. It is because they are spokesmen for oppressed or dissenting sections of the population that their work tends to be seized on abroad as a focus for campaign work and public appeals; nothing — with the possible exception of symbolic public acts of defiance — speaks more clearly or directly across national frontiers than a poem of protest or an open letter of dissent. The creative writer or artist thus occupies a position of public eminence not for his art alone, but for what it represents to large sections of the population. For some, there is no contradiction between the two: their art and their public dissent are inseparable, and they combine the two with a force that political spokesmen are unable to emulate. For others, this function is thrust upon them and sits uncomfortably on their own more private task of creation.

Poets or writers in exile have a difficult task of adjustment. They are released from the dual pressure of public expectation and official displeasure, but to a large extent it is these which have given their work its force and expressive power. Once the initial excitement of their arrival in exile has worn off, they are confronted with a more subtle kind of adversity: cut off from their roots and their 'constituency' at home, their work can no longer voice the direct aspirations of their people; it is often in a language alien to the host community; it may revert to a private expression of this isolation, or seek comfort in the self-reinforcement of the exile community, with its accompanying tendency to over-compensate for the loss of public support and sense of community which exiles experience.

The practical problems of exiled artists are no more easy to resolve. They will share with other refugees the difficulties of finding somewhere to live and work. And while a number of writers and artists may benefit from the assistance of friends and fellow-exiles during this period of adjustment, as a group they are less well catered for than are other professional categories with well-established structures for aiding each other.

While it may in principle prove easier for the writer or artists (except in the performing arts) to enter the United Kingdom as a self-employed person (see below), there is usually neither the financial security nor the

130

work opportunity to make this practicable. The exiled artist, whether admitted as a refugee or under normal immigration procedures, is often obliged to seek regular employment, or to fall back on social security benefits. This expedient, while more socially acceptable, is usually far from satisfactory as a means of pursuing his or her own programme of work, and may contribute to the sense of frustration and isolation encountered in adjusting to a new and not always friendly community.

The particular needs of writers and artists are frequently neglected, or dismissed as inessentials. This is especially so in Britain, where provision for exiled creative artists is far from adequate, a failure which demonstrates a profound lack of understanding for their needs — for workspace, materials, social and commercial outlets, a sense of cultural community — and perhaps because it is felt that the nature of their work is ephemeral, even frivolous. New arrivals need help and encouragement in pursuing their chosen task. The deep-seated need that these poets, writers and artists have fulfilled in their own countries as spokesmen for the communities they represent, giving a public voice and identity to their aspirations, might well serve as an example for the central role their art can play in society.

One particular professional sanction which can cripple a writer's career is his exclusion from the means of publishing his work. In a number of countries, the national Writers' Union exercises a quasi-official control over writers' outlets, and expulsion of non-conformist members are from time to time signalled in connection with human rights activities or sympathies. On 5 April 1977, *Le Monde* carried news of the exclusion from their respective Writers' Unions of two Soviet writers, one Russian, the other Georgian, as well as an item concerning a letter of allegiance to the ruling party from the East German Writers' Union, which had earlier banned from its committee a number of writers sympathetic to the exiled poet Wolf Biermann.

Because of the semi-official character of a number of the national writers' unions, the international bodies on which they are represented are largely inhibited from taking action on behalf of expelled writers. The International Writers' Guild (105 Carlton Street, Toronto M5B 1M2, Canada) is constitutionally unable to engage in any activity which may be construed as political.

Protest action — with the notable exception of International PEN — has accordingly been largely left to individual initiatives. A number of prominent writers — authors and playwrights especially — have lent their names and their expertise to public interventions on behalf of imprisoned writers. Their participation, especially in letter-writing campaigns, can help to draw public attention and sympathy to such cases. A recent visit by a prominent British playwright to human rights campaigners in Moscow, and the subsequent publication of his account of the visit in the Sunday press, was followed soon after by the release of the detainee whose case he had described. Whether coincidental or not, there is little doubt that the public sympathy his story attracted contributed significantly to the pressure of external opinion on the Soviet authorities to release him.

Those wishing to enlist the support of writers to their cause should contact International PEN or Writers & Scholars, and keep abreast of letters published in the daily press.

The trusts and societies which exist to help writers and artists and to protect their rights are not primarily concerned with exiles as refugees. Along with other applicants, their claims will be considered according to their literary or artistic merit; subsidiary considerations, such as extreme need, may be taken into account, but will not be determining factors.

For young writers and artists arriving from abroad, this naturally poses the further problem of gaining acceptance. If they have had no material published, or exhibited in this country, they may need some form of sponsorship. An informal system of individual advice and assistance does operate through the usual artistic and literary channels, and this is invaluable, not least in the moral support it provides. With such informal contacts, however, there is always the danger that new arrivals may — though inadequate English, demoralization, or other inhibitions — fail to find this kind of assistance and simply fall through the net.

Closer cooperation between the refugee organisations and the literary associations may be called for to avert this possibility. Greater awareness of the needs of refugee writers and artists could be stimulated in this way. A more systematic method of individual sponsorship might be adopted, for example by keeping a central register of persons willing and able to help (with money, accommodation, references, contacts, advice), as well as a brief record of past cases of such help extended to refugee writers and artists.

Index on Censorship *see under* **Writers and Scholarship Educational Trust**, pp. 136-7.

International PEN
English PEN Centre
The Sketch Club,̌ 7 Dilke Street
London SW3
Tel: (01) 352 9549
Cable: Lonpenclub London
International Secretary: Peter Elstob
International President: Mario Vargas Llosa

PEN stands for the principle of unhampered transmission of thought within each nation and between nations, and members pledge themselves to oppose any forms of suppression of freedom of expression in the country and community to which they belong. PEN declares for a free press and opposes arbitrary censorship in time of peace.

from the PEN Charter

Aims

PEN is a worldwide organisation which brings together writers, editors and translators in many countries, and takes action on their behalf at an international level. Through its *Writers in Prison Committee* it works closely with other humanitarian organisations in making known the situation of oppressed writers, and assists them in whatever way it can. Through its *Foundation PEN Emergency Fund* it is able to help a number of writers (50 during 1976) in various parts of the world who are imprisoned or otherwise persecuted for what they have written.

Scope for public actions — letters to the press, representations to governments and publicity on particular cases — is restricted to a category of 'writers' which would include literary critics and literary journalists but probably exclude reporters and sub-editors. There is some debate within the organisation as to the limitations imposed on its humanitarian activities by the need to maintain PEN's continued standing as a 'non-political' organisation (a debate by no means confined to professional assocations. The International Secretary of PEN approaches this question with some circumspection: with members throughout the world potentially at risk from repressive governments, the acceptability of International PEN as a non-political organisation is an essential prerequisite for its continued presence in a number of countries where it performs an irreplaceable function in bringing writers together.

Structure

PEN Clubs exist in every corner of the world, including some of the communist-bloc countries. International PEN is not based solely on national representation, but as an informal meeting-place for writers with common interests it reflects local cultural identities: the Catalan Centre has been revived and there are currently moves afoot to initiate centres for the Basque and Galician writers in Spain, just as there already exist Flemish- and French-speaking committees in Belgium. The working languages of International PEN are English and French, though its membership in the English-speaking world tends to be more active than the Francophone sections; the election of the Peruvian writer Mario Vargas Llosa as International President has provided a boost to the Spanish-speaking PEN Clubs in Latin America, an area where the writers' task often involves considerable personal danger.

In addition to the established PEN-Clubs within these countries, PEN also incorporates a *Writers in Exile Centre* with branches in New York, Hamburg, Paris and London. Most of these are composed of Eastern Europeans (even where officially-acknowledged PEN-Clubs exist in their country of origin), though in recent years Latin American writers have swelled the ranks of the exile community; unwilling to accept the anti-communist tenor of the Eastern European Writers in Exile Centre, these are being encouraged to set up their own exile groups. In this way, PEN encompasses the interests of writers from all walks of life — and of varying, not to say opposing, political points of view.

Finance

PEN Clubs finance themselves through donations and fund-raising campaigns. The Swedish, Belgian and American branches are particularly enthusiastic fund-raisers, the latter making special provision for writers in financial difficulties (including exiled writers) in the USA.

Apart from cases of severe financial hardship, PEN does not give material encouragement to writers who have difficulty in getting published — simply because these problems are common to too many creative writers. Of course, this does not prevent its taking an active interest in the plight of writers who are persecuted for what they have written and who may be prevented from writing or publishing.

Considerable funds are directed to international interventions on behalf of imprisoned authors and their families. Cases are referred to PEN directly by local members or friends of the prisoner's family. Distribution procedures are necessarily discreet.

PEN Writers in Prison Committee
C/o PEN
7 Dilke Street
London SW3
Chairman: Michael Scammell
Secretary: Mrs K. von Simson

Writers as a class are mistrusted by ideological regimes of every tendency, and by despots of every sort . . . Literature is by nature a critical exercise and rulers do not like criticism.

Maurice Cranston, former Chairman of WIPC

The *Writers in Prison Committee* was set up by PEN in 1951 with the aim, quite simply, of getting writers out of prison.

Like its parent body, the Committee prefers discreet intervention to well-publicised action which may provoke the imprisoning authorities into hardening their position (though some recent initiatives by human rights organisations, notably on behalf of dissidents in the USSR, have demonstrated that sustained publicity can effect a backing-down by the authorities). Since it works on behalf of a relatively small number (80 during 1976) of writers imprisoned for the expression of unwelcome opinion, the Committee is well aware that in defending those writers is risks associating PEN too closely with the opinions expressed. It therefore strives to attain a balance between its low-profile activities and the necessary work of information which can testify to its political impartiality.

A further difficulty arises when, as quite often happens, out-of-favour writers are imprisoned on civil or criminal charges, more often than not trumped up by the authorities to take the offending writer out of circulation in society. In assessing such cases, the Committee works closely with seasoned human rights organisations like Amnesty International and draws on its own experience in evaluating each case and adopting the appropriate courses of action. These may include 'adoption' as honorary members of national PEN Centres and varying degrees of publicity, though as yet PEN's policy tends to vary from country to country and no hard-and-fast procedures have been adopted.

The Writers in Prison Committee has taken action on a number of well-known cases, including those the poet Kim Chi Ha (South Korea), Valentyn Moroz (USSR), Kofi Awoonor (Ghana), Mihajlo Mihajlov (Yugoslavia), Samad Ismail and Samani Amin (Malaysia), Husain Jahiedin, Azmi Mahmud and Said Zahari (Singapore).

Royal Literary Fund
11 Ludgate Hill
London EC4M 7AJ
Tel: (01) 248 4138
Secretary: Victor Bonham-Carter

The purpose of the Royal Literary Fund is to assist authors and their families who are in want or distress. Before these needs can be considered, all applicants must have published work of approved literary merit and thus clearly established their literary standing.

The Royal Literary Fund, established in 1790, exists specifically to assist writers undergoing some hardship which prevents them from writing or earning a living in other ways through, for example, illness, incapacity, or financial difficulties. Its committee will consider applications from exiled writers in the United Kingdom if they can furnish evidence that their work is 'of approved literary merit'. This involves sponsorship by at least two members of the RLF Committee, who will be asked to investigate an application and report on the literary status and financial situation of the writer concerned. Applications take some six weeks to process.

Assistance takes the forms of interim grants and pensions. During 1976-7, over £70,000 was spent on aid to writers and their dependants, and covered a wide range of literary specialisations.

Society of Authors, Playwrights and Composers
84 Drayton Gardens
London SW10 9SD
Tel: (01) 373 6642
Secretariat: George Astley, Philippa MacLeish, Victor Bonham-Carter

---

The Society of Authors is a non-profit making organisation. Its purpose is to promote the interests of authors, and defend their rights whenever and wherever they are challenged.

The Society, which dispenses legal advice to its members and lobbies on behalf of authors' rights and legal protection, administers a number of awards for writers and translators. It maintains an *Authors' Contingency Fund* for short-term emergency grants totalling £4,000 during 1976. Technically, writers only qualify if they have had work published in the United Kingdom; they must be of British or Commonwealth nationality.

Writers and Scholars Educational Trust
21 Russell Street
London WC2B 5HP
Tel: (01) 836 0024
Director: Michael Scammell
Assistant Director: George Theiner

WSET's primary objective is to raise the level of debate on issues of censorship and freedom of expression throughout the world. These aims encompass a wide variety of practical activities: the publication (in association with the Trust) of the magazine *Index on Censorship*,[1] the commissioning

---

[1] Published six times a year and distributed by Oxford University Press (Journals).

of research papers on current topics related to press freedom and the exchange of information, the collection and classification of documents, books and news items on censorship throughout the world, which are available for consultation by interested persons. The emphasis is international, and encompasses the visual and performing arts as well as the written word.

Since 1975, a small *Emergency Aid Fund* has been in existence to help writers, scholars and artists who experience hardship as a result of their expressed views or published works, for example, writers who may be prevented from working or who are subject to harassment by the authorities in their country; or who, because of this, are obliged to leave as refugees and require help in establishing themselves (and their professional standing) elsewhere.

While the resources of the Emergency Aid Fund are as yet very limited, the Trust can provide assistance by publishing banned works in *Index*, a procedure which may give proscribed authors considerable moral encouragement and modest payment for their work. Providing contact with a wider literary community through the pages of the magazine, and occasionally in person, it recognised by WSET as an essential element of this work.

Writers Guild of Great Britain
430 Edgware Road
London W2 1EH
Tel: (01) 723 8074/5/6
General Secretary: Elaine Steel

The Writers Guild is a TUC-affiliated union, working to 'protect writers' ethical and material interests'. It is largely concerned with activities on behalf of its British members, but has despatched cables of protest against the harassment and imprisonment of writers overseas (most recently in the case of the Charter 77 signatories in Czechoslovakia).

The Guild administers a benevolent fund for its members in financial straits, but there is no precedent for disbursements to refugee non-members in need. It is occasionally approached by writers in difficulty overseas (or on their behalf by various organisations), and can assist with advice and contacts in the United Kingdom.

Chapter 12

VISUAL AND PERFORMING ARTS

Since they work in the public eye actors and musicians are particularly vulnerable targets for repressive regimes. They are by definition public figures, and readily associated with the potentially 'dangerous' ideas they — quite literally — represent. In Uruguay recently, a performance of *Julius Caesar* was broken up, its actors and director imprisoned and subsequently exiled. But more often the ideas portrayed are their own: the emotive force of words and music rendered subversive when they reach the hearts and minds of large audiences. Pop-singers, folk-singers, popular theatre can attract popular support on a scale many a political demagogue would envy, and there may indeed be an element of professional jealousy in the ruthlessness with which singers and actors have been attacked. How else does one begin to explain the elimination of a troupe of actors in Uganda, or the vicious way in which the Chilean singer Victor Jara was mutilated and murdered?

Performing artists are represented in their own countries by national unions and through these by the international union confederations. This inter-union structure supports them and represents their interests when they are in danger or difficulty; however, such action tends to be restricted, by reason of the non-political stance of the unions, to risks incurred in the course of their work or union activity: a theatre director, say, imprisoned for his political opinions, might fall outside the scope of union rescue activity.

Performing artists arriving in the United Kingdom do not enter under the self-employed heading which governs the entry of writers, poets and visual artists. If they do not apply for asylum, they will need to furnish evidence that they can support themselves by their work. In either case, union support will probably be needed before they can work in this country. As a matter of general policy, the British performing artists' unions take a sympathetic view of refugee cases, and have a good record of relaxing their protective stance to allow actors, dancers and musicians from repressive regimes to work here alongside British union members.

There is no special provision of exiled artists as such. They may often find themselves in the same position as authors, having to establish themselves in this country before being able to qualify for assistance.

ACME Housing Association
43 Shelton Street
London WC2H 9HJ
Tel: (01) 240 0540
Director: David Panton

ACME is a housing trust which provides low-rent studio space and accommodation for artists; the ACME Gallery in Covent Garden provides the possibility for these and other artists to exhibit their work. The ACME Housing Association is a practical and non-political venture, dealing solely with visual artists; its interest is determined by circumstances of the applicant, whose major qualification must be a commitment to his or her work as an artist. Given this emphasis on the personal needs of the artist, ACME has been able to assist a small number of refugee artists over the difficult initial period following their arrival.

ACME began as a self-help organisation for artists in 1972. It takes over vacant properties on a short-term basis from the Greater London Council and the London boroughs, and these in turn attract studio conversion grants from the Arts Council. Artist-tenants are responsible for their own conversion work, and rarely pay more than £4 a week in rent. Needless to say, there is a very heavy demand from artists for the kind of facility tht ACME can provide.

ACME was able to help one exiled Russian printmaker whose work had proved unacceptable to the Soviet authorities, and who arrived in London with the single-minded idea of getting on with his own work unhampered by bureaucratic censure. He had little money when he came and no English. The Arts Council referred his case to ACME, who listened sympathetically to his story and were able to give him priority on their housing list. In addition to working and living accommodation in the East End, artist contacts were able to offer some teaching and access to cheap etching plates. The ACME Gallery put on a one-man show of his work – an event of some importance both psychologically and in establishing his credentials as a self-supporting artist with the immigration authorities. He is now living and working in a small community of artists in South London.

ACME's success in providing practical assistance at this level may prove a useful example to organisations working with refugees and exiles in other areas.

Artists' General Benevolent Institution – Burlington House, Piccadilly, London W1V 0DJ. Tel: (01) 734 1193 *Secretary:* Miss Dorothy P. Laidman

The Institution provides financial relief to professional artists and their dependants in time of misfortune who have earned their living by their arts and whose work is known in the United Kingdom.

United Kingdom

Arts Council of Great Britain — 105 Piccadilly, London W1. Tel: (01) 629 9495 *Secretary General:* Roy Shaw

The Council runs award schemes for artists but these are open only to British subjects or to those resident in this country for five years. It does provide some advice on where to turn for help.

Arts Service Grants Ltd — **SPACE Provision** — 125-9 Shaftesbury Avenue, London WC2H 8AD. Tel: (01) 936 1754

The group deals with studio accommodation, providing 18 studio buildings for some 260 visual artists who are full-time professionals: no special provisions for exiles exist, but their special interests may be taken into account. SPACE also provides a free information service concerning setting up and running an independent studio. It is a non-commercial venture, a charity funded by the Arts Council and the Greater London Arts Association.

British Actors' Equity
8 Harley Street
London W1N 2AB
Tel: (01) 636 6367
Cable: Britequity London W1
President: Hugh Manning
General Secretary: Peter Plouviez

Equity helps actors in difficulty on a strictly humanitarian and non-political basis. It works closely with the International Federation of Actors (FIA), now based in London (see below), checking information on cases with the Foreign Office, the British press and other non-political organisations.

Like the Musicians' Union, Equity is concerned to protect the livelihood of its British members, but is prepared to make exceptions in urgent cases of humanitarian need. It would view membership applications from refugee actors and dancers favourably, and would if necessary endorse their entry into the country by stating its non-opposition to their settling and working here. As for foreign performers already in this country and seeking asylum, most are professionals with union status as 'visiting artists'; they would not necessarily have to be affiliated to Equity before action could be taken on their behalf. In the case of members of the cast of the black musical *Ipi-Tombi* who were unwilling to return to South Africa, Equity issued a press statement indicating its support for their request to be allowed to stay in this country, and its favourable view of their continuing to work here.

Equity has also lent its weight to actors in trouble overseas. Its public protest over the arrest in South Africa of John Kani and Winston Ntshona, combined with interventions from their professional colleagues and friends in the United Kingdom, may well have contributed to their subsequent release. Equity may hear of these cases directly, or they may be referred to them by the FIA from one or other of its national affiliates. In the case of the six actors reported murdered in Uganda, Equity pursued its own enquiries through official and non-official sources in London, but was unable to establish any detailed confirmation of the report. Equity also played an important part in the campaign to allow the ballet-dancers Valery and Galina Panov to leave the Soviet Union.

No emergency funds are available, though where appropriate Equity will back requests to the FIA Solidarity and Aid Fund.

Federation of British Artists – 17 Carlton House Terrace, London SW1Y 5BD. Tel: (01) 930 6844 *Secretary-General:* Maurice Bradshaw

The Federation cannot provide funds, but may assist artists in getting their work exhibited through its 22 affiliate art societies.

International Federation of Actors
30 Thayer Street
London W1M 5LJ
Tel: (01) 487 4699
Secretary-General: Gerald Croasdell

The International Federation of Actors, now in its 25th year, has 48 member unions in 38 countries around the world (East and West, with an important Latin American contingent). It represents the interests of all performing artists (with the exception of musicians) before the inter-governmental organisations, and coordinates union action at international level. In this regard its awareness of human rights issues is of crucial importance.

On human rights questions, its terms of reference, in keeping with its constitution, are strictly defined in professional terms as non-political humanitarian interventions where the vital interests of actors and theatre directors *as such* are at stake. Where performing artists are persecuted for non-professional reasons, the FIA will consider carefully before taking action. The FIA recognises the difficulty of distinguishing between what is 'political' and 'non-political' in this respect, but is reluctant to jeopardise the limited but effective influence it enjoys with governments by even appearing to adopt a politically-motivated stance.

This strictly professional approach has tended to concentrate FIA rescue activities in the Southern Cone of Latin America, where the performing arts are the target for deliberate policies of cultural repression. Initiatives on behalf of Chilean actors and the Chilean affiliate union were effective largely because FIA's intervention was recognisably within its professional scope. It has also been successful in mobilising member unions to help bring actors in Chile to live and work in Europe (offers of work, approaches to governments on entry-visas and work-permits, and so on). The FIA is now very much concerned with the position of actors and directors in Uruguay and Argentina.

The FIA is cautious about employing publicity in defence of actors at risk, when it has reason to believe that this may only increase the danger of persecution of potential victims.[1] Information — such as the list of imprisoned Chilean actors distributed by FIA — is only disseminated after careful checking. But on occasion (such as the arrest of the Uruguayan Vice-President of the FIA) all-out publicity initiatives are undertaken through member-unions.

The FIA disposes of a small *Solidarity and Aid Fund*, which can provide assistance to actors and theatre directors in an emergency, when national affiliated unions are unable, for whatever reason, to assist. This has mostly taken the form of grants to refugee actors once they have arrived in their actual country of exile and, additionally, some help is often given by affiliated national unions and their members.

Musicians' Union
29 Catherine Place
Buckingham Gate
London SW1E 6EH
Tel: (01) 834 1348
General Secretary: John Morton

The Musicians' Union has for many years been committed to opposing discrimination in all its forms and wherever it occurs. The Union has maintained an embargo on engagements in Southern Africa for almost twenty years, and has undertaken industrial action in this country against racial discrimination. As a leading member of the International Federation

---

[1]   Though it is worth noting that, in AI's experience, immediate publicity on torture cases may have considerable effect in stopping torture sessions.

of Musicians,[1] the Union pursues cases of persecution of musicians abroad through that organisation. In recent years, such cases have been raised in respect of Uruguay and Chile.

The Union has assisted musicians coming to this country as refugees or seeking asylum once they are here. These have included refugees from Nazi Germany, South Africa and most recently Chile. In such cases, the Union's basic concern to protect the jobs of its British members is waived, and members are authorised to work with refugee musicians. A policy decision was made by the MU's Executive Committee in anticipation of a limited number of Chilean refugee musicians arriving in this country; these would be advised to contact the MU with a view to eventually being admitted to membership; Union members would then be authorised to work with them and the Union would advise the Department of Employment that work permits for the refugees would not be opposed.

Although this policy was confined to Chileans, it will presumably stand as a precedent where refugees from other countries are concerned.

---

[1] Kreuzstrasse 60, CH-8008 Zurich, Switzerland.

Chapter 13

JOURNALISTS

IPI protested against the ten-year sentence imposed in Taiwan on Huang Hua, managing editor of the *Taiwan Political Review*. Huang, aged 37, who had been in detention since July, was sentenced to ten years imprisonment by a military tribunal on 8 October on charges of allegedly using the magazine to propagate rebellious throughts and attempting to instigate an armed revellion.

IPI Report, December 1976

Of over 1,000 journalists accredited in 1973 by the Colegio de Periodistas (Chilean Journalists Association), only 300 are practising their profession under the present regime. Some 400 are unemployed or have other jobs. About 300 have had to leave the country.

AI, Journalists and Writers in Prison, 1977

As commentators and critics on current events, journalists in repressive or unstable societies often place themselves knowingly at risk. Many have shown great courage in pursuing their stories in the midst of civil conflict or under threat or intimidation from political opponents who fear the full force of publicity about unsavoury truths for which they may be responsible. As with other public professions, journalists are exposed to attack both for what they say and for what they represent. Many journalists are persecuted as a result of working for politically-oriented newspapers, or providing what are construed as political comments by the authorities; but it is often the mere fact of exercising their professional duties, of bearing unwelcome witness to events, that lands the journalist in trouble. The IPI Annual Review of World Press Freedom (1977) reports that '1976 was a depressing year. Restraints on the media and the persecution of journalists throughout the world intensified to an unprecedented degree'.

Foreign journalists are in large measure protected by their nationality, and the publicity and resources which their home newspaper can afford them. When on occasion they are captured, arrested or put on trial, the publicity generated by the international press corps (a professional freemasonry with its own strong sense of solidarity) will usually cause sufficient discomfort to the imprisoning authorities — if only at the superficial but sensitive level of their public image — that the offending journalist is released; more often, the risk is of expulsion, and here the home newspaper or news agency will bear the cost. Such instances are nowadays so numerous as to be considered an occupational hazard, though they still raise serious questions about the freedom of journalists to exercise their professional curiosity.

It is often at the national level that journalists are less well protected. From South Korea to Uruguay, with many stops in between, newspapers have been closed down, editors and journalists subjected to harassment, intimidation and strict censorship of copy, some tortured in reprisal for their courageous reporting of events. International opinion is better informed than ever before of such outrages; the public outcry over many arrests of journalists in India, Singapore and South Africa amongst others, has in all probability hastened the release of the imprisoned journalists. But apart from the small emergency fund set up by the IFJ, there is no standing provision for endangered journalists to pay for defence costs, support families of imprisoned journalists, or pay travel expenses where national journalists' unions are unable to help.

Note: since organisations which exist to champion press freedoms are by and large concerned with the rights of newspapers to publish, we are confining this section specifically to those organisations which take action on behalf of journalists and editors at risk.

Institute of Journalists
1 Whitehall Place
London SW1A 2HE
Tel: (01) 930 7441
General Secretary: R.F. Farmer, FCIS

The Institute of Journalists has around 200 overseas members (just one-tenth of the total membership) in 51 countries, and will intervene on their behalf if they are in trouble. A list of these is maintained by the Institute's Overseas and International Committee, which is also responsible for liaising with journalists' associations overseas.

The Institute awards its Gold Medal as occasion demands to non-journalists who have spoken out on behalf of press freedoms or otherwise worked to amend laws, reduce risks and break down barriers to freer exercise of journalists' professional duties; and to 'journalists who have been prepared to suffer for the freedom of the written word, and whose courage and devotion have been eminently inspiring'.

International Press Institute
c/o The City University
280 St John Street
London EC1V 4PB
Tel: (01) 251 2525/6
Telex: 25950 IPILON
Cables: PRESSINT London EC1
Director: Peter Galliner

IPI defines its brief as

> The furtherance and safeguarding of freedom of the Press, by which is meant: free access to the news, free transmission of the news, free publication of newspapers, free expression of views

It is concerned with press questions at all levels of production – journalists, editors and newspaper management. The membership – around 1,900 individual members in 62 countries – favours those with editorial or policy responsibilities in the printed press, news agencies and broadcasting systems; individual journalists and academics are eligible for associate membership. Most are grouped in National Committees which promote issues of press freedom in the local context.

The IPI, now in its 27th year, runs a programme of research into press and media questions, publishes studies on these matters in conjunction with other organisations, organises regional seminars and conferences (including, for example, encounters between Spanish and Portuguese editors and their Western European counterparts); it is currently reviving its training programmes for journalists in Asia and Africa.

The IPI has a good record, particularly in recent years, of representations on behalf of imprisoned journalists throughout the world. These will be of a public or private nature depending on the likely reaction of the government in question, and the extent of IPI's formal and informal contacts in the country concerned (including their own National Committee, if one exists). Between May 1976 and May 1977, IPI intervened on some 35 occasions where the professional freedom of editors and journalists was under evident threat; the areas thus covered represented all shades of political opinion, though for obvious reasons, Latin America, India, and South Africa figured prominently. IPI has also demonstrated its awareness of the situation in less well-publicised countries, such as Malaysia and Taiwan.

The results of IPI's monitoring of press freedoms throughout the world are reported in its *Annual Review of World Press Freedom*, which provides a detailed factual account of the restraints encountered by newspapers and by individual editors and journalists. The information on which this

146

Report and IPI's interventions are based comes largely from press sources and newspaper contacts. IPI also maintains good contacts with other organisations, such as the FIEJ (International Newspaper Publishers Federation) and Amnesty International.

IPI is funded through membership fees (through its National Committees), together with donations from publishing companies and grant-making Foundations (for specific projects). The organisation does not publish its annual accounts in the United Kingdom.

National Union of Journalists
314 Gray's Inn Road
London WC1
Tel: (01) 278 7916
General Secretary: Kenneth Ashton
Deputy General Secretary: Charles Harkness

The NUJ has despatched many urgent cables and protest letters to governments and embassies over the years on behalf of journalists in difficulty with the authorities. Protest action covers all aspects of the repression, harassment and imprisonment of journalists, regardless of their political views or ethnic origin. In some cases — Peter Niesewand in Rhodesia, Anthony Grey in Peking — NUJ intervention appears to have been decisive in securing their release (at least in the view of the journalists concerned). Representations on behalf of journalists are not confined to those of British origin, but cover every area where journalists are reported to be in trouble. Letters and cables are phrased according to the sensitivity or insensitivity of the government in question, and will be sustained over a long period where official responses are unforthcoming.

The NUJ hears of individual cases through the journalists' unions in the country concerned — often through the International Federation of Journalists, of which it is the biggest constituent member; also, through news stories, professional colleagues and the family and friends of the journalist concerned. Action by the union is initiated by its International Committee with the approval of the National Executive. Where necessary, the NUJ will coordinate its activities with other groups and organisations which they are convinced are actively striving to alleviate conditions for journalists, and regardless of their political credentials (though wary of political identification with any one quarter, since this cooperation is purely on a humanitarian basis).

The NUJ will publicise cases through its national branches and chapels and through its own paper, *The Journalist*. Press releases may be put out on journalists with a British connection (such as Grey and Niesewand).

United Kingdom

While the NUJ is well-placed to encourage journalists to give publicity to those cases which would benefit from it, it recognises that the British press is notoriously ill-attuned to such questions, unless there is a British connection. Where journalists are concerned, it has proved difficult to break through in anything other than the trade press.

The NUJ has cooperated with Amnesty International in circulating Urgent Action cases and other letter-writing campaigns for journalists to its branches and chapels. Some of these have also participated in the Chilean adoption programme run by Chile Solidarity Campaign and the Chile Committee for Human Rights. While it has no standing funds for journalists in trouble overseas, NUJ members have offered informal help to Chilean refugees in finding work and accommodation.

Chapter 14

POLITICAL PARTIES

Politicians in many countries run the risk of being imprisoned. In some societies, it may even be termed an occupational hazard. The convenience to the governing faction of removing one's political opponents from the public arena may only be offset by the inconvenience of their political martyrdom in prison. Amnesty International lists 62 known cases of Parliamentarians imprisoned or 'disappeared' in mid-1977;[1] numerous other politicians, whether democratically elected or not, may be undemocratically disposed of in this way (not to mention the widespread use of murder as a political weapon in societies as otherwise dissimilar as those of Central America and Central Africa).

While this survey does not seek to concern itself with the political parties as policy-formulators, they have all to some degree involved themselves in human rights work. Their representations on behalf of individuals at risk can prove crucial where there is informal personal contact with like-minded politicians or parties in power in the country in question. The parties' stand on particular issues can exert a strong influence on related institutions — the close relationship between the Labour Party and the trade unions is the most obvious case in point — and at the international level in conjunction with their colleagues in other Western European parties. We have given a brief outline of these operational resources below.

Perhaps the most important attribute of the political parties for human rights work is their access to political leaders. The part played in obtaining releases of individuals or their right to emigrate by informal behind-the-scenes contacts is considerable, and only rarely — as in the Corvalan-Bukovsky exchange — are these private approaches given publicity. Secrecy is, perhaps, a key element in the success of such undertakings since, unlike public protest, they permit the imprisoning authorities to acquit themselves without public loss of face; moreover, since these dealings may be of a straightforward transactional nature, the suggestion that political prisoners or émigrés are being 'bought out' may prove unpalatable publicity for the political leaders initiating the 'deal' who are sensitive to their public image at home. The pragmatic nature of this approach, which has in the past proved successful with otherwise unyielding regimes, adds a new complexion to the arguments over continuing trade links with oppressive regimes.

---

[1] Amnesty International, *Parliamentarians in Prison*, 31 July 1977.

As for public interventions, for all the advantages that these can bring to work on individual cases, there are clear dangers in human rights work being too closely identified with one or other political point of view. The implication is always present, whether warranted or not, that the case is being taken up in order to make political capital out of it; and this in turn may prompt political rivals to press home the implied association, to the detriment of the individual whose case is being fought over in this way. The Russian dissidents in particular have found themselves caught in the political crossfire, with potentially damaging effect on their own precarious position in Soviet society.

Communist Party of Great Britain
16 King Street
London WC2E 8HY
Tel: (01) 836 2151/5
Cables: Communal Rand London WC2
General Secretary: Gordon McLennan

The Communist Party has no special machinery for dealing with human rights cases. Where these concern countries other than Britain, they come under the work of its International Department. South Africa, Namibia, Zimbabwe, Northern Ireland and Chile have been key issues in recent years. The CP has picketed the Chilean Embassy, campaigned on behalf of Chilean leaders Luis Corvalan (since released) and Victor Diaz (disappeared), and protested to the BBC at its coverage of events in Chile. It has also taken up cases in Uruguay and Brazil (though not to date on Argentina), as well as in the US (the Wilmington Ten), Dominica (Desmond Trotter), Guyana and St Vincent. The CP has protested about human rights violations in Turkey, Israel, Ethiopia, Sudan, Cyprus, Iran, Spain; and about political discrimination in the Federal Republic of Germany against personnel employed by public bodies on the ground of their political views and affiliations.

The British Communist Party, in company with the French and Italian Parties, has recognised the rights of those holding dissenting opinions in Eastern Europe, particularly the Charter signatories in Czechoslovakia. However, there are signs of a split between the substantial majority who support this 'Euro-communist' position and the hardliners who share with the Eastern European and Soviet parties the view that the dissidents represent counter-revolutionary forces.

The CP can give publicity to human rights issues in its fortnightly journal *Comment*. The *Morning Star*, while not an official party organ, has provided consistent coverage of human rights stories even when these are not carried by other national newspapers.

In addition to its own independent activity on human rights, the CP is represented, or has one of its leading officials, on a number of committees, such as the Anti-Apartheid Movement, the Chile Solidarity Campaign, SATIS (for South African Prisoners), TAPOL (Indonesian Prisoners), etc. It also gives support to such bodies as the Union of Turkish Progressives, League for Democracy in Greece, and others, which take up human rights cases in the particular country for which they are concerned.

Labour Party
Transport House
Smith Square
London SW1P 3JA
Tel: (01) 834 9434
National Executive Human Rights Chairman: Rt Hon Shirley Williams MP
Secretary: Tony Humphries

While the Labour Party's National Executive Committee has established a Human Rights Sub-Committee, this is primarily concerned with internal civil rights, including race and immigration questions and a statutory Charter of Human Rights guaranteeing observance under United Kingdom law of the rights determined by the European Convention on Human Rights. International human rights questions are dealt with by the Party's International Committee at Transport House.

The Labour Party occupies an advantageous position in three respects: it is able to press its government colleagues for action, whether public or informal, on particular issues and cases; it can use its own influence through its international contacts with political colleagues, including those in the Eastern European communist parties; and through its close working relationship with the British labour unions.

Labour Party cooperation with the unions on human rights issues is two-way. It will advise unions on appropriate actions to take on behalf of individual cases, and itself investigate and take action on such cases brought to its attention by union members and individual supporters. At a more general policy level of course, the interaction is constant, many unionists also being Labour Party members. The International Committee of the Labour Party tends to work with individual members from the unions who are especially active on human rights issues, some of whom are at the same time members of the Party's National Executive Committee. It finds this direct day-to-day contact more speedy and effective than working through the intermediary of the Trades Union Congress.

151

United Kingdom

The Labour Party has been able to impress human rights considerations on its own colleagues in government in two main areas: on the question of military and civilian aid to repressive regimes, it has advised a selective approach in part determined by the human rights record of the recipient country; and on the admission (or prevention of deportation) of political refugees it has urged a more comprehensive attitude in the light of the known risk of persecution if the refugee is returned home. Labour's 1976 programme thus urged a review of the British aid programme to Indonesia (the largest outside the Commonwealth countries), and argued, against existing government commitments, that arms sales to certain repressive regimes should be curtailed. The International Department has in recent years stepped up its research on Latin America, and seeks to provide a more detailed background analysis for policy decisions; it will urge a more comprehensive intake of refugees from countries in addition to Chile (in particular, Argentina).

On individual refugee cases — two recent examples being the student leader Tan Wah Piow and lawyer Frances Koo from Singapore — the Labour Party again has the advantage of by-passing officialdom for direct representations at ministerial level. Through its Parliamentary and union contacts, it has been able to sponsor individual refugees — mostly Chileans to date — to help secure entry visas and obtain support in getting them settled in this country; to this end, it works closely with the younger generation of refugee organisations: WUS, the Joint Working Group, Chile Solidarity and the Chile Committee for Human Rights. Overseas Development Minister Judith Hart and NEC member Alex Kitson (of the T&GWU) have both played a central role in obtaining a degree of official recognition (albeit a limited recognition) of the Chileans' special needs.

At the international level, informal interventions with Eastern European politicians have on occasion benefited individuals subject to harassment or persecution — Soviet Jews, members of national minorities, Polish and Czech dissidents — although, as is usual in such cases, it is virtually impossible to prove cause-and-effect. Because much of this work takes place behind the scenes, the Labour Party is sometimes accused of adopting 'double standards' in its human rights work, a charge which it rejects in the light of these interventions, which often incur the displeasure of their Eastern European official contacts. More publicly, delegations have addressed themselves to the Czech ambassador in London on the treatment of Charter 77 signatories, and to Soviet labour leader Boris Ponomaryev during his 1976 visit to London.

The International Committee of the Labour Party has a wide geographical coverage on human rights issues, with the accent on the English-speaking Commonwealth and Eastern Europe. The expansion of its work on Latin America has resulted in the Party's commitment to 'speak out more strongly against the violation of basic liberties by authoritarian regimes and their supporters' in Latin America.

152

Limited solidarity funds exist for Southern Africa. No funds are available, however, for individual relief in human rights cases.

See also *Labour's Programme 1976* and *Argentina, Chile and Brazil*, statement by the NEC of the Labour Party, July 1977.

Liberal International
1 Whitehall Place
London SW1A 2HE
Tel: (01) 839 5905; 839 3311
Secretary General: Richard Moore

The Liberal International, which brings together like-minded liberal democrat parties from Western Europe, India, Israel and Sri Lanka, including the British Liberal Party, places a high priority on human rights concerns. It is a small organisation but with its party members, there exists a large nominal membership spread throughout Western Europe and including Canada and Israel. It serves to bring issues to the attention of member-parties, some of which take a more active interest in human rights issues than others; on occasions it issues statements in its own right. One of these, adopted without opposition by its 1972 Annual Congress, condemned oppression of minorities (in Uganda, Burundi and Southern Africa), of political dissenters (in Eastern Europe, Greece, Spain and Portugal), of intellectuals, religious and national minorities (in the Soviet Union), and the practice of torture and political killing (in Brazil, Syria and the Central African Republic) — which gives a fair idea of the scope of its approach to human rights issues.

The Liberal International does not always respond by publicity and public statements, but may resort to informal initiatives by individual European members who may be highly-placed government officials. The Liberal International also has been at the centre of recent moves amongst a number of democratic parties to set up concerted action on human rights initiatives within the European context.

The Liberal International incorporates a Committee of Liberal Exiles (at the same address, above), which organises meetings on Central and Eastern Europe. Its membership includes such organisations as the Polish Liberal Group in Great Britain, the Estonian Liberal Democratic Group in Sweden, and the Hungarian Liberal Group in Switzerland, each of which is politically active amongst political exiles from their own country.

United Kingdom

Liberal Party Organisation
1 Whitehall Place
London SW1
Tel: (01) 839 4092
Spokesman on Human Rights: Lord Avebury

The Liberals have adopted respect for civil liberties and human rights, as the cornerstone of their approach to foreign policy issues. They are anxious to avoid human rights issues being used as a political pawn, and aim at an across-the-board consensus to take precedence over considerations of long-term strategy or short-term political advantage. Because of this, the Liberals have been at pains to stress their position as human rights all-rounders, supporting the rights of cultural and national minorities as well as individual cases.

The Liberals seek to strengthen the role of the European human rights machinery (Court of Justice and Human Rights Commission), and to make human rights considerations one of the criteria for enlarging the European community. A draft resolution for possible debate at their September 1977 Assembly also pressed for an improvement in the (far from adequate) UN machinery on human rights, and the appointment of a UN High Commissioner for Human Rights; for the British government to ratify the 1966 Optional Protocol to the UN Covenant on Civil and Political Rights, and to withhold military and development aid to 'regimes which indulge in a consistent pattern of gross violations of human rights'.

Earlier Assembly resolutions have condemned such violations in a wide range of countries, have urged respect for national minorities such as the Kurds, and have called for unrestricted right of entry into the United Kingdom of 'refugees and uprooted persons'. The Liberal Party also supports proposals for a British Bill of Rights.

As with the other parties, human rights work is usually undertaken by a few active party members. Cases are taken up on an *ad hoc* basis as they are brought to the Party's attention. Both Lord Avebury, the Liberal spokesman on immigration and refugee questions, and Jeremy Thorpe as its Foreign Affairs spokesman, have taken part in Amnesty missions in recent years.

Socialist International
88a St John's Wood High Street
London NW8
Tel: (01) 586 1101
Telex: 261735
Cables: INTESECON
Secretary General: Bernt Carlsson

As a grouping of political parties (with 39 member parties throughout the world and a further 15 consultative parties, mostly in exile), the Socialist International does not view its human rights work in terms of protest action, but as an integral part of its political task of setting standards and working at a political level to see them implemented. Human rights thus figured strongly in the keynote speeches at the Socialist International's 13th Congress in November 1976.

The Socialist International is serviced by a small secretariat in London, which also acts as a clearing-house for information between member parties. These are most strongly represented in Western Europe and the pro-Western world, though there is a small contingent from Asia (India, Japan, Korea, Malaysia), Africa (Senegal), and Latin America (Argentina, Chile, Costa Rica, Dominican Republic).[1]

Representing particular socialist principles (as proclaimed at Frankfurt in 1951 and Oslo in 1962), the Socialist International sees its relationship with many Third World parties as one of contact and support, but not direct affiliation. In the same way, it is concerned with the mode of application of fundamental and universal human rights in Third World countries whose political, economic and cultural patterns may preclude or inhibit the traditional Western guarantees of legal process and constitutional protection. Both topics are currently under discussion by the Socialist International and its member parties.

---

[1] It must be stressed that all approaches on Human Rights cases must be channeled through the constituent national parties, and not directly to SI.

Chapter 15

TRADE UNIONISTS

The right of everyone to 'form and to join trade unions for the protection of his interests' is guaranteed under article 23 of the United Nations Universal Declaration of Human Rights. It is clear, however, that many governments do not implement this guarantee. In April 1977, Amnesty International listed 283 individual cases of trade unionists imprisoned (or 'missing') as a result of their union activities. This represented an increase of 72% over the number of individual cases known to AI in the previous year. And these figures in turn can only account for a small proportion of those harassed by police, sacked from their jobs or forced into exile or clandestine activity as a result of having attempted to organise their work-force outside, or in defiance of, official structures.

Harassment, imprisonment and also torture of trade unionists is particularly evident throughout Latin America. In South Africa, many union officers have been banned as a direct result of their union work, while in Rhodesia a considerable number of black unionists are held under the Emergency Powers in connection with their presumed political sympathies. Indonesia has held large numbers of unionists without trial for over a decade as a result of their affiliation to the former communist-oriented union federation (outlawed in 1965). In all, 21 countries figure on Amnesty's list, which is far from exhaustive.

International solidarity with unionists at risk has a long history, and the international movement is well-structured to respond through the international trades confederations. The union movement is essentially concerned with the defence of democratic and economic rights as the pre-condition for trade union rights and the existence of the union movement throughout the world. While this approach includes human rights in the narrow sense employed in this survey — the right of association, of free expression, freedom from arbitrary arrest and torture, etc. — it is equally concerned with the wider concept of social and economic rights: the right to a living wage, protection at work, security of work, the right to strike, etc. Union action on human rights cases must be viewed in the wider context of fostering union activity and establishing inter-union solidarity.

The unions are essentially responsive bodies, and will react to the many approaches made to them by human rights organisations and support groups, or by the national or international confederations. They will react especially when a member of their own trade is directly involved overseas. This argues for a better supply of information to the unions about human rights cases, and closer cooperation with the campaigning organisers.

The British Labour Movement has a strong tradition of international solidarity with anti-fascist struggles and campaigns for union rights overseas. In recent years it has come in for a degree of criticism for its dilatory approach to concerted action on Southern Africa and Latin America. The speed of the response to the ICFTU's 1976 call for a union boycott of South Africa, and the effectiveness of the Chile campaign in mobilising practical support at all levels of the union movement have helped redress this impression, though doubts are still expressed in some quarters as to the unions' willingness to extend this action to other less well-known areas of repression.[1]

The most frequent criticism levelled at the Labour Movement is that of adopting double standards in its attitude towards human rights violations in Eastern Europe. This criticism fails to take into account the frequent private approaches that have been made to officials in the Eastern bloc, not to mention the public stand taken on a number of occasions towards the rights of dissenters in those countries. The response to outside demands for union involvement in human rights cases from the Eastern bloc may be illustrated by a report from the debate on Eastern Europe and the USSR at British Amnesty's Trade Union Human Rights Conference at Eastbourne in May 1977:

> The debate that ensued took the form of an attempt by two of the trade unionists (who shall be nameless) to assert that breaches of human rights did not occur in the USSR and that stories to that effect were the work of the CIA . . . The majority of the other trade unionists present were frustrated by this attempt to block any useful action and reacted sympathetically to what we had to say. They had to warn us, however, that similar arguments were bound to arise in their own unions should we seek help on Soviet cases from them. We emphasised that we were only asking for the opportunity to place the evidence before them. Industrial workers' representatives thought there was a good chance that their members might take action over the suppression of workers involves in strikes. Professional union representatives felt that if they could avoid compromising the non-political image of their unions they might do useful work for POCs.

The actions undertaken by the individual British unions are too many to list in detail here. A good outline of the union record on Chile is to be found in *Chile and the British Labour Movement* (available from Chile Solidarity Campaign); this includes details of the prisoner adoption scheme (in conjunction with the Chile Committee for Human Rights), refugee reception (with the Joint Working Group), and the blacking of Chilean products. One recent initiative which resulted from the increased union interest in Latin America was a clandestine mission sent by the National Union of Mineworkers to investigate the situation of a number of Bolivian mineworkers imprisoned in Chile, as well as conditions for

---

[1] In fairness many union officials are simply too busy to concern themselves with large numbers of international appeals.

miners and unionists in Bolivia itself. Other unions which have shown a strong interest in human rights issues are the T&GWU, the NUR, National Union of Seamen, and Union of General and Municipal Workers.

While the TUC represents the union movement as a whole in the UK, individual unions have been able to react more speedily when directly approached by human rights organisations and support groups, or in response to appeals put out through the international trades secretariats or the international bodies such as the WFTU or the ICFTU. In contrast to their European counterparts, however, they have proved on the whole less spontaneous in expressing solidarity with unionists at risk overseas, though not from any lack of sympathy, rather for lack of time and adequate information.

The International Trade Secretariats (ITS) and International Trade Union Confederations — International Confederation of Free Trade Unions (ICFTU), World Federation of Trade Unions (WFTU), and World Confederation of Labour (WCL) — often serve as a clearing-house for information on violations of human and trade union rights, and may intervene with governments and intergovernmental bodies on behalf of union members deprived of these rights. As confederations of national unions and union federations, they can call on their affiliates at short notice on specific fund-raising appeals. Many have standing funds: the ICFTU, for example, has an 'International Solidarity Fund' based on voluntary contributions pledged by affiliated organisations, both for emergency aid and for longer-term projects (though not restricted in its application to human rights cases or victims of persecution).

Trades Union Congress
Congress House
23-28 Great Russell Street
London WC1
Tel: (01) 636 4030
General Secretary: Rt Hon Lionel Murray, OBE

The TUC has, through its Congress resolutions, a firm general commitment on human rights issues on the international level. It has adopted resolutions, given publicity and made representations to government or union counterparts overseas. Where there is no formal union structure (e.g. in Latin America, where these may be banned or operating secretly), it maintains contact with labour leaders in exile. Elsewhere, it may back international calls for action, such as the recent blacking of South African goods and services. In contrast to these public gestures, the TUC accepts the argument that behind-the-scenes approaches may prove more effective in certain circumstances, and has made use of its Eastern European and Soviet contacts to this end. (These are not always cases directly related to union activity — for instance, interventions have been made on behalf of individuals who have lost their job as a result of their political stance.)

Because of this dual public/private approach, the TUC has been accused of adopting double standards. But the TUC believes that it is reacting in different ways, each appropriate to the different circumstances of the case.

The TUC acknowledges the important role played by local union branches, chapels and trades councils in the Chile adoption and refugee resettlement campaign as a possible precedent for future actions. It does not undertake much education work at this level, leaving this to the individual unions and to the Labour Party structure (local-level initiatives often depend for their effectiveness on local union or trades council activists who may also be Labour Party members). Union or trade journals can often provide more extensive coverage than can the TUC's *Labour Journal* in reaching the shop floor.

Funds

As a result of the Hungarian refugee influx after 1956, a precedent does exist for specific fund-raising for refugee reception. Chile is now the only area for which there is a standing fund, from which money is channeled to the exiled CUT in Paris. Affiliate unions may be encouraged to donate funds to other causes, such as Medical Aid to Vietnam. The TUC itself has few funds, and acts as a clearing-house for its wealthier affiliates and for the ICFTU.

III Refugees

Chapter 16

ADMISSION OF REFUGEES

Mr K., a South African, applied for asylum at the port of entry. He was interviewed at least three times by two different immigration officers. He was refused and was told that he would be returned to South Africa within 24 hours. A South African organisation contacted UKIAS, which interviewed him at length. Eventually after much negotiation and some publicity he was permitted to remain in the UK as a refugee. The official interviews failed to clarify his actual status, and he was in danger of refoulement. The intervention of outside bodies had been a matter of chance.

Mr A was to be deported for having contracted a marriage of convenience. He appealed explaining that he feared persecution. The Home Office did not investigate his fears, and instead simply stated that he had produced no proof. It is the view of UKIAS and of the UNHCR that he almost certainly is a refugee. He is at present in prison while the Home Office reconsider his case. They have refused to release him.

Mr N sought asylum at the port of entry. He was interviewed on board a vessel of the country from which he was seeking asylum, and apparently informed that he could be interviewed in English or remain on board ship until an interpreter could be found. He chose English, although he speaks it poorly. He was refused asylum and held in jail. His appeal was dismissed. Eventually he became so distressed at his reception that he gave up and asked to be allowed to go to a third country.

Case-studies from *An Outline of the Current Procedures for Refugees and Asylum-Seekers in the UK*, UKIAS, June 1977

Introduction[1]

Refugee work is central to human rights activities in the United Kingdom, which has traditionally been looked to as a country of asylum. A refugee is defined by article 1 of the 1951 UN Convention on Refugees as

a person who, owing to a well-founded fear of being persecuted for reasons of race, religion, nationality, membership of a particular social group or political opinion, is outside the country of his nationality and is unable or, owing to such fear, is unwilling to avail himself of the protection of that country.[2]

Unlike other migrants, the refugee makes a particular moral demand on

---

[1] We are indebted to Ms Sue Ashtiany of UKIAS, Dr Guy Goodwin-Gill of the UNHCR London Office, and Ms Nancy Rice-Jones of the Standing Conference on Refugees for their assistance in compiling this section.

[2] *Convention relating to the Status of Refugees*, 1951, extended by the 1967 Protocol. See Cmd. 9171, June 1954.

the country from which he seeks asylum, since he claims to have nowhere else to go.

The extent to which governments and voluntary organisations have responded to this demand is beyond the scope of this survey. The following chapters aim to show how the British system of reception and settlement has adapted to the needs of new categories of refugees in recent years. The voluntary organisations have largely come to recognise that the refugee phenomenon does not begin and end at the port of entry; but the immigration machinery under which refugees are admitted and the lack of proper eligibility procedures have in too many instances denied the asylum-seeker any benefit of doubt. Britain's traditional claim to be a country of asylum has come to look rather threadbare, and in view of this it is important to understand why many individuals in fear of persecution still turn to this country for refuge.

British contact with incoming refugees until the 1950s was almost exclusively European in character. The arrival of Russian and Eastern European Jews at the end of the century was followed in the interwar years by the influx of refugees from Nazi persecution; the Second World War saw the resettlement of some 250,000 displaced persons, and during the 1950s the first refugees from communist regimes in Eastern Europe, notably the Hungarians after 1956, the Czechs after 1968. A refugee was seen typically as someone who was unlikely to return to his country of exile. The British could pride themselves with some justification on their tradition of asylum, and point to the contribution made to national life by refugees who had successfully integrated.

The refugees who began to arrive after the 1960s departed radically from this established stereotype. They came increasingly from outside the familiar European cultural tradition. Many were from newly-independent African and Asian countries, at a time when immigration from these areas was creating hostile undercurrents in the host community. And during the mid-1970s the pattern changed still further with the arrival of significant numbers of Latin American refugees. In the words of one refugee organisation, the British Council for Aid to Refugees,

> Ten years ago it was the exception to have a refugee referred to us who had not come from Europe. In 1974/75 we were called on for help to refugees from Latin America (mainly Chileans), from Africa (Ethiopians, Rhodesians, Ugandans and Southern Africans), from Indochina (Vietnamese, Cambodians and Laotians) as well as Kurds.[1]

Between October 1975 and September 1976 , the BCAR alone assisted with 517 refugee cases (1,017 individuals) from some 30 countries. As well as emergency intake from well-publicised areas of civil or international conflict, there is a steady trickle of individuals and small groups of

---

[1]   British Council for Aid to Refugees, *Annual Report 1974/75.*

asylum-seekers reaching the UK.

The British government, as a signatory to the 1967 Protocol to the 1951 Convention, subscribes to an undertaking to supply refugee statistics on request, but to date has appeared reluctant to maintain any. Refugee questions tend to be overshadowed in the press and Parliament by the debate on immigration in general. Refugees form only a tiny proportion of the immigrant population, and are governed by the same entrance regulations. But because refugees have explicit reasons for wanting to enter or remain in this country, there are strong arguments for urging fuller consideration of their problems, in relation not only to the capacity of the host community to absorb them, but to the political and human rights issues surrounding their flight.

The lack of any firm distinction between political refugees and other immigrants has reduced the chances of acceptance for potential refugees. In Britain, where there is no distinct legal status for refugees, the onus is on the incoming refugee to prove to the Home Office's satisfaction that he is not just an immigrant. Protectionist policies on immigration have resulted in entry refusal for *de facto* refugees who are covered by the 1951 UN Convention on Refugees and its 1967 Protocol (to which the UK subscribes), but not recognised as such by the British government (e.g., Cypriot refugees). Yet their 'well-founded fear of persecution' remains as urgent as those of their fellow refugees whose needs are formally recognised.

A further new element in defining refugee problems has been the recognition that many foreign workers, students and visitors prefer to stay in this country owing to a well-founded fear of persecution if they return home. A student may find that a coup in his country has left him without political or financial support at home; a migrant worker may fear reprisals at home for his political activity while overseas. These 'hidden' refugees prefer not to declare themselves as such when applying for an extension of their entry permits, because they do not wish to draw attention either to themselves, or to their families and friends at home. If they overstay their entry permission, they are liable for deportation without appeal. The recognition that disguised refugees now exist in significant numbers throughout Europe has prompted a number of voluntary organisations to press for more adequate official protection for them;.[1]

A further important feature of refugee intake in recent years has been the recognition that many refugees see their exile as a more or less temporary period of preparation for their eventual return, and are accordingly anxious to pursue their political activities while in exile. The reception and resettlement of Chilean refugees in particular has prompted a reassessment of the nature of their refugee work by some of the

---

[1] See *Asylum in Europe, a handbook for refugees and exiles*, prepared by Anne Paludan for the International University Exchange Fund and World Student Christian Federation, October 1975. A second edition, which includes the UK, is to be published in 1978.

voluntary organisations, who see them not so much as a strain on the country's social services, as a positive asset to this country and capable of contributing to their own country's development on their eventual return home. (The fact that many of the Chileans are academics or professionals of course encourages this approach.) It is likely that this long-term perspective on refugee work marks an irreversible trend for the organisations concerned with refugees.

The problems of these new types of refugee — the temporary exile, the undeclared refugee, and the *de facto* refugee — argue strongly for a more comprehensive understanding of the local conditions which have given rise to their fears, and for a greater degree of public and official awareness of the issues at stake. It is here that human rights organisations can contribute their expertise in supporting the refugee's request for asylum.

International Instruments

Britain is a signatory to the 1951 UN Convention relating to the Status of Refugees and its 1967 Protocol extending the 1951 dateline indefinitely. Article 14 of the Universal Declaration of Human Rights, to which Britain subscribes, states that 'everyone has the right to seek and enjoy in other countries asylum from persecution'. This right is not generally interpreted as comprising the right to *obtain* asylum: all states reserve their own sovreign rights in admitting refugees. Thus refugees recognised by the UN High Commission for Refugees as falling within its mandate — 'Mandate' or 'Convention' refugees — may have a stronger backing in their request than refugees not covered by its terms, but have no automatic access to refugee status in the eyes of government officials.

The Convention commits signatories to extend to refugees in respect of property, work, association, education, welfare benefits and freedom of movement, facilities which are 'as favourable as possible and, in any event, not less favourable than [those] accorded to aliens generally in the same circumstances'. The contracting states undertake not to penalise refugees entering the country illegally as their first country of asylum, provided they present themselves to the authorities without delay and 'show good cause' for their illegal entry.

Article 33 of the Convention elaborates the principle of *non-refoulement*, which means that no refugee is returned to 'territories where his life or freedom would be threatened'.[1] The principle is therefore not confined to returning the refugee to the country from whence he came.

There have been attempts in certain countries to circumvent the *non-refoulement* rule by claiming that the unsuccessful applicant had not formally 'entered' the territory at the time of being turned away. At the January 1977 diplomatic Conference on Territorial Asylum, the

---

[1] Exceptions are made in the case of war-criminals, and those convicted of serious crime, or considered a threat to national security.

principle of *non-refoulement* was reinforced on the basis of proposals from the non-governmental organisations present which may be interpreted as constituting an absolute obligation by contracting states not to turn away asylum-seekers at the frontier. The proposed draft Convention restates the principle so that no refugee 'shall be subjected to measures such as rejection at the frontier, return or expulsion, which would compel him to remain in or return to a territory with respect to which he has a well-founded fear of persecution, prosecution or punishment . . .'.[1]

In addition to the formal legal instruments, certain rules of thumb are observed by the European states in admitting refugees. One is that asylum is usually granted only in the first country at which the refugee arrives on leaving his own country. Usually when a refugee has stayed for a specified length of time in another country 'en route', this is considered his or her first country of asylum.[2] While in Britain exceptions have been made to this rule, notably in the case of large-scale movements of refugees (e.g. from Uganda), this is treated as a special dispensation, and not as a precedent. The UKIAS has attempted to persuade the United Kingdom authorities that an applicant for asylum should not be refused simply because he could have sought it elsewhere and didn't. Certain other European countries – Belgium, Holland, Sweden in particular – have already dropped the 'first-country' rule of thumb, and consequently accept refugees refused entry by the UK.

Resettlement in third countries may be attempted through the intermediary of the UNHCR Office, but this is a lengthy procedure, which normally requires prior written confirmation from the country in question that it will accept the refugee.

Acceptance

The nature of immigration control into this country is different from that in most other countries in our reliance on control before or at entry. Inquiries to establish personal acceptability take time but they are completed as quickly as resources allow.

Merlyn Rees, Home Secretary, to the House of Commons
23 December 1976

The United Kingdom applies a different philosophy to its refugee vetting procedures from many other Western European countries. While these

---

[1] The Convention on Territorial Asylum was adjourned and there have been serious doubts expressed as to whether it will be reconvened in the foreseeable future. Despite the greater protection afforded by the above amendments to article 3 on *non-refoulement*, and a proposed new article on the facilitation of family re-unification, article 2 was re-phrased so as to place the admission of asylum-seekers at the discretion of states and, by implication, on their interpretation of the 'definite possibility' of persecution on the refugee's return.

[2] Certain countries, however, such as Italy and Austria, are in effect transit countries, and refugees are resettled from them.

have long land frontiers which are often too unprotected to allow for tight entry controls on arrival, the UK has been able to adopt this approach. which might be qualified, in both senses of the word, as insular. Once allowed in, it is claimed, the refugee is relatively free from the constant surveillance and police harassment which is the lot of foreign residents in a number of continental countries.

This approach has been increasingly called into question for its inflexibility in coping with emergencies, and the lack of understanding displayed towards certain categories of refugees. The situation of the Chilean refugees at risk in Argentina is a case in point. While awaiting clearance from Britain — a process which can take up to 7 or 8 months — refugees may be kept waiting for visas in circumstances of extreme danger. At least one person is known to have undergone torture in the interim. Similar delays have meant that political detainees in Chile who can opt for exile have remained in prison for longer than necessary.

The UK offered in June 1976 to take 75 cases urgently needing resettlement from Argentina. 109 cases were quickly submitted. These refugees had all been detained and ill-treated in Argentina, and were mostly under threat of expulsion to their own countries of origin. By February 1977, the UK authorities had cleared only a small proportion of these cases, of which only 16 have come here. The rest had already been received by other countries.

These dilatory procedures may prove dangerous to the refugees and damaging to Britain's reputation abroad. They contrast poorly with the 48 hours' emergency clearance employed by Sweden and security-conscious France. Furthermore, the knowledge that British identity-checks are conducted through CIA sources has done much to discourage would-be applicants.

Persistent lobbying by voluntary organisations for the government to extend its visa provisions to other nationals at risk in Argentina (i.e. in addition to Chileans) has so far met with little success. To date, only about twenty Uruguayan refugees (7 visas) have been admitted from Argentina. There is no evidence as yet that any precedent has been created for the admission of refugees in a similar plight in Latin America or elsewhere in the world.[1]

While admission procedures and subsequent controls vary considerably amongst other European countries, it is safe to say that most of these have adopted procedures which give the benefit of the doubt to refugees who are unable to provide evidence to the full satisfaction of the authorities in support of their fears of likely political persecution. In Holland (experimentally) and in Denmark, a distinct category — 'B-status' — has been created to accommodate *de facto* refugees who cannot provide

---

[1] See leader article, 'We Should Say What We Mean', in *The Times*, 29 January 1977.

adequate proof (and thus cannot qualify as Convention refugees), but who are likely to run a risk on being returned to their own country. This intermediate status also affords a wider interpretation of what constitutes a legitimate fear, and might, for example, afford protection for draft-evaders from certain countries. Sweden, which like Britain has no clearly distinct status for refugees but allows them in 'for special reasons' under its immigration laws, has earned a great deal of respect and sympathy overseas for the generous interpretation it has displayed in implementing these regulations to the benefit of refugees and draft-evaders.

Asylum

The UK Immigration Act makes provision for refugees within the context of normal immigration proceedings.[1] Its Immigration Regulations allude to article 1 of the 1951 Convention and to 'well-founded fears of persecution' as the key to any definition of refugee status. There is no formal reception structure for incoming refugees as a separate category; any appeal against refusal of entry or leave to stay has to be lodged with the normal immigration appeals procedures.

The United Kingdom does accept a few individuals as 'refugees'. However, this is often difficult to tell as there is no formal identification for refugees as a distinct category. Indeed, official sources will always refrain — presumably for diplomatic reasons — from mentioning 'asylum' when refugees are allowed to stay. It is clear from the Immigration Rules that political asylum is used only as a last option for admission to the country when the applicant does not qualify on any other grounds. The majority of refugees will, if admitted, be allowed to stay in the UK under other categories on 'compassionate grounds'; residence under these terms is not indefinite, but subject to renewal and review in the same way as other categories of stay.[2]

Since there is no interim status of 'asylum-seeker', such as has been established in some other European countries, and no set procedures for refugee reception, the admission of refugees is dependent on three elements: the discretionary powers of immigration officials, the persistance of the applicants, and the ability of the advisory bodies to intervene quickly and assist them.

The work of the port immigration officials is so defined that their task is to sift out and send away anyone they are not satisfied has a valid claim to enter. This would appear to be entirely inappropriate as a means for

---

[1]   See the Immigration Act (1971) and the Statements of Immigration Rules for Control on and after Entry (for Commonwealth and Non-Commonwealth citizens), 25 January 1973, HC 79, 80, 81, 92.

[2]   While the British government is under a statutory obligation to supply Convention Travel Documents to refugees, many who are admitted under these alternative headings or as self-employed, may not be granted one by the Home Office.

evaluating the claims of asylum-seekers. The Home Office has argued that the discretionary powers employed by its port officials permit a greater flexibility of approach when evaluating the 'compassionate grounds' on which refugees may be allowed to enter the country. However, it has been argued that such discretionary powers can cut both ways, and restrict the opportunity allowed to the refugee to state his or her case. This is especially so when officials have understandably only a limited comprehension of the circumstances which have caused the refugee to flee.

By virtue of the provisions of the law, it is always up to the applicant to show that he or she is liable to persecution for political, racial, religious or other reasons on returning home. These arguments can only be supported publicly when the refugee appeals against the refusal of entry. The stage at which the advisory agencies can contact the applicant with legal advice may therefore be crucial; it is not known how many potential refugees are turned away without exercising their right of appeal.

The situation is complicated by the fact that many *de facto* refugees are unwilling to declare themselves as such, for fear of drawing undue attention to themselves or to their relatives and friends at home, and therefore fail to gain admittance as immigrant workers, students or visitors. Even those who do then put forward political reasons for their application may incur the suspicion of immigration officials because of their attempts to obscure personal details for similar reasons. In a system which employs discretionary powers to *refuse* admission, requests for asylum on political grounds may also be viewed with suspicion by officials as a back-door attempt to circumvent the normal immigration hurdles.

If a refugee seeking asylum on entry is refused immediate leave to enter the country but not sent away,[1] he or she may be detained pending a decision by the Home Office. In such cases, the refugee is seldom held for more than a month or two, although some cases have taken up to 7 or 8 months for further decision.

In some instances, applicants are detained in prison. They have the statutory right to apply for bail, and to consult with lawyers and representatives of the UKIAS. The voluntary organisations are also concerned at this stage; they, and UKIAS, are anxious that refugees should be contacted and given legal advice on how best to appeal an unfavourable decision *before* the formal appeal procedures get under way.

The UN High Commission for Refugees, through its London office, is advised of cases concerning political asylum on appeal. As an international agency, the UNHCR does not play an active part in initiating appeals proceedings. The UNHCR may submit evidence to the adjudicator, along with refugee and human rights organisations, that the appellant is liable to suffer persecution if returned home. Such arguments may be difficult to put when 'persecution' has taken the form of continued harassment over

---

[1]   See note on admissions, below.

a period of time, or when no precise acts of persecution have been committed against the appellant. The onus is on him to convince the adjudicator of the serious possibility of persecution on his return.

Procedures

The Home Office Immigration and Nationality Department which deals with refugees contains a Commonwealth and an Aliens section, and each of these are subdivided into 'case work groups'. Refugees are handled by special groups. When an application is submitted it will go to the normal case working group. They will decide if it is a matter of asylum or refugee status and refer it to the special group if they think it is. Sometimes if asylum is not formally requested, the case will de dealt with under the ordinary machinery. Thus for example a Czech who went to the Home Office explained that he did not intend to return to Czechoslovakia, and wished to settle in the West, was not treated as someone who could be seeking asylum.

A number of aspects of the present system are striking:

— the Home Office relies on non-specialist, untrained or inappropriately trained people to interview an applicant;
— it is quite possible that someone who is seeking asylum will be treated as not seeking asylum;
— because of the rules, asylum will be brought into consideration only where a person does not otherwise qualify to remain;
— decisions are sometimes not reached for 8 months or more and the applicant has no special status during this period;
— the Home Office does not usually inform any agencies about a case, except that the address of the UKIAS is given to people who have a right of appeal.

A particular difficulty is raised by people who do not have an effective right of appeal. These are: refugees applying to enter the UK from abroad; people being turned down at a port of entry who do not have visas; people who are in this country and who for one reason or another do not have a right of appeal (including over-stayers).

In the first category above, it is at least possible for the applicant to contact UKIAS. The second and third are more worrying. The Home Office can — and there is evidence that it does — decide that an asylum seeker is not a refugee and simply send him away without reference to any agencies for a second opinion. This causes concern because it is known that interview procedures leave something to be desired. In a significant number of such cases known to UKIAS, the Home Office were intending to send away (refouler) a refugee and changed their assessment only after intervention by the voluntary organisations and UKIAS.

United Kingdom
ADMISSION

Application from Abroad

In common with many other countries, the United Kingdom does not generally grant asylum to persons overseas, whether still in their country of origin or in some country of first or temporary asylum. There is thus no provision in the immigration law making the status of refugee a ground for the issue of an entry clearance. Where the United Kingdom does respond to emergencies abroad (for example, after an appeal by the United Nations High Commissioner for Refugees), then it implements its response outside the immigration law, as an exceptional exercise of discretion. The consequence for the individual refugee is that, if his application to come to the UK is turned down, he has no effective right of appeal.[1] The terms of the law are against him, and make no provision for his questioning the exercise of this discretionary competence.

Applications by Refugees in the United Kingdom

A refugee may apply for asylum either at the port of entry or, subsequent to his admission, at the Home Office.

At a Port   The immigration rules provide that a passenger who does not otherwise qualify for admission shall not be refused entry if this would mean his going to a country to which he is unwilling to go owing to a well-founded fear of persecution. At a port such claims are considered by immigration officers, who may refuse admission (after reference to a Chief Immigration Officer) if they are not satisfied that the claim to asylum is established. If the asylum-seeker arrives without a visa (either because he has not applied for one or because nationals from his country do not require them) he may only appeal against the refusal of entry *from abroad*. Thus he may find himself returned to the country of persecution from which he has escaped. There is no settled practice of temporary asylum or temporary release, or reference to the London Office of the UNHCR.

If the asylum-seeker arrives with a visa then he can pursue his right of appeal while still in the UK. The existence of this right does prevent immediate 'refoulement' to a country of persecution. Papers in such cases are now referred to the London Office of the UNHCR, so enabling the Representative to decide whether or not to exercise his right to become a party to the appeal proceedings (see below).

After entry   After entry an asylum-seeker may apply for an extension of stay on the ground that he has a well-founded fear of persecution in his own land. He may also resist an intended deportation order on the same

---

[1]   To an adjudicator or to the Immigration Appeal Tribunal, under the provisions of the Immigration Act 1971.

grounds. In both cases the decision rests with the Home Office Immigration and Nationality Department. There is a right of appeal against an adverse decision only if the asylum-seeker still had permission to be in the UK at the time of the decision and providing that he is not the subject of a deportation order made after recommendation by a court on conviction. In such cases the asylum-seeker may do no more than submit representations on his own behalf, either from himself or from other interested parties, such as MPs and interested organisations.

Where a right of appeal exists, then the asylum-seeker may put his case to an adjudicator and then to the Immigration Appeal Tribunal. He may be represented by a solicitor or by the Refugee Counsellor from UKIAS, and the UK Representative of the UNHCR may elect to become a party to the proceedings. However, in the 28 months from 1 January 1975 until 30 April 1977 no appeal by an asylum-seeker was successful and in view of this the UNHCR withdrew its active participation in appeals proceedings (*see* p. 187). Strong representations have since been made to the Home Office by the refugee agencies on the inadequacies of the appeals system with regard to refugee cases.

Appeals

Appeals are heard by adjudicators appointed by the Home Office. The adjudicator is empowered to refuse admission if he considers the appellant to be an illegal entrant, i.e. not to satisfy the exact terms of the Immigration Regulations. This decision may be appealed to the Immigration Appeal Tribunal.

While the legal basis for the adjudicator's decisions have never been formally questioned, publication of the findings in two cases dismissed on appeal have cast grave doubts on the fairness of appeals proceedings.[1] The two instances are not typical of all adjudications, but the fact that the interpretations given by the two adjudicators in question displayed strong political bias has prompted concern about a system in which judgements may be passed which go against official policy, and over which there is no control or review. Other adjudicators have shown themselves more sympathetic to refugee claims; but the allocation of hearings to well- or ill-disposed adjudicators must add a further arbitrary element to the existing hazards of refugee entry.

---

[1]   The cases in question concerned Chilean refugees, former Socialist Party members, who were referred to disparagingly (and inaccurately) as 'communist agitators' and for whom one adjudicator 'could see no marked compassionate circumstances special to the appellants'. See Immigration Act (1971), Determinations of 9 November 1976 and 10 December 1976; reported in the *Guardian* and *The Times* of 4 February 1977, *New Statesman*, 11 February 1977. Amongst others, the Labour Party's National Executive Committee has since urged the government to ensure that the adjudicators are politically unbiased in their recommendations.

United Kingdom

As for the 'hidden' refugees, their situation is no easier than that of all other temporary immigrants, who are liable for deportation if they break the Immigration Laws. Following a recent ruling by the Court of Appeal, immigrants have no right of appeal against deportation orders if they have failed to apply for an extension of their visas before these expire. In other words, they are liable for deportation if they are found to have overstayed their leave of entry, even though this may be the result of ignorance, sickness or . . . fear of deportation.

Professionals and Freelancers

Under the Immigration Regulations, certain categories of professional people do not require work permits, although they do need to satisfy the immigration authorities that they have adequate means of support while in the country. These categories include: churchmen and missionaries 'coming to work as such', doctors and dentists 'to take up professional appointments', and self-employed persons such as artists and writers who 'may be admitted if the Home Office is satisfied that they do not intend to do work for which a work permit is necessary and that they will be able to support themselves and any dependants without recourse to public funds'.

Since many *de facto* refugees fall into these professional categories, there is a clear case for setting up a system of sponsorship, either through 'adoption' techniques organised by professional associations etc., or through the establishment of funds which can ensure that such categories can be supported until they find employment here.

Chapter 17

REFUGEE RECEPTION AND SETTLEMENT

The reception, counselling and integration of refugees into the British host community has traditionally been left to voluntary effort. Apart from a Home Office grant to the Joint Working Group towards its Chilean programme, and Overseas Development Ministry funds to WUS for Latin American and Vietnamese students, this effort is carried on entirely through voluntary and non-governmental initiatives.

As in other areas of humanitarian work, a division of responsibilities has developed amongst the voluntary refugee organisations. This corresponds to the different needs of refugees — for counselling, material assistance, interim accommodation, placement in work and study, English language classes, vocational training and so on. And given the differences of approach to government, to the nature of their work, and to the refugees themselves, there are also political divergences which correspond to what might be called a generation gap.

The new pattern of refugee influx over the last few years has given rise to the creation of 'parallel' structures in all the European countries.[1] These are characterised by a refusal to shy away from political issues connected with their work, either domestically in their relations with the government departments handling refugee cases, or internationally in their support for the political aspirations of the refugees they seek to assist. Against this, the more 'traditional' refugee organisations may be seen as less critical in their dealings with the government departments — more 'establishment-minded' — and unwilling to consider their refugee work in other than purely charitable humanitarian terms.

This difference of approach also means a wider range of options for the refugees themselves. The newer refugee organisations will deal with *de facto* and 'hidden' refugees whom the traditional structures, working only with Convention refugees, may not acknowledge. Moreover, recent refugees may tend to distrust the bureaucratic approach of the traditional agencies and prefer the informality of the 'parallel' organisations, with which they can identify more readily in terms of life-style and political attitudes.

However, this generation difference does not amount to a decisive split. The injection of a related but distinct political element into voluntary refugee work has proved a positive asset in promoting more

---

[1]   See *Report on the Problems of Refugees and Exiles in Europe*, Anne Paludan for IUEF, Geneva, September 1974.

thoroughgoing debate on refugee issues, including lobbying, without necessarily jeopardising contacts and cooperation with the relevant government departments.

The work involved in counselling and assisting new refugees is time-consuming and costly. As well as the perennial difficulties of adapting to a new culture and society, refugees have in recent years encountered additional problems in competing for work, study, and accommodation with the rest of the population. The morale of unemployed refugees may drop sharply, especially when relatives and friends at home are still known to be in danger or detention; language-classes are often full, and transport difficult to arrange; local social security staff are often sympathetic but overworked; psychiatric help for traumatised or depressed refugees is hard to obtain.

The local structures set up in response to the Chile emergency have provided a valuable lesson in alleviating many of these difficulties by devolving these tasks onto local reception groups. Refugees are dispersed throughout the country after a spell — usually three weeks — in a reception centre; this reduces the chances of despondency and dependence on available services. Local groups help to arrange work and accommodation, establish contact with local social and medical services, with schools, unions and places of higher education, and provide the necessary continuity and moral support which a centralised agency, however well-staffed, cannot always provide.

However, the important achievements of the Chile campaign, while affording many useful examples for future work, cannot be allowed to detract from the strongly felt need for more adequate official provision for refugees, especially in meeting future contingencies. The voluntary organisations have persistently (but to no avail) pressed the government for help in establishing permanent reception facilities for incoming refugees such as exist in other European countries. At a time when private sources of funding are running low, official financial assistance in this area may prove crucial to the future effectiveness of refugee resettlement in the United Kingdom.

Chapter 18

REFUGEE ORGANISATIONS

British Council for Aid to Refugees
35 Great Peter Street
London SW1P 3LR
Tel: (01) 799 3087
Chairman: Mr P.G. Barber CBE
General Secretary: Mrs N.V. Morley-Fletcher

Founded in 1950, the BCAR is the only British refugee organisation operating solely in this country. It also undertakes casework and has a separate section for the reception and settlement of new arrivals granted admission to the UK and a section for dealing with the general welfare problems of refugees who have been in this country for some time but need special support because of age, physical or mental handicap.

It works with the major refugee, humanitarian and development aid organisations twenty-two of which, including Christian Aid, Catholic Women's League, Central British Fund for Jewish Relief, the Ockenden Venture, UKIAS, UNA and WUS, are represented on the Council. BCAR is also associated with the British Red Cross Society, WRVS and the UNHCR office in London and cooperates with some twenty-eight exile groups, mostly of Eastern European origin; the two most recent additions are the Ethiopian Refugee Self-Help Organisation and the British-Kurdish Friendship Society. Representatives from the Home Office Immigration and Nationality Department and from the Department of Health and Social Security are observers on the Council.

BCAR's expenditure for the year 1975/6 amounted to £183,945 – a 23.6% increase on the previous year's total which reflects both the effects of inflation and an increased caseload. This sum, however, excludes the £62,500 Government Grant (to BCAR) made specifically for the reception and settlement of refugees from Chile by the Joint Working Group, a separate body, formed in summer 1974, of which BCAR is a founder member.

The work and special programmes for refugees from other countries are financed from legacies, donations, subscriptions, interest on investments and the residue from earlier appeals. Very recently the Home Office has agreed to make a grant as a contribution towards BCAR's Headquarters' administration expenses.

The BCAR is a strictly non-political organisation and devotes its energies entirely to the practical problems of resettlement and welfare work of refugees irrespective of the refugees' political, racial or social background. It refrains from lobbying activities, as this is felt to be the task of the Standing Conference, of which BCAR is a member.

BCAR's caseload consists largely of Convention refugees (those recognised by the UNHCR as falling within its mandate) but includes some *de facto* refugees who need assistance while waiting for clarification and recognition of their refugee status. It helps individual refugees with their material needs while their appeals are being considered. Its terms of reference preclude it from assisting refugees or displaced persons who hold British passports on arrival in the UK, but it continues to assist those who have acquired British nationality since coming to Britain if their circumstances are such that they have not integrated into the community owing to lack of English or for other reasons, resulting from their status as refugees.

Between October 1975 and December 1976, a total of 1,228 refugees from some thirty-four countries were referred to BCAR for resettlement.[1] Cases are referred to them by the Home Office, local Citizens' Advice Bureaux, Social Services Departments, UNHCR office in London, other voluntary agencies, national exile groups and by individuals. This referral system is not automatic, as is shown by the variety of sources involved. In addition to the newcomers, BCAR cares for over 1,300 elderly refugees, some of them in homes and hostels provided by the Council. Some of these hostels can also provide interim employment for newly arrived refugees.

Casework is carried out independently of other refugee organisations, though there is close cooperation with voluntary agencies, Government Departments and statutory bodies concerned. BCAR can provide help with temporary accommodation for incoming refugees, language classes, referral to local government and social security offices and counselling on housing, employment, vocational training and study. This work is increasingly hampered by housing shortages, the tight labour market (especially where language difficulties are involved), and delays in obtaining social security benefits. While voluntary organisations are obliged to rely to a large degree on local authority assistance in these key areas of resettlement work, BCAR's experience has led it to increase its own initiatives in obtaining lodging and jobs. The two refugee Housing Associations formed by BCAR provided accommodation for over 325 families in the year 1975/6 plus hostel accommodation but their present housing stock is insufficient to meet the ever-growing need for accommodation. This and the lack of response from local authority housing departments has meant that for the majority of new arrivals BCAR has to find housing through the private

---

[1]   Just under half this total were Chileans, and most were dealt with by the JWG. In 75 cases, Chileans sought help direct from BCAR's Settlement Section.

178

sector which is expensive and often inadequate. In September 1976 BCAR set up its own English language courses for refugees,[1] which served also as a means of occupation, socialisation and mutual reinforcement for newcomers who are often depressed, lonely and demoralised.

BCAR recognises the crucial importance of moral support to refugees during the waiting period — often a long one — before they are established. This is particularly so when the supporting community of refugees is small or non-existent. BCAR maintains close links with the national refugee groups which can afford a degree of political and cultural reinforcement.

Christian Aid
240/250 Ferndale Road
London SW9 8BH
Tel: (01) 733 5500
Director: Rev Dr Kenneth Slack

Christian Aid undertakes some casework directly from its London office. Although the caseload is low, and in many instances referred to more spcialised agencies, Christian Aid has access to the WCC's worldwide contacts, and is thus particularly helpful in arranging the resettlement of refugees in third countries.

In some cases, Christian Aid may distribute travel loans, paid by the World Council of Churches and by the Inter-Governmental Committee for European Migration (ICEM)[2] in Geneva, to move anyone from what is considered 'an intolerable situation' — this applies to non-Convention refugees as well as those recognised by the UNHCR; travel in this context does not necessarily mean coming to Britain — in many cases, refugees are helped to travel to third countries, such as Canada, Australia, New Zealand and the United States.

Christian Aid may also distribute small interim grants from an emergency fund of around £3,500; in addition, some small discretionary grants are available through the office of the Director of Christian Aid (these totalled £2,500 in 1974; in 1975/6, Christian Aid channeled £4,614 to its refugee work in this country for refugee expenses, and £2,724 in direct grants).

A wide variety of cases are referred to the Christian Aid office, either through the churches in exile in London (who often hear at first-hand of asylum-seekers from Eastern Europe) and through WCC's worldwide

---

[1] In conjunction with the Neighbourhood English Classes (85A Highgate Road NW5).

[2] 16 ave Jean Tremblay, 1211 Geneva 19.

network of churches. The WCC contacts are used independently of ICEM and International Social Service[1] to reunite families forced apart because one of their number is a refugee.

It should be mentioned in this context that both Christian Aid and the WCC in Geneva are involved in largescale refugee resettlement programmes around the world. In many areas, particularly in Africa and SE Asia, the problems of refugee populations are on such a large scale that these operations are closer in character to development aid projects than to the Western 'rescue' type of procedure. During 1975, the WCC Refugee Office assisted the movement of 4,820 refugees from 20 different countries of first and second asylum, and spent some £450,000 on these operations in five continents. Christian Aid spent some £177,000 on earmarked refugee projects during 1975/6 – and possibly as much again when one includes contributions devoted to more general projects involving refugee work. Both pursue a policy of decentralisation wherever possible: Christian Aid, for example, channels most of its African refugee aid through the All-African Council of Churches and the South African Council of Churches. Neither international body would wish to draw a clear distinction between its refugee programme and its development aid projects or its human rights work (such as relief for the families of political prisoners) since all are, to their way of thinking, inextricably linked by their common concern for social justice.

See also page 38 on voluntary overseas aid organisations.

International Social Service of Great Britain
Cranmer House
39 Brixton Road
London SW9 6DD
Tel: (01) 735 8941
Cables: Migranto London
Director: Miss W.I. Rouse
Refugee Worker: Miss Ruth Black

Though not primarily a refugee organisation, International Social Service is involved in some casework with refugees and exiles as part of its overall task of assisting with family problems across international frontiers (e.g. family reunion, children separated from parents, etc.). ISS increasingly acts as a go-between in contact with national social service departments. The main area in which it can assist refugees and exiles is in reuniting broken families. It does not, however, act as a lobby on behalf

---

[1] Cranmer House, 39 Brixton Road, London SW9.

of refugees, and will refer this aspect to the UNHCR office in the country concerned.

ISS coverage is worldwide, and includes Eastern Europe. Its funding is through subscriptions, donations, grants and revenue from an annual spring fair. The organisation's headquarters are in Geneva.

Jewish Refugees Committee
(Caseworking Committee of the Central British Fund for
Jewish Relief and Rehabilitation)
Woburn House, 5th floor
Upper Woburn Place
London WC1H 0EP
Tel: (01) 387 5461
Cables: Migrate London
Joint Secretary: Miss E. Aronsfeld

The Jewish Refugee Committee, the caseworking committee of the Central British Fund, undertakes the Fund's resettlement activities for Jewish refugees in this country. It had its origins in the massive effort to bring over Jewish refugees, most of them in transit, from prewar Nazi-controlled Germany and Austria. At its prewar peak, JRC staff numbered 600, but its activities had so tailed off by the mid-1950s that it seemed destined to be wound down, until the Hungarian and Suez crises of 1956, both of which produced a new emergency intake of Jewish refugees. The JRC accounts for around 10% of the Central British Fund's £210,000 annual budget (1974/5) — not counting further donations and legacies which it receives directly.

Like the other refugee organisations, the JRC takes on cases from many countries, recently from Iraq, USSR and Argentina. It concerns itself solely with Jews, but does not restrict itself to Convention refugees (particularly since anti-Semitism may manifest itself in more subtle ways than outright political persecution); however, the Committee has to be convinced that applicants have suffered genuine persecution before it will consider them for support. The JRC will assist potential refugees only if it feels that they have a good case for being eligible for social security benefits: the Committee is anxious to avoid the possibility of subsidising their long-term upkeep from the Fund when more pressing cases may present themselves.

The JRC grants sums to individual refugees for a wide range of interim purposes — as bridging loans for housing, supplements to social security benefits and wages, help with heating bills and holidays; in one recent instance, they helped finance the studies of one Latin American refugee who did not qualify for a WUS grant. This assistance inevitably includes advice, counselling and contacts, for elderly refugees as well as for the new arrivals.

See also **Central British Fund for Jewish Relief and Rehabilitation,** page 55.

Joint Council for the Welfare of Immigrants
44 Theobald's Road
London WC1X 8SP
Tel: (01) 405 5527
General Secretary: Vishnu Sharma
Deputy General Secretary: Ian Martin

As its name implies, the JCWI is primarily concerned with the problems of immigrants already in this country or arriving here under the Immigration Act. It has the advantage of working closely with immigrant organisations in the United Kingdom, and acts to a large extent as their spokesman in matters concerning immigration policy.

A small proportion of JCWI's work involves *de facto* refugees, many of whom are already living in this country as students, tourists or temporary immigrants. Some two or three *de facto* refugees 'surface' in this way each month, usually when their entry permits are about to expire; JCWI will advise them on how to proceed, handling the immigration aspect of their problems and referring them to specialised organisations where appropriate (especially UKCOSA, WUS on student affairs and UKIAS Refugee Unit on questions of asylum). For many, the difficulty is to prove that they are at risk of being persecuted on their return home, and not just as members of a persecuted minority.

Because JCWI deals largely with *de facto* refugees who are not afforded the full legal protection of Convention refugees, the organisation adopts a fairly militant stand in pressing for their rights. It has cooperated with the Danish Refugee Council in preparing a report on *de facto* refugees for submission to the United Nations. It has been particularly concerned with refugees from the Cyprus conflict, and with Rhodesian students unwilling to return home. It also actively opposes the recent ruling which has deprived short-stay immigrants of their rights of appeal against refusal of permission to remain if they fail to renew their entry permits before these expire.

JCWI, which is itself acutely short of funds, has no standing funds for refugees. It does dispose of a small emergency fund of £1,500 for immigrnts with serious short-term problems through its related body, the Immigrants' Aid Trust. It is dependent on private trust funds — Cadbury, Rowntree, Gulbenkian and others — and donations to finance its £29,000 annual budget (1975).

Joint Working Group for Refugees from Chile in Britain, *see* pp. 79-81.

Ockenden Venture
Ockenden
Guildford Road
Woking, Surrey GU22 7UU
Tel: (048 62) 72012/2
Executive Chairman: Miss Joyce Pearce, MBE, MA

Through its homes, set up since 1955 to provide educational care for some 800 young displaced persons from Eastern Europe, the Ockenden Venture has expanded its community to take in refugees from a variety of backgrounds as well as a number of British children under care. Programmes for British children would include shortstay alternative education and intermediate treatment facilities. The emphasis throughout is on the young (32 of the 58 refugees at present with Ockenden are children) and on the creation of alternative community values based on interdependence and self-help.

From its early concern with displaced persons after the war, to its present intake of young refugees from Third World countries, Ockenden's progress has reflected the changes in the refugee population in Britain over the past twenty years. In addition to the long-term members of its community, Ockenden provides some short-term accommodation for newly-arrived refugees. It is also closely involved with helping refugee re-settlement overseas, on the principles of localised self-help; it assists Tibetan and Bihari refugees in India, Vietnamese and Cambodians in Thailand and the Philippines, Chinese refugees in Macao.

The Ockenden Venture works closely with BCAR and the Standing Conference, on both of which it is represented. For many, it epitomises the traditional spirit of selfless voluntary effort. Its 1975/6 budget of £250,000 — raised entirely from donations, subscriptions and covenants — went towards the upkeep of its 12 community homes, holidays and help for elderly refugees, emergency reception of the Vietnamese orphans airlifted from Saigon in 1975, and assistance to the overseas settlement projects mentioned above.

Standing Conference on Refugees
(formerly the Standing Conference of British Organisations for
Aid to Refugees)
International Development Centre
Parnell House
25 Wilton Road
London SW1V 1JS
Tel: (01) 828 7616/2626
Secretary: Miss Nancy Rice-Jones

The Standing Conference on Refugees (SCOR) brings together some 33 British-based organisations involved in refugee work at home and overseas. It serves as a focal point for the exchange of information on refugee matters, discussion on policy issues and representation of common interests to Government, as well as providing a link with international bodies, such as the United Nations High Commissioner for Refugees (UNHCR), the United National Relief and Works Agency (UNRWA) and the International Council of Voluntary Agencies (ICVA).

The Standing Conference works mainly through five Regional Committees: Africa, Asia, Europe, Latin America and Middle East; and Working Groups set up to consider special issues, such as *de facto* refugees; appeals procedure; unaccompanied refugee children.

Membership includes: Amnesty International (British Section), British Council for Aid to Refugees (working only in the UK), Catholic Fund for Overseas Development, Christian Aid, Friends Service Council, International Social Service of Great Britain, International University Exchange Fund (London office), Joint Council for the Welfare of Immigrants, the Ockenden Venture, Oxfam, Save the Children Fund, UK Immigrants Advisory Service, United Nations Association, War on Want, the UK branches of the World YMCA and YWCA; with the British Red Cross Society, The Order of St John and the Women's Royal Voluntary Service as observers.

In addition to the membership of the main Conference, a number of agencies specialising in one area or subject belong to one Regional Committee only. In all, therefore, the Standing Conference represents a wide range of interest and influence.

One of the most important functions of the Standing Conference is to make approaches to the Government on issues which are of concern to several agencies. Recent instances have been concerned with

— improving means of cooperation and exchange of information between the voluntary organisations and the government departments dealing with refugees (Home Office, Foreign Office, DHSS, Department of Education and Science) not only regarding current refugee cases, but

also on the Government's contingency plans for future refugee emergencies.
- the establishment of a permanent reception and reorientation centre for refugees in the United Kingdom which, in the view of the voluntary agencies, is an essential component of refugee work.
- adaptation of international legal instruments to the needs of refugees, including *de facto* refugees.
- the manner in which the admissions regulations are implemented (for example, with regard to Latin American refugees from Argentina, Greek and Turkish Cypriot refugees, and Asians from Rhodesia). A new Working Party of SCOR's European Committee has produced a report on current appeals procedures for asylum-seekers.
- need for revision of the Appeals Procedure.
- detention in Pentonville Prison pending decisions on asylum.

United Kingdom Immigrants Advisory Service
Brettenham House, 7th floor
Savoy Street
London WC2
Tel: (01) 240 5176
Refugee Unit: Maureen Connelly and Alistair McGeachy

Since May 1976 the UNHCR has financed a full-time Refugee Unit based with UKIAS, the statutory body working on behalf of incoming immigrants. The Refugee Unit now comprises two full-time counsellors, a secretary-interviewer and one secretary, with support from 9 UKIAS representatives at the ports of entry and major cities.

The idea of basing a refugee office within the overall service for immigrants is a reflection of the current status of refugees, whose terms of entry are governed by the Immigration Act. While some criticism has been voiced at the quasi-official nature of this arrangement, the refugee workers concerned would argue that this facilitates the necessary access to Home Office officials without inhibiting their critical independence towards inadequacies in the admission procedures.

The refugee worker assists refugees with legal advice in connection with their application for asylum, and with appeal procedures. The effectiveness of this work depends on whether individual refugees can contact UKIAS in good time. There is no formal system of referral. However, asylum-seekers whose applications have been rejected are given an opportunity to contact UKIAS' Refugee Unit which can assist with appeals. UKIAS has good contacts with Home Office officials, but remains critical of the lack of any formal admission procedure of reception structure for incoming refugees, and the failure to provide an interim status of asylum-seeker, as in other European countries.

The refugee counsellor's caseload over the first year was 334 — not all of them political refugees (many were fleeing civil conflict in the Lebanon and Cyprus). Some apply for asylum on arrival; others surface as 'hidden' refugees after they have been in the country for some time. Of the 334, 150 were appeal cases, on refusal of their initial application (65 of these overseas). Roughly 10% of these appeal cases were heard by an adjudicator, though none have succeeded. The other cases may be taken up with the Home Office, in conjunction with the UNHCR, and settled out of court; these are usually cases which the refugee counsellor considers to fall clearly within the definition of 'refugee'.

UKIAS works closely with the office of the UNHCR on refugee cases, both in the practical details of supporting requests for asylum and arranging resettlement, and at the level of pressing for a more liberal application of existing legislation. UKIAS may supply the UNHCR office with information on the basis of which it can make representations to the British Government at a higher diplomatic level on the shortcomings of present policies in regard both to general refugee work, and particular cases.

UKIAS cooperates with most of the voluntary agencies working in this field, both the 'established' bodies such as the British Council for Aid to Refugees, and with human rights organisations and support groups. These can often supply well-authenticated background information in support of th refugee's plea for asylum. Some can provide material assistance — ACTTs, Equity and the Musician's Union especially (see page 142) have all responded positively in extending facilities to refugees from their respective professions.

United Nations High Commission for Refugees, London Office
36 Westminster Palace Gardens
Artillery Row
London SW1P 1RR
Tel: (01) 222 3065/6
UK Representative: Mr Jean Heidler
Legal Officer: Dr Guy Goodwin-Gill

The Office of the United Nations High Commission for Refugees (UNHCR) in the United Kingdom sees its work as securing protection and assistance for refugees arriving in this country. It does not provide financial aid, but does give legal advice and assistance. It seeks to ensure that the legal provisions for asylum and the safeguarding of rights and benefits after admission are fully implemented and, where possible, improved. As the direct representative of the UN High Commissioner for Refugees in Geneva, the UNHCR London Office operates at a diplomatic level, liaising with UKIAS, voluntary bodies and Home Office departments, initiating actions, and ensuring that individual refugee cases receive appropriate assistance. The UNHCR in Geneva also funds the Refugee Unit at UKIAS.

Individual appeal cases are now referred to the Office of the UNHCR systematically by the Home Office; individuals and voluntary agencies will also turn to them for legal advice and support, which is provided free of charge. The UNHCR's Legal Officer may assist the UKIAS refugee worker in arguing the appellant's case before the adjudicator or immigration appeal tribunal. Where the case falls clearly within the terms of the UNHCR Mandate, or where the individual concerned does not have a right of appeal, the UNHCR may choose to take it up directly with Home Office officials, circumventing the appeals machinery.

However, the number of cases which the UNHCR considers as falling within its mandate appears to exceed the numbers of those admitted to this country as refugees by the Home Office. Out of 23 cases appealed before adjudicators between January 1974 and April 1977 at which the UNHCR was present, or submitted written observations attesting to the UNHCR's reasons for considering the individuals concerned to be within the terms of the Convention, not one had succeeded. In the light of this, the UNHCR Representative decided no longer to participate in appeals proceedings for the time being.

In addition to providing supporting evidence for refugees requesting admission, the UNHCR will also seek to persuade the Home Office to issue Convention Travel Documents to refugees admitted to this country. The British Government is under statutory obligation to provide such travel documents to refugees, but in some instances where the refugee is admitted to the country under another heading, e.g. as a student or self-employed person, they may find themselves without the Convention Travel Document which must serve as their passport. The UNHCR will then back their request for a CTD on the grounds that the refugee in question falls within the terms of the Convention.

The Office of the UNHCR will also help individuals refused asylum in this country to obtain admission to third countries with more flexible admissions policies; this is done through the UNHCR office of the country concerned.

The UNHCR deals almost exclusively with the problems of refugees on arrival. Problems arising after admission are normally referred to settlement agencies, such as the British Council for Aid to Refugees, and Ockenden.

At the diplomatic level, the UNHCR as an inter-governmental agency conducts negotiations with governments over questions of policy, such as the implementation of national legislation on refugees and the provision of more generous entry quotas; this is the main function of the UNHCR Representative in this country, who works in tandem with direct approaches made by the Geneva head office. A recent example was the High Commissioner's appeal to signatories of the Convention to provide for an emergency intake of Latin American refugees at risk in Argentina.

The UNHCR Office does not feel that working in close consultation with government departments compromises its stance in seeking to ensure adequate protection for refugees. The UNHCR is in a unique position in being able to provide legal and technical advice to governments from an international vantage-point. In this, it serves as a useful ally to the national voluntary organisations. UNHCR accepts the need to work closely with officials on individual cases; but this has in no way impaired its critical stance towards aspects of British Immigration Regulations when applied to refugees.

One major limitation of the effectiveness of UNHCR is that it can only handle individual cases which are covered by the UN Convention on Refugees. The UNHCR is in general concerned about the problems of *de facto* refugees, and seeks to encourage governments to adopt a more liberal interpretation of existing refugee and immigration legislation in order to afford them greater protection.

The work of the United Kingdom Office of the UNHCR is of course only one small element of the UNHCR's work on behalf of refugees throughout the world. An estimated 2.3 million refugees, mostly in Africa and Asia, fall within its purview. In Third World countries with high refugee populations, UNHCR operates large-scale settlement and training programmes in addition to its legal and diplomatic approaches to governments. Emergency relief schemes are also in operation in areas of civil conflict, such as Cyprus, Angola and South-East Asia (Thailand).

Chapter 19

CONSCIENTIOUS OBJECTORS

On 21st August Mr A, an 18 year-old Asian resident in Rhodesia, came to Britain to study and to avoid being called-up by the Rhodesian army. He was refused entry. Forty-seven days later he signed a statement that he had agreed to be sent back to Rhodesia. During all that time he had been held in custody in a detention centre in London Airport and a number of attempts by people in Britain, including a Member of Parliament, to have him released and permitted to remain in Britain failed.

How the British Government Forces British Subjects to
Fight for the Illegal Regime in Rhodesia
JCWI Circular, February 1977

Many countries, including all those in the Arab world, make no alternative provision for conscientious objection to compulsory military service. In such circumstances, conscientious objectors may be liable for severe punishment, including harsh prison terms, forcible induction into the armed services and even execution. In Greece, where other basic rights have once again been recognised in law, refusal of military service is not acknowledged amongst them, and conscientious objectors have been called up on their release from prison only to find their refusal once again resulting in heavy terms of imprisonment.

In most countries, penalties are much lighter, but some which provide alternative forms of community service for conscientious objectors have penalised them by making such alternatives of much longer duration than military service (as in France, or recently Spain, where objection is only countenanced on religious grounds). Efforts to explain alternative provisions to new recruits in posters and publications have been suppressed (France) as have pamphlets directed at regular military personnel (Great Britain).

Conscientious objectors who seek asylum are in a more difficult position than many other refugees, since their claims to 'wellfounded fear of persecution' may prove difficult to substantiate, and their arguments, whether moral or political, prove unacceptable to the authorities concerned. While there are no formal provisions for COs in any relevant European entry regulations, a clear distinction can be discerned between those governments which adopt a liberal interpretation of their immigration and refugee legislation in favour of COs, and those which do not.

As with other asylum-seekers, COs may base their arguments on political and philosophical grounds, which do not carry much weight with officialdom. British Government officials tend to make a further distinction

189

between COs with 'rooted moral objections' and draft-evaders who may seek to enter the UK as students or visitors. Most fall into the latter category.

Only a handful of COs arrive in Britain in any one year, the numbers fluctuating according to circumstances. The case of draft resisters from Rhodesia/Zimbabwe is causing particular concern and their numbers are thought likely to increase. Some five or six Rhodesians have been refused entry into the UK when the alternative for them is armed service for the government of an illegal regime. These were all of Asian origin; most white Rhodesians arriving in Britain are not subject to close immigration control.

The attitude of immigration officials tends, as with other refugees, to be restrictive. COs have been held for up to two months at Harmondsworth detention centre (Heathrow), and only granted 'temporary release' after the intervention of concerned MPs and voluntary workers. In some instances, COs have been sent away before they were able to consult with lawyers and voluntary organisations — proof that vigilance from voluntary organisations and refugee workers is urgently needed.

Conscientious Objectors Advisory Team
Blackfriars Hall
Southampton Road
London NW5
Tel: (01) 485 8977
Secretary: Sue Dowell

COAT is an informal group set up in November 1976 to help and advise COs coming to this country. It comprises members from Pax Christi, the Peace Pledge Union, Friends Peace & International Relations Committee, UNA and WUS and individuals concerned with peace and human rights issues who are experienced in counselling work. It has no organised structure for these activities, apart from occasional meetings. Nor does it seek to become any more permanently structured, unless CO problems in this country should attain more significant proportions.

COAT aims to keep a watching brief on individual cases, and may liaise with UKIAS and voluntary organisations such as JCWI, approach embassies and Home Office officials, lobby MPs and provide some counselling and much-needed moral support to COs. COAT is also concerned with developments affecting COs abroad; it participates in campaigns on behalf of imprisoned COs, keeps abreast of new legislative measures affecting CO status, and presses governments to view conscientious objection with greater sympathy and understanding.

Peace Pledge Union
6 Endsleigh Street
London WC1H 0OX
Tel: (01) 387 5501
Secretary: Jan Melikar

The Peace Pledge Union acts as a campaigning organisation, disseminating information about COs imprisoned in various countries through its bulletin *The Pacifist* and intervening on their behalf by means of letters and representations to embassies and governments. It may occasionally advise individual cases in this country. Through its linked with War Resisters International (35 rue van Elewijck, Brussels), it may supply information on COs overseas; however, its brief has traditionally been peace work within Great Britain and since the ending of conscription in this country, the emphasis placed on conscientious objection has been relatively low.

Part B

The United States of America

I Voluntary Organisations

Chapter 1

HUMAN RIGHTS ORGANISATIONS

Ad Hoc Committee on the Human Rights and Genocide Treaties
25 East 75th Street
New York NY 10021
Tel: (212) 535 3700
Chairman: Arthur J. Goldberg
Executive Secretary: Betty Kaye Taylor
Washington Chairman: Hyman Bookbinder

The Ad Hoc Committee on the Human Rights and Genocide Treaties supports efforts to advance the UN Charter purpose of promoting and encouraging human rights and fundamental freedoms for all without discrimination. The Ad Hoc Committee will continue to press for early ratification of the conventions on slavery, forced labour, political rights of women and genocide. Simultaneously, the Ad Hoc Committee recommends that its member agencies study and endorse the other international human rights conventions adopted by the United Nations and its specialised agencies — the Convention on the Elimination of all Forms of Racial Description, the Convention Against Discrimination in Education and the ILO Conventions on Discrimination in Employment and on Equal Pay for Equal Work.

Americans for Democratic Action
1411 K Street, NW
Washington, DC 2005
Tel: (202) 638 6447
National Director: Leon Schull

ADA was founded in 1947 and has 65,000 members, 20 state groups and 50 local groups. It is an organisation of professional and businessmen, labour leaders, educators, housewives, political leaders and others interested in liberal political ideas. Its purpose is 'to formulate liberal domestic and foreign policies, based on the realities and changing needs of American democracy; enlisting public understanding and support of these policies; seeking to put them into effect by political action through major political

195

parties'.

ADA has consistently given leadership in the efforts to bring about reductions of US aid to governments guilty of consistent and gross violations of human rights. ADA along with Clergy and Laity Concerned, took the lead in organising the Human Rights Working Group of the Coalition for a New Foreign and Military Policy. Mr Bruce Cameron (Foreign Policy Legislative Representative), who is also the Legislative Coordinator for the Human Rights Working Group, has, over the past 2 years, authorised at least ten amendments which have been sponsored by Members of Congress. ADA has presented testimony on the relationship between human rights and security assistance before the Senate Foreign Relations Committee and House Appropriations Committee. ADA chapters and individuals have consistently raised the issue of human rights and US foreign policy with their Members of Congress.

Publications: *Legislative Newsletter*, semimonthly (when Congress is in session); ASA *World* monthly; and a variety of pamphlets and reports including *Action on Human Rights*; *Human Rights and Security Assistance: Proposal for Reform*; and *Human Rights and US Foreign Policy: A Response by Non-Governmental Organizations to the State Department Reports on Argentina, Haiti, Indonesia, Iran and the Philippines.*

American Friends Service Committee
1501 Cherry Street
Philadelphia, Pa. 19102
Tel: (215) 241 7000
Chairman: Wallace T. Collett
Executive Secretary: Louis B. Schneider

The American Friends Service Committee was established in 1917 and now has 10 regional groups in the United States. It was founded by and related to the Religious Society of Friends (Quakers) but is supported and staffed by individuals of all major denominations.

It attempts to relieve human suffering and to find new approaches to world peace and nonviolent social change. Work in some 17 countries includes refugee relief and rehabilitation, peace education, and community development. The AFSC sponsors off-the-record seminars around the world to build better international understanding. It also conducts programmes with US communities on the problem of minority groups, such as housing, employment, and denial of legal rights. AFSC sponsors the Washington Public Affairs Program, which conducts informal, off-the-record meetings for members of Congress and federal officials. It offers summer voluntary service opportunities for young people. And it seeks to build informed public resistance to militarism and the military-industrial complex.

AFSC is carrying out work on the issue of human rights in all three of its programme divisions: the Community Relations Division, the International Division, and the Peace Education Division. The latter two place particular emphasis on challenging United States support to governments that carry out policies which grossly violate human rights.

A co-recipient of the Nobel Peace Prize, AFSC programmes are interracial, interdenominational and international.

Publications: *Quaker Service Bulletin*, 3/year; *Annual Report*; programme literature and booklets.

Amnesty International USA
2112 Broadway
New York NY 10023
Tel: (212) 787 8906
Six E Street, SE
Washington, DC 20003
Tel: (202) 544 0200
Executive Director: David Hawk
Press Officer: Larry Cox
Washington Director: Stephanie Grant
Assistant Director: Ginger McRae

Western Regional Office
3618 Sacramento St
San Francisco CA 94118

Amnesty International is a worldwide non-governmental organisation working for the release of prisoners of conscience. AI strives for the observance of the Universal Declaration of Human Rights, the UN Standard Minimum Rules for the Treatment of Prisoners and UN Declaration on the Protection of All Persons from Torture and Other Cruel, Inhuman or Degrading Treatment or Punishment.

AI works through groups of citizens, called adoption groups, who come together to work for the release of individual prisoners of conscience assigned to them by the Research Department of AI's International Secretariat in London.[1] These small groups send informed and continuous appeals to the imprisoning government urging the prisoner's release. In addition, fact-finding missions are sent to countries where human rights violations are thought to be occurring. At times, AI may also send jurists to observe controversial trials or to plead for the life of a sentenced victim. Since 1972, AI has also conducted an international campaign for the abolition of torture.

---

[1] See also pp. 7-12.

United States of America

On the basis of its missions and other research, AI has published reports and background papers on over 28 countries. AI also publishes an annual report on the organisation and the state of human rights around the world.

Center for Civil Rights, University of Notre Dame Law School
University of Notre Dame
Notre Dame, Indiana 46556
Director: Donald P. Kommers

The Center for Civil Rights of the University of Notre Dame Law School was established in 1973 under a grant from the Ford Foundation. One of its purposes is to develop a major research and documentation centre in the areas of domestic civil and international human rights. The Center has begun a bibliographical service for the benefit of scholars in the area of international human rights broadly defined to apply to studies of human rights in individual countries as well as to the problem of securing human rights on a transnational basis. Thus far, the Center has produced two detailed bibliographies, one covering the period 1970-76 and the other 1965-69. Among future plans of the Center is to extend these bibliographies back to 1948, the year of the United Nations Universal Declaration of Human Rights, covering important works in French, German and Spanish as well as English. In April 1977, the Center held a Conference on 'US Foreign Policy and Human Rights', the proceedings of which are forthcoming in a volume by the University of Notre Dame Press in autumn 1978.

Center for International Policy
120 Maryland Avenue NE
Washington, DC 20002
Tel: (202) 544 4666
Director: Donald L. Ranard

The Center for International Policy (CIP) is a non-profit research organisation that critically examines the complex nature of US political, economic and military relations with the third world. The focus is the US foreign assistance programme, the financial vehicle used to reflect the priorities of and execute US foreign policy. Center reports detail the flow of aid through US military and economic assistance programmes and the international financial institutions such as the World Bank, to assess the effect on the status of human rights in the recipient countries. The impact of aid is analysed on the context of development, political, and social problems and national security considerations.

The Center produces carefully researched, incisive studies for use by Members of Congress, the press, US government officials, and activist organisations involved in education and lobbying around human rights issues. Topics examined in these reports include: the 'backdoor' forms of aid which often escape Congressional and public scrutiny yet contribute significantly to the overall aid picture; the Overseas Private Investment Corporation (OPIC), a US government agency which insures the investments of multinational corporations in the third world; the links between the advance of human rights and programmes designed to meet basic human needs; and many others. The most in-depth and well received project was a two-volume survey of the relation of human rights and US foreign assistance in four Latin American and East Asian countries. An updated version is currently being prepared which will be commercially published next autumn.

The Center's director is Donald Ranard, a 30-year veteran of the US Foreign Service with extensive experience in Asian affairs. Frustrated by the failure of the US government to respond to evidence that the South Korean government was orchestrating a plan to buy influence in the US Congress and to the increasingly repressive and corrupt nature of the Park Chung-hee regime, Mr Ranard retired from the State Department and brought his case to the public. He has played an instrumental role in bringing the facts of the bribery scandal to light as well as alerting the American public to the denial of basic human rights and freedoms in South Korea.

The Center intends to continue evaluating the US commitment to advancing human rights by measure of its performance and results. Greater emphasis will be placed on the question of economic rights and the development policies needed to insure that the poor majorities benefit from economic development.

The Center is a project of the Fund for Peace and depends solely on the contributions of individuals and foundations in support of the work.

Central Committee of Correspondence
3414 Spring Garden Street
Philadelphia, Pa 19104

A non-profit collective, the Central Committee of Correspondence was founded in 1966 to oppose the Vietnam War; it is now chartered as

Community Publishing, Inc. It publishes *Mailing List of Movement Organizations*, which is designed to help build communication among grassroots groups working for peace, human rights, and radical social change. The List contains the names and addresses of several thousand groups throughout the US, and of some international organisations.

Coalition for a New Foreign and Military Policy
110 Maryland Avenue, NE
Washington, DC 20002
Tel: (202) 546 8400
Coordinator: Brewster Rhodes

Founded in 1976 (as a merger of the Coalition on National Priorities and Military Policy, founded 1969, and the Coalition for a New Foreign Policy, founded 1973 and formerly Coalition to Stop Funding the War), the Coalition has some 8,000 members. It is a coalition of 40 national religious, labour, civic, peace and public interest organisations. Its purpose is to mobilise and focus nation-wide grassroots pressure on Congress to develop an open, humanitarian, non-interventionist foreign policy for the US. Recent areas of interest include: building nation-wide support for Congressional amendments to transfer funds from the military budget to programmes addressing pressing human needs; pressing for effective arms control and disarmament measures; promoting majority rule in Southern Africa; human rights legislation and cutting economic and military aid to repressive governments; normalising relations with former enemies (e.g. ending the Vietnam trade embargo and recognising the new governments in Indochina). The Coalition provides information on priorities and foreign policy legislation in relation to ending US intervention abroad; it provides information that is 'current and accurate' about bills, amendments, and sponsors an evaluation of who are the 'swing' members of Congress; it organises suggestions about how best to develop a local pressure campaign. It communicates with Congressional members.

The Human Rights Working Group of the Coalition, which includes many organisations that are not themselves part of the Coalition, was established on the initiative of Clergy and Laity Concerned and Americans for Democratic Action in an effort to maximise the impact of non-governmental organisations on the formulation of public policy in the field of international human rights. The HRWG meets once a month as a full body to plan strategy and to implement common activities around the following goals: the extension and implementation of the human rights provisions in the bilateral US military and economic assistance laws; the extension of effective human rights provisions to the replenishment bills for the international financial institutions; the ratification of pending UN human rights covenants and the implementation of human rights through international organisations and treaties; to get changes in US refugee policy more consistent with human rights standards; and to monitor spying at home and abroad.

The HRWG helps to reduce the duplication of efforts and maximise the degree of coordination among groups working on human rights at the national level by monitoring human rights legislation in Congress and its implementation in the Executive branch, targeting key legislation for HRWG support or opposition, facilitating lobbying for organisations in the HRWG that lobby, disseminating information on human rights violations and US policy towards repressive regimes to Congress, the Administration and the Public, producing and distributing common materials for public education, identifying issues needing additional research and providing direction for citizen action at the local level.

Publications: *Citizen's Action Guide*, 2nd edition 1978; briefs and legislative action alerts; reprints, pamphlets, articles.

Commission to Study the Organization of Peace
866 United Nations Plaza
New York, NY 10017
Tel: (212) 688 4665
Executive Director: James Frederick Green
Secretary: Margaret Olsen

The Commission to Study the Organization of Peace was originally founded as a research body to study the reorganisation or replacement of the League of Nations. Since that time, however, the scope of the Commission's interests has continually grown and now includes: the pacific settlement of disputes, maintenance of international peace and security, disarmament, trusteeship and human rights. The membership of the Commission is comprised of scholars, lawyers, businessmen and civil leaders throughout the country who all work together on the Commission's occasional reports.

The Commission has published 24 reports and 20 special recommendations; those pertaining to human rights are *Draft International Bill of Human Rights* (February 1947); 18th Report, *The United Nations and Human Rights* (August 1967); 20th Report, *The United Nations: The Next Twenty-Five Years* (1970); and 25th Report, *New Aspects of the International Protection of Human Rights* (1977).

Council on Hemispheric Affairs
30 Fifth Avenue
New York, NY 10011
Tel: (212) 673 5740
1735 New Hampshire Avenue, NW
Washington, DC, 20009
Tel: (202) 332 8860

The Council on Hemispheric Affairs is a non-profit educational organisation supported by contributions from foundations, organisations and individuals. It was established in 1975 to focus interest and mobilise new voices on regional affairs; and it seeks to monitor the full spectrum of US-Latin American relations, and to enlarge public and governmental understanding and concern with current Latin American realities. Among the Council's concerns are: advancing respect for human rights; upholding civil rights and religious freedoms; the position of women in Latin America, and opportunities for them and for minorities; and supporting the right of Latin American trade union movements to organise and function freely.

Through its media releases, its studies and its meetings with policy makers, the Council conveys to specialists and the general public current information and analyses of the economic, social and political forces affecting democratic life in the Americas. It also liaises with embassies, congressional and executive agencies and offices, and other groups and individuals. In June 1978 a report was published on the human rights record of 22 Latin American countries. Argentina was rated the worst offender. Other reports concern US military aid programmes, and the activities of regional lending agencies and other aspects of US-Latin American financial and trade relations.

The Council houses a repository of case histories of persecuted religious figures and political dissidents in Latin America. By conveying this information to both the Latin American and US press and others, the Council brings attention to the plight of thousands of defenceless and innocent people who oppose dictatorial regimes in their own nations or who are victims of anti-Semitism or other forms of religious discrimination.

The staff of more than 15 consists of full-time volunteers and professionals. On average, 3 research papers are published each week. A newsletter is in preparation for the public, and a special information service will be introduced for legislators.

Freedom House
20 West 40th Street
New York, NY 10018
Tel: (212) 730 7744
President: John Richardson, Jr
Executive Director: Leonard R. Sussman

Freedom House is concerned with freedom and individual liberty through-out the world. The organisation, since its inception in 1941, has logged the status of freedom and dictatorship in its yearly Comparative Survey of Freedom, an assessment of the level of political and civil liberties in every country. Freedom House also maintains the Freedom House/Books US programme, which distributes over 120 different books to students in the countries of Asia, Africa and Latin America; and, the Helsinki Watch, which monitors compliance of the signatories to the Helsinki Accords.

Freedom House publishes a bi-monthly periodical entitled *Freedom at Issue*, which also carries the annual Comparative Survey of Freedom. Freedom House also publishes occasional papers as the need arises.

Fund for Free Expression
201 East 50th Street
New York, NY 10022
Tel: (212) 572 2276
Executive Director: Ms Jeri Laber
Chairman of the Board: Robert L. Bernstein

The Fund for Free Expression is an organisation concerned with protect-ing the right to free expression throughout the world. It was begun in 1975 by a group of individuals who were alarmed by the growth of intellectual repression in diverse parts of the world and were determined to do what they could to protect the rights of writers and of all human beings to speak out without fear of harassment, arrest, imprisonment, torture or death.

On the Fund's Board are writers, editors, publishers, journalists and other public-spirited people. Equally opposed to dictatorships of the right and of the left, their only ideological commitment is to free expression, which they consider basic to all human freedoms. They know that the number of 'free' nations in the world is dwindling, that unless we exercise our own freedom to speak out in defence of others, we may find, too late, that *we* have lost that right, too.

United States of America

As part of its programme, the Fund for Free Expression acts as a clearing house for various human rights groups, especially those concerned with the protection of intellectual freedom. It also offers advice to dissident writers exiled abroad and tries to help them find publishers for their works. In addition, the Fund is seeking to enlarge the US readership of *Index on Censorship*, a London-based human rights periodical, the only one of its kind in the world.[1] Members of the Fund's Board serve as a US Advisory Committee to *Index*.

Index has two functions, one political and one literary: it provides a forum in which truths can be told about dictatorial regimes, and it offers space where 'silenced' writers may publish literary works censored in their own countries. Its message is both grim and optimistic, pointing to the often unbelievable atrocities practiced by 'civilised' governments, yet proving, at the same time, that even under such conditions the human will to bear witness, to create and to be heard often manages to survive.

The Fund for Free Expression is supported exclusively by private donations. Contributions are, of course, tax deductible.

Human Rights Internet
1502 Ogden Street, NW
Washington, DC 20010
Co-chairpersons: Laurie S. Wiseberg and Harry M. Scoble

The Human Rights Internet is a communications network of scholars, activists, and policy-makers in the human rights field. Established in March 1976 as a sub-section of the International Studies Association, it was separately incorporated in November 1977 as a not-for-profit organisation.

Its main organ of communication is the *Human Rights Internet Newsletter*, published nine times a year. The newsletter is an attempt to fill the vacuum which existed between human rights organisations — so that one group knows what other groups are doing; between academics and activists in the human rights field — so that activists know what research is being carried out and scholars are aware of what activists are doing; and between both these groups and policy-makers. Thus the *Newsletter* reports on the campaigns and programmes of human rights organisations, on research in progress and published material, on conferences held and planned, on courses being taught in the human rights field and on teaching resources, and on major policy decisions of inter-governmental organisations and governments.

Membership in the Internet is open to any individual or organisation

---

[1] See p. 136. Distributed to US and Canadian bookstores by Random House.

204

professing a commitment to the principles elaborated in the United Nations Universal Declaration of Human Rights. The Internet, however, has no action programme apart from that of communication and coordination in the human rights field. To a limited extent, the Internet has been functioning as a clearing-house on human rights, responding to the specific needs of students, scholars, activists or policy-makers seeking information. It hopes to be able to expand on this function in the coming year.

While US-based, the Internet has attracted the participation of a significant number of people in other parts of the world and has been making a particular effort to improve its non-American sources of information. While its linkages with major human rights organisations in Western Europe are well-established now, linkages with the Third World and the Socialist World are still weak. This will, therefore, remain a major focus of concern for the coming year.

Inter American Association for Democracy and Freedom
20 West 40th Street
New York, NY 10018

The Inter-American Association for Democracy and Freedom aims to promote democracy in the Americas; to defend human rights, and protect and investigate violations of civil and political liberties; to oppose dictatorship of both left and right in the Americas; and in all ways to further juridical stability for social, economic and political democracy.

A member of the International League for Human Rights, it assists other organisations in securing asylum and employment for political refugees from countries under dictatorships, and conducts conferences and classes for discussions of Inter-American problems, and has a reference library. It investigates problems of human rights as they occur and acts to protest where necessary; it also may supply legal assistance.

International Association of Educators for World Peace
P.O.B. 3282, Blue Springs Station
Huntsville, Alabama 35810
Secretary General: Dr Charles Mercieca

The aims of International Association of Educators for World Peace are to foster international understanding and world peace, using education

205

as a medium, further the application of the Universal Declaration of Human Rights through the promotion of social progress, broaden international communications at personal level; and to assist the development of peaceful co-existence. It holds periodical meetings, seminars and workshops throughout the world to discuss a family or community problem of national or international relevance; practical action based on personal contact is outlined and put into practice immediately and details of this action are submitted to the organisation's *Newsletter*, with a view to informing other members.

The IAEWP has consultative status with ECOSOC and UNESCO.

Members of Congress for Peace Through Law
201 Massachusetts Avenue, NE, Suite 201
Washington, DC 20002
Tel: (202) 544 4250
Chairman: Rep Charles W. Whalen, Jr (for the 95th Congress)
Executive Director: Sandford Z. Persons

Members of Congress for Peace Through Law is a bi-partisan bicameral organisation of Members of Congress which aims to enhance the capacity of the Congress to evaluate policy and to create institutional links between lawmakers and outside thinkers and practitioners. MCPL's work is done through its eight issue committees which are: Arms Control and Military Affairs; African Affairs; Food, Population and Natural Resources; Human Rights and Foreign Policy; International Development; International Institutions and World Order; Middle East Peace; and Law of the Sea and Oceans Policy.

On key issues, MCPL arranges briefings, conducts seminars, holds forums, provides background papers, prepares testimony, mobilises support for legislation, coordinates on- and off-floor legislative strategy and in general serves as a catalyst among the ideas institutions, organisations and individuals which have impact on international peace. The Human Rights and Foreign Policy Committee to MCPL is chaired by Representative Toby Moffett (D-Conn); Vice Chairmen of this committee are Representative Tom Harkin (D-Iowa) and Senator John Heinz III (R-Pa) for the 95th Congress.

Publications: the MCPL Human Rights committee has published a *Directory of Human Rights Organizations* and a *Guide for Congressional Human Rights Investigations Abroad*. In addition, a bi-monthly newsletter is published and a weekly *Legislative Alert* for MCPL members. *A Human Rights Directory* of US-based international human rights organisations is due in November 1978.

United States Institute of Human Rights − 200 Park Avenue, New York, NY 10018. Tel: (212) 973 4752 *President:* Louis Henkin

The United States Institute of Human Rights was formed a number of years ago in loose affilitation with the International Institute of Human Rights at Strasbourg, France, which was started with the aid of President René Cassin, who donated a generous portion for the purpose out of his Nobel Peace Prize award money.

The United States Institute has been sponsoring seminars, in conjunction with the American Society of International Law, sending students to the annual teaching session of the International Institute at Strasbourg, and sponsoring the publication of the monthly periodical *Checklist of Human Rights Documents*, published at the Tarlton Law Library of the University of Texas Law School, at Austin, since January 1976.

World Without War Council
National Office:
175 Fifth Avenue
New York, NY 10010
Tel: (212) 674 2085
President: Robert Pickus
Executive Vice-President: Lowell Livezey
Midwest Regional Office:
67 East Madison, Suite 1417, Chicago, Ill. 60603
Northern California Regional Office:
1730 Grove Street, Berkeley, California 94709
Northwest Regional Office:
1514 NE 45th Street, Seattle, Washington 98105
Other Office:
1838 SW Jefferson, Portland, Oregon 97201

The World Without War Council was founded in 1958. It is not a membership organisation but functions as a joint effort of leaders of national and regional peace, labour, business, religious, veterans, educational, and public affairs organisations interested in progress toward the nonviolent resolution of international conflict and constructive global systems change. The principle purposes and functions of the Council are (1) to establish the goal of ending war as a guiding force in American life; (2) to clarify the elements of understanding and belief and to define the strategies and tasks essential to achieving the goal; (3) to engage mainstream organisations and institutions in appropriate work through their own constituencies to translate these ideas into national policy; (4) to offer, through national and regional centres of thought and activity, the catalytic, training, model-building, programming and coordinating services and resources needed; (5) to provide a continuing overview of peace efforts by voluntary organisations with the purpose of aiding in the development of common standards and priorities for more effective work; and (6) to articulate the moral and political values which provide the motivation needed for a sustained engagement in that work. Thus the Council works to build public understanding and support of alternatives for the US government which do not involve the surrender of democratic values.

To these ends, the Council coordinates the work of its affiliated but independent regional councils. It distributes material for discussion and action through channels of mass constituency organisations and affiliated councils. It provides background material on world issues; conducts national intern work/study programmes; develops materials and speakers for schools and community programmes; conducts organisational consulting, war/peace issues and State Department/Independent Sector programmes. It also manages the International Conflict and American Organizations Project, a common work process for leaders of major stable organisations in the field and 'intermestic' philanthropy programmes.

During the past year, the Council and its regional affiliates have held public forums and workshops on international human rights and has published an *International Human Rights Kit* intended for students and citizens interested in human rights. The Midwest Office runs a World Without War bookstore and has published a resource list on international human rights.

Publications: *Perspective*, quarterly.

Chapter 2

CHURCHES AND RELIGIOUS ORGANISATIONS

American Jewish Committee
The Jacob Blaustein Institute for the Advancement of Human Rights
165 East 56th Street
New York, NY 10022
Tel: (212) 751 4000
Chairman: Philip E. Hoffman
Programme Consultant: Sidney Liskofsky
President: Richard Maas
Executive Vice-President: Bertram H. Gold

The American Jewish Committee, founded in 1906, is the oldest human relations agency in the United States. It has 42,000 members organised in chapters around the US, and 28 offices in the US, Israel, Europe, and South America. The Committee sponsors research, education and social action as a means of safeguarding Jewish security, enhancing inter-religious and racial harmony, and promoting human rights for all.

The Jacob Blaustein Institute for the Advancement of Human Rights is an arm of the American Jewish Committee. Established in 1971 to encourage undertakings in those areas with which Mr Blaustein was most closely identified during his lifetime — Blaustein played a leading role at the 1945 San Francisco Founding Conference of the United Nations in seeking inclusion of forceful human-rights provisions in the Charter — the Institute works to further understanding and implementation of international human rights. Among the major human rights projects initiated by the Blaustein Institute were the Uppsala Colloquium on the Right to Leave and the Right to Return, held in 1972 under the joint auspices of the International Institute of Human Rights (Strasbourg) and the Faculty of Law of the University of Uppsala (the proceedings and papers of which have been published), and the McGill International Colloquium on Judaism and Human Rights, held in 1974 (the papers of which are shortly to be published). The Blaustein Institute also provides a number of fellowships to enable Americans to attend the teaching session at the International Institute of Human Rights and has sponsored Jacob Blaustein lectures at these sessions. Presently, the Jacob Blaustein Institute is sponsoring a textbook on the International Covenant on Civil and Political Rights, which will interpret the provisions of the Covenant to help safeguard its libertarian and humanitarian spirit and intent. In all its activities, the Blaustein Institute 'seeks to maintain the highest standards of scholarship and objectivity, and encourages the participation of qualified scholars and statesmen, theoreticians and practitioners without distinction as to race, religion or nationality'.

Publications: *Commentary* (journal), monthly; *Present Tense* (journal), quarterly; and *American Jewish Yearbook*, annual. Also publishes books, articles, bibliographies and other material.

B'Nai B'Rith – 1640 Rhode Island Avenue, Washington, DC 20036

The aims of B'Nai B'Rith are to coordinate the work of its various constituents in their fight for human rights and against discrimination on grounds of race, religion or origin; to help refugees and migrants in their integration; and to develop Jewish culture in youth and student groups and through adult education.

Centre for Religion and Human Rights in Closed Societies – 475 Riverside Drive, New York, NY 10027

CRHR publishes a journal, *Religion in Communist Dominated Areas*, which is the only scholarly publication on the American continent to specialise in publishing and analysing documents on religious situations and anti-religious propaganda in all Communist countries, paying particular attention to violations of religious freedom and other human rights in all closed societies.

Church Committee on Human Rights in Asia
Institute on the Church in Urban-Industrial Society
5700 South Woodlawn Avenue
Chicago, Ill 60637
Coordinator: Linda Jones
Chicago Staff: Joyce Overton

The Church Committee on Human Rights in Asia is an ecumenical group of concerned Christians who work on behalf of those struggling for human rights in South Korea, the Philippines, and Indonesia. It does this by providing programmes and resources for local study/action groups; carrying the needs and concerns expressed by Asian Christians to US legislators and policy-makers; working with the local media to carry human rights stories coming out of Asia; and challenging locally-based corporate interests with subsidiaries in Asia to abide by decent wage and living standards for Asian workers.

The Committee was founded three years ago. To keep its members informed of developments, it started a newsletter in 1977. In addition, it has speakers, side shows, films and literature to share with interested groups and individuals.

Clergy and Laity Concerned
198 Broadway
New York, NY 10038
Tel: (212) 964 6730
CALC Human Rights Coordinating Center
Washington, DC

CALC, with over 40 chapters and affiliates around the United States, was organised in 1965 as an ecumenical grassroots network to work for justice and peace. It originally consisted of Roman Catholic, Jewish, and Protestant clergy and lay people pledged 'to push unequivocally toward termination of American intervention in Vietnam' and 'to stand with young men of draft age who cannot in conscience fight in Vietnam', Since then, CALC has broadened its scope into various areas of social justice and presently has several nationally-coordinated programmes: Human Security – Peace & Jobs; Politics of Food; Vietnam – Reconstruction & Reconciliation; and US Power and Repression – International Human Rights. The focus of the human rights programme is upon countries which receive US bilateral and multilateral aid.

CALC maintains the Human Rights Coordinating Center in Washington, DC, which has been an active participant in the Human Rights Working Group of the Coalition for a New Foreign and Military Policy. Through its network, CALC has concentrated on supporting US policies to ratify the UN Human Rights Covenants, expose private banking and corporate support to countries which violate human rights, and end economic and military[1] aid as well as arms sales to gross violators of human rights. Another aspect of their work is their efforts to recognise and correct domestic human rights violations.

Publications: CALC *Report*, monthly magazine; special reports and pamphlets including a booklet on torture and long-term detention for the US Catholic Conference, 'If You Want Peace, Defend Life', 1976.

---

[1] Except in such cases where such aid directly benefits the needy people.

United States of America

Friends Committee on National Legislation
245 Second Street, NE
Washington, DC 20002
Tel: (202) 547 4343
Executive Director: Edward F. Snyder

Founded in 1943, the FCNL is an appointed committee of the Religious Society of Friends and of 15 other Friends' organisations in the United States. It functions autonomously but seeks to 'keep responsive to concerns of Quakers generally'. It is the Quaker lobby in Washington and has three full-time lobbyists who spend their time talking with members of Congress and staff aides, helping draft bills and amendments, testifying before Congressional committees, working with other civic-minded organisations, and alerting FCNL's constituency about when to contact legislators.

Its current priorities include human rights (in the US and internationally, civil and political), cutting military spending, disarmament and economic conversion, meeting basic human needs, strengthening world institutions, and American Indian affairs. FCNL maintains collections of current materials and documents on war and peace and human rights in the United States.

FCNL works closely with the American Friends Service Committee and has used the AFSC's expertise at home and abroad to develop testimony before Congressional committees and to draft policy provisions. Thus, while the AFSC was conducting nationwide public education campaigns against the Vietnam war, FCNL was tackling the same issue on Capitol Hill. The FCNL also took leadership on issues of recognition of the People's Republic of China, opposition to conscription, support for world disarmament and human rights. FCNL strongly believes in the utility of working through coalitions. Thus, FCNL has joined with the Coalition for a New Foreign and Military Policy, including its Human Rights Working Group. It has also made substantial contributions to the Interreligious Task Force on US Food Policy (a group of people from Protestant, Catholic and Jewish backgrounds working on food issues).

Publications: the organisation publishes a monthly newsletter, 11/year, FCNL *Washington Newsletter*, reporting on the status of federal human rights legislation. On an irregular basis, it publishes *Action Bulletins* and papers and booklets on topics of concern to Friends.

Jacob Blaustein Institute for the Advancement of Human Rights, see under **American Jewish Committee**, p. 209.

212

Chapter 3

COMMITTEES AND SUPPORT GROUPS

American Committee on Africa
305 East 46th Street
New York, NY 10017
Tel: (212) 838 5030
Executive Director: George M. Houser

The American Committee on Africa, founded in 1953, is devoted to supporting the African people in their struggle for freedom and independence. It grew out of an *ad hoc* committee to give support for a campaign of peaceful protest in South Africa against unjust laws in 1952. When that campaign was finally suppressed by repressive measures in South Africa, it was decided that there should be a support organisation in the United States to provide assistance whenever possible to liberation movements in Africa and to provide information about conditions in Africa generally.

Thus the ACOA informs Americans about significant African issues, mobilises public support for African freedom, and works for US policies which will strengthen this aim. ACOA also provides a forum for African representatives through public meetings, news media, conferences, speaking tours and arranges meetings with African leaders and reports on decisions reached.

Since the mid-60s ACOA has concentrated on Southern Africa. It actively opposes specific instances of US corporate collaboration with apartheid through bank loans, trade and investments. In the aftermath of Steve Biko's death, ACOA helped initiate the formation of the Committee to End Bank Loans to South Africa which has attracted the participation of more than 50 organisations throughout the United States. In 1972, ACOA and the boards of several Protestant churches jointly sponsored the Washington Office on Africa, which represents the aim of ACOA to the Congress and in other ways in Washington. Members of ACOA and of the Washington Office on Africa frequently testify before Congressional Committees and UN committees and lobby to end government policies which foster colonial and white minority rule.

Associated with ACOA, but an independent tax-exempt organisation, is the Africa Fund, which supports schools, hospitals, medical and social services in Angola, Mozambique, Guinea-Bissau and Cape Verde Islands. Africa Fund also aids those from South Africa, Namibia and Zimbabwe who have been the victims of political persecution through education and family assistance, legal defence and refugee aid. It provides research and literature on economic, social and political developments in southern Africa.

Publications: the ACOA publishes occasional books, pamphlets, fact sheets and in-depth reports. In July/August 1977, it also initiated the ACOA *Action News* as an occasional newsletter. ACOA also helps distribute the publications of the Africa Fund, the Washington Office on Africa, and other similar groups.

Ann Arbor Committee for Human Rights in Latin America
P O Box 7426
Ann Arbor, MI 48107

The Ann Arbor Committee defines itself as a politically non-partisan community organisation modelled after Amnesty International. It was established in the summer of 1976 as a result of a growing concern about the plight of political prisoners, the treatment of minority groups, and the role of US business and government in several Latin American nations. The Committee works with all individuals and groups having similar concerns.

The Committee seeks to meet the challenge of ameliorating conditions in oppressive and repressive Latin American nations in a variety of ways. Its main activity is publicising widespread abuses of human rights, US complicity with repression, and the general political situation in such countries as Chile and Argentina.

In November 1976 the Committee organised a teach-in on the subject of right-wing terror in Latin America, for which more than thirty speakers from nine nations came to Ann Arbor. The Committee also sponsored a series of speakers, showed films, arranged cultural events and took part in demonstrations. It has adopted a Chilean student, campaigning for his release from prison, and a 'disappeared' person, whose case it is publicising.

Argentine Commission for Human Rights
Information Bureau, P O Box 2635
Washington, DC 20013
Tel: (202) 296 8340
Washington Representatives: Gino Lofredo and Ms Olga Talamante

---

The Argentine Commission for Human Rights is a non-profit, non-governmental international organisations (with permanent representatives in Geneva, Rome, Paris, Mexico City and Washington, DC) working for the defence of human rights and the restoration of democracy in Argentina. The Commission was formed by a group of Argentine lawyers who had become increasingly aware of the need for a permanent national and international organisation to defend human rights in their country. It was constituted in response to the dramatic events which followed the military coup of March 24, 1976.

The Commission has submitted testimony to the House Subcommittee on International Organizations, and the Senate Subcommittee on Foreign Assistance. It has also provided regularly to members of Congress up-to-date information on developments in Argentina. In addition, the Commission has testified before the European Parliament, the UN Commission on Human Rights, the UN Subcommission for the prevention of discrimination and UNESCO.

Chile Legislative Center
120 Maryland Avenue, NE
Washington, DC 20002
Tel: (202) 544 3067
Center Coordinator: Sally Dinsmore
Staff: Nena A. Terrell

The Chile Legislative Center represents a broad network of church, labour, academic, community and women's organisations as well as individuals concerned with the restoration of fundamental human rights and democracy in Chile. The CLC is action-oriented, non-profit educational resource centre for both the Congress and the public. It aims to carry on an extensive education campaign; to lobby effectively on relevant legislation; and to establish good working relationships with Congressional staff. It also monitors the activities and policies of Congress and the Administration regarding Chile and tries to ensure that information stemming from this is disseminated nationally to non-governmental interest groups, including solidarity committees, religious and local civil organisations.

215

In addition it sponsors visits to Congressional offices by former Chilean parliamentarians, government officials and other prominent Chileans.

In May 1976 CLC held a national legislative conference on Chile to seek the cut-off of US military and economic aid to the Chilean military junta and the allocation of funds for the resettlement of Chilean refugees.

Publications: the CLC produces the *Chile Legislative Center Bulletin.*

Chinese Human Rights Society
P O Box 55,
Shrub Oak, NY 10588
President: Prof S.K. Chang, University of Illinois at Chicago Circle
Dept of Information Engineering, College of Engineering, Box 4348
Chicago, Ill 60680

The Chinese Human Rights Society (CHRS) was founded to uphold human rights in China and Taiwan as well as to promote the civil rights and liberties of ethnic Chinese throughout the world. It is a non-profit organisation, independent of any government, political party, religious, regional or professional group.

From the beginning of its activities, the Society has continuously urged both the governments in Peking and Taipei to respect human rights and fundamental freedoms. It has, on numerous occasions, taken a public stand for the defence of individuals and groups accused of political crimes.

Formosan Association for Human Rights – P O Box 1094, Woodside Station, Flushing, NY 11377

The Formosan Association for Human Rights distributes information on political repression by Nationalist China in Taiwan. This includes news of activities affecting Church organisations, publishers and students, and of cases of torture.

Friends of the Filipino People
110 Maryland Avenue, NE
Washington, DC 20002
Tel: (202) 543 1517
Washington Staff: Severina Rivera

The Friends of the Filipino People was formed in October 1973, just over

216

a year after President Marcos declared martial law in the Philippines. It is concerned with US military and economic aid, multilateral funding, political prisoners, 'runaway shops' and their effect on US labour, and US bases in the Philippines. Particular emphasis has been placed on the Congress Education Project, the principal body within FFP charged with informing the Congress of the full range of US-Philippine relations. In this regard, FFP has testified before numerous Congressional hearings. FFP also acts as a resource for various Congressional offices, other human rights organisations, academic and church institutions and the media.

Among FFP's publications is *Human Rights and Philippine Political Prisoners* (Congressional testimony). It also publishes the *FFP Bulletin.*

Indigena
P O Box 4073
Berkeley, CA 94704

Indigena is an information centre on the Indian peoples of the Americas. It seeks to develop the exchange of information among Indian peoples and organisations throughout the Western hemisphere, and to educate non-Indians about the living conditions of Indian peoples, their struggles against racialism and discrimination and their attempts to gain social and cultural justice and human rights. Its special focus is on Latin America.

Indigena produces a bilingual (English/Spanish) publication, *Indigena Newsletter*, which covers the above subjects.

Khronika Press
505 8th Avenue
New York, NY 10018
Tel: (212) 722 9120
Editor-in-Chief: Valery Chalidze

Khronika Press is a New York-based organisation which factually and objectively documents the human rights movement in the USSR through the publication of *A Chronicle of Human Rights in the USSR* (in Russian and in English), the printing of *A Chronicle of Current Events* (in Russian), as well as through the publication of books and documents written by members of the human rights movement such as A. Sakharov, A. Marchenko, V. Turchin and many others. Khronika Press, now in its fifth year of existence, was initiated by Edward Kline and Peter Reddaway

(Edward Kline, Valery Chalidze, and Pavel Litvinov are now its three editors, Peter Reddaway is the London correspondent) as a supplement to the Moscow-based *Chronicle of Current Events* (*A Chronicle of Current Events*, begun in April 1968, suspended its publication in October 1972 due to intense KGB pressure and resumed publication in 1974).

Khronika Press focuses on the mainstream human rights movement. It supports civil rights, freedom of expression, association, and movement. The role of specialised English-language journals such as *A Chronicle of Human Rights in the USSR* is to supply full texts, background information and accurate details to the press, to human rights organisations, and to interested government officials, scholars and students. Replies to specific inquiries, press releases, research papers, and so forth, are natural extensions of this function.

Khronika Press has received direct or implied requests to provide supplementary services for the individuals and groups whose works they publish, including: copying and circulating *samizdat*, which does not warrant printed publication; arranging for English-language publication of *samizdat*; supplying information on the human rights movement and encouraging Western support for its goals; assisting Western efforts to defend dissenters from persecution by the Soviet authorities. Mr Chalidze has sought to limit Khronika Press involvement in welfare and other collateral activities, but real and present needs exist; Khronika Press and its editors individually have devoted substantial time to such activities when they have been unable to locate other organisations prepared to meet these needs. Khronika Press is a non-profit organisation which does not accept support from any government or political organisation, and which continues to try to meet the needs of a growing amount of *samizdat* reaching the West.

Medical Mobilization for Soviet Jewry, *see* p. 233.

National Conference on Soviet Jewry
2025 Eye Street, NW
Washington, DC 20006
Tel: (202) 293 2262
Washington Representative: Marina Wallach
Public Information Officer: Jonathan Schenker

The National Conference on Soviet Jewry is the major nation-wide co-ordinating agency for American activity and policy on behalf of Soviet Jews. Thirty-eight national member agencies and over 200 local affiliated councils, federations and committees comprise the NCSJ constituency.

The NCSJ reaches nearly every corner of organised Jewish life in the United States, and maintains international ties.

The Conference has the same two missions it had at its founding: to help all Soviet Jews who wish to emigrate leave the Soviet Union for Israel and elsewhere and to help Jews in the Soviet Union as Jews with all the rights and privileges and freedoms accorded to other groups in the USSR.

A *News Bulletin* is published bi-monthly and occasional papers are prepared on request.

North American Coalition for Human Rights in Korea
100 Maryland Avenue, NE
Washington, DC 20002
Tel: (202) 488 5600
National Office:
Room 1538, 475 Riverside Drive
New York, NY 10027
Tel: (212) 678 6260
Executive Director: Sang Ho Kim
Co-Director: James Sinnott
Washington Associate: Mike McIntyre

The North American Coalition for Human Rights in Korea mobilises the concerns of people in North America for human rights in Korea, facilitates their concerned action in advocacy of these rights, enables the sharing of information and analysis about the immediate emerging situation and its causes, and seeks to support those whose human rights have been violated in Korea.

Because North Americans have current relationships with South Korea, this Coalition will initially concentrate on South Korea, but it will not ignore human rights and other issues in North Korea. Because human rights depend upon a just, independent, and developed Korea, the wider problems, including reunification, will also be considered.

The Coalition brings together citizens, Christian and other religious agencies, and other bodies in Canada and the United States (with the understanding that strategies/actions will be modified as appropriate for each country); it maintains relations with similar groups in other countries and, especially, with those involved with the human rights struggle in Korea.

219

United States of America

Of Human Rights
Box 648
East Campus, Georgetown University
Washington, DC 20057
Tel: (202) 638 7497; 965 0360
Chairman: Mrs Elena Mederos Gonzalez
Executive Secretary: Mr F. Calzon

Of Human Rights draws attention to political prisoners held in Cuba. A newsletter is published twice each year which is a digest of articles and reports from newspapers and international organisations. Other information which may be received from Cuban political prisoners and their families is passed on to appropriate bodies. OHR is a non-profit organisation registered in Washington DC and financed solely by individual contributions.

Office for Political Prisoners and Human Rights in Chile
339 Lafayette Street
New York, NY 10012
P O Box 40605
San Francisco, CA 94140

The main objectives of the Office for Political Prisoners and Human Rights in Chile are to ensure that all Chilean political prisoners, especially thousands of little-known workers and students, are adequately represented in political prisoner campaigns; to provide as much current information as possible on prisoners and the conditions they endure; and to relay and make accessible current information about the over-all human rights situation in Chile.

The Office publishes twice yearly the *Ophrich Bulletin.*

Palestine Human Rights Campaign
1322 18th Street, NW
Washington, DC 20009

The Palestine Human Rights Campaign was formed in May 1977, and publishes the *Palestine Human Rights Bulletin.* According to its second issue, of August 30th, 1977, 'Since Israel's continued violations against Palestinian human rights receive little or no attention in the United States,

220

the PHRC was formed . . . to: promote the investigation, publication and understanding of these incidents of human rights violations; lend support to the victims and their attorneys; and secure the enforcement of existing internationally recognized norms of human rights and fundamental freedoms for the Palestinian people.'

Society for the Protection of East Asians' Human Rights – P O Box 1212, Cathedral Station, New York, NY 10025 *Directors:* Seng Chang and Richard Sorich

The Society for the Protection of East Asians' Human Rights is a non-partisan international organisation which seeks to encourage respect for, and publicise the state of, human rights in all of East Asia, with primary emphasis placed on China, Korea and Taiwan.

It publishes *Spearhead*, a semi-annual journal of articles, book reviews, documentation and chronology of recent events.

Solidarity Committee with the Argentine People – 41 Union Square West, P O Box 1037, New York, NY 10003 *Secretary:* Harry Maurer, *International Affairs:* Jorge Ramirez, *Domestic Affairs:* Jorge Sabez

Solidarity Committee with the Argentine People is a volunteer organisation designed to gather and supply information to the American people about the present military government of Argentina. SCAP is working for the restitution of humanitarian and civil rights for all Argentina.

SCAP publishes the bi-monthly *Argentina's Newsletter on Human Rights*.

Southeast Asia Resource Center
(formerly the Indochina Resource Center)
P O Box 4000 D
Berkeley, CA 94704

The Southeast Asia Resource Center, founded in 1971 to provide expert information on the Indochinese War and people, has responded to the post-war situation by broadening its focus from Indochina to the Southeast Asia region. The Center follows and interprets events in the new societies of Vietnam, Laos and Cambodia, and also covers Thailand, the Philippines and Indonesia. Its primary function is to co-ordinate and disseminate information on the countries and issues of Southeast Asia and on US involvements there. It has worked around the issue of human rights since 1971, and in September 1977 published a special issue of the *Southeast Asia Chronicle* entitled 'Human Rights in Southeast Asia'.

The Center issues the *Southeast Asia Chronicle* six times a year, each issue being devoted to a specific subject matter. It also occasionally publishes book-length works of general interest and produces and distributes information for broadcast and print media.

The Center maintains a mail-order service, specialising in books, articles and audio-visual materials on Southeast Asia. Many of these materials are not normally available in local outlets, and they include government studies, foreign publications and unpublished academic research, as well as many out-of-print works on the Indochina war.

Washington Office on Africa
110 Maryland Avenue, NE
Washington, DC 20002
Tel: (202) 546 7691
Director: Edgar Lockwood

The Washington Office on Africa (WOA) is a coalition office of nine Protestant church agencies and the American Committee on Africa. It was established in 1972 to advocate and work for a United States policy towards Southern Africa which would support majority rule. The WOA is an active lobby in Congress on bills that directly concern Africa; it also works to build constituency support and concern about these measures.

Publications: the WOA publishes a quarterly newsletter on US Southern Africa policy entitled *Washington Notes on Africa*. WOA also prepares *Africa Action* bulletins on particular legislative issues and background material on relevant bills for members of Congress and their staff.

Washington Office on Latin America
110 Maryland Avenue, NE
Washington, DC 20002
Director: Joe Eldridge

The Washington Office on Latin America was established in 1974 by a coalition of religious and academic groups because of their concern for the economic, political and social conditions in Latin America. The Office focuses on human rights in Latin America and on US policy towards that region, and serves as a liaison between Latin Americans and the US institutions affecting foreign policy, such as churches, the press, non-governmental organisations, and the executive and legislative branches of government. It collects, evaluates and reports matters of importance; and publishes a bi-monthly newsletter, *Latin American Update*, to inform its constituencies on current Latin American issues.

II Professional Organisations

Chapter 4

SCIENTISTS

American Association for the Advancement of Science
Clearinghouse on Persecuted Scientists
1515 Massachusetts Avenue, NW
Washington DC 20005
Human Rights Coordinator: Bruce A. Kiernan

The Clearinghouse provides information about, and advocacy on behalf of, foreign scientists whose human rights or scientific freedom have been violated. It publishes a newsletter with information on current activities. The Clearinghouse has been able to advise the National Academy of Sciences, the Federation of American Scientists, Amnesty, Committee of Concerned Scientists and the International Congress of Scientific Unions.

Between May and July 1978 the Clearinghouse referred 8 cases of violations of Human rights to appropriate organisations; some details of these cases appear in the newsletter.

The Clearinghouse at present has 33 participating organisations, among whom are the following: American Anthropological Association, American Astronautical Society, American Geological Institute, American Institute of Chemists, American Mathematical Society, American Philosophical Society, American Physical Society, American Political Science Association, Institute of Electrical and Electronic Engineers, Linguistic Society of America, National Association of Social Workers, National Society of Professional Engineers.

Committee of Concerned Scientists
9 East 40th Street
New York, NY 10016
Executive Director: Mark S. Hellmann

CCS responds to the need felt by a part of the scientific community to mobilise the entire community for the challenge that faces international science. It attempts to develop and coordinate effective programmes to aid oppressed colleagues. At the same time it provides the informational resources necessary to effectuate such programmes. A significant portion of CCS' recent work involved responding to attacks on the personal and scientific freedom of scientists in the USSR, Argentina and elsewhere.

Co-Chairmen provide general guidance and direction along with divisional vice-chairmen. The vice-chairmen serve as the first and most important contact for efforts within their respective scientific disciplines. Although CCS is not organised along chapter lines, in many areas informal groups have emerged on campuses and in communities. CCS has also been co-operating with other scientific organisations in America and with committees which have similar goals in other countries.

Federation of American Scientists – 307 Massachusetts Avenue, NE, Washington, DC 20002. Tel: (202) 546 3300 *Director:* Jeremy J. Stone

The Federation of American Scientists highlights cases of infringement of human rights in its monthly *Public Interest Report*, and is considering an annual country-by-country survey of human rights problems as they affect scientists. It makes frequent public interventions (especially on Soviet cases), and subscribes to an Amnesty-based adoption scheme on behalf of imprisoned scientists throughout the world.

National Academy of Sciences, Committee on Human Rights
2101 Constitution Avenue, NW
Washington, DC 20418
Tel: (202) 389 6226
Chairman: Robert Kates, Clark University
Staff: W. Murray Todd, National Academy of Sciences

The National Academy of Sciences has over the years taken many private initiatives in defence of individual scientists and their freedom of information and movement. In 1976 it formed the Committee on Human Rights, out of concern that the human condition is absolutely diminished by deprivations of basic rights whenever, wherever and to whomever they may occur. The special sense of responsibility felt towards colleagues, and limited resources, have restricted the Committee's activities to drawing attention to selected cases of scientists and scholars whose situation is particularly grave and well documented. The Committee sees the plight of those few on whose behalf it is able to speak and act as symbolic of that of many others from all walks of life, and expresses its hope that in seeking to alleviate the conditions of colleagues its actions will benefit those others as well.

The Committee produces no publications, but does issue periodic releases and statements on behalf of individuals. In April 1977, the

Academy pledged its active support for eight scientists in three countries whom it described as 'victims of grave official harassment for political reasons': two were Soviet scientists, five were Argentinian physicists, and one a Uruguayan mathematician. At the same time the Academy announced a 'human rights drive' to pressure the three countries concerned and to signal its 'concern' for all humanity repressed and tortured.

Chapter 5

LAWYERS

American Association for the International Commission of Jurists
777 United Nations Plaza
New York, NY 10017
Tel: (212) 972 0883
Executive Secretary: Nicole Bourgois

The International Commission of Jurists (ICJ) is a non-governmental and non-political international organisation which holds consultative status with the United Nations Economic and Social Council, UNESCO, and the Council of Europe. Its headquarters are in Geneva, Switzerland. It draws support from judges, law teachers, practitioners of law, and other members of the legal community and their associations (*see also* p. 262).

National sections of the ICJ have been established in over 50 countries. The American Association for the ICJ is such a national section. These sections supply the International Secretariat with material on legal development in their respective countries, undertake research on matters of particular concern to their members or country, hold local and regional meetings, organise public lectures and occasionally hold joint sessions with other Sections to discuss matters of common interest. In a number of countries, they have taken the initiative in putting forward and elaborating proposals for law reform which have subsequently been adopted into the law of their country.

The ICJ makes private interventions on the behalf of political prisoners and sends missions to different parts of the world to observe important political trials. A fundamental aspect of the ICJ's work in the promotion of human rights is the collection, preservation and dissemination of material on the Rule of Law and human rights. The headquarters in Geneva continues to act as an international centre for information on the international protection of human rights. In 1978, the ICJ received funding to, and has established, a Centre for the Independence of Judges and Lawyers in Geneva. (See p. 263.) The AAICJ will be mobilising support from members of the American Bar for this Centre.

Recent projects of the AAICJ include a study of the question of the legal rights of mental patients; an analysis of the International Covenants on Civil and Political Rights and Economic, Social and Cultural Rights, in relation to US Federal and State laws to assist the US Congress in its ratification of these Covenants; and a briefing for Canadian officials on the

United States' human rights policy.

Publications: AAICJ has initiated a periodic Newsletter, first issue December 1977.

Commission for International Due Process of Law – 105 West Adams Street, Chicago, Ill. 60603

The Commission for International Due Process of Law aims to achieve firm international legal methods and orderly international judicial procedures in preserving and guaranteeing individual human rights against unlawful custody and imprisonment, and related violations of the basic charters of human rights.

International Project, Center for Law and Social Policy – 1751 North Street, NW, Washington, DC 20036

International Project is a law firm, funded by foundations, which represents individuals and groups before the courts and federal agencies in connection with various foreign affairs matters, including international human rights issues.

Lawyers Committee for Civil Rights Under Law
(Southern Africa Project)
733 15th Street, NW, Suite 520
Washington, DC 20005
Director: Millard W. Arnold

Under the Southern Africa Project, the objective is to ensure that all individuals in Southern Africa, whose fundamental rights have been denied, receive a fair and impartial trial and are represented by a competent attorney of the individual's own choosing. The method by which this is usually done is to provide legal and financial assistance to Southern African attorneys and to refer individuals to attorneys. Resources for these purposes come from the UN Trust Fund for South Africa and Namibia as well as from private and corporate donations.

A number of publications are available which deal with South African Statutes and with deviations from the rule of law. These include *South Africa's Internal Security Act, No. 44 of 1950* (the effects of its banning provisions on organisations and individuals); *Deaths in Detention in South Africa* (a list of individuals and a history of their activities prior to death); *The Inquest into the Death of Stephen Bantu Biko* (a report by Dean Louis Pollack, University of Pennsylvania, observer to the inquest); and

United States of America

Human Rights – The Role of Law and Lawyers by Patricia Derian, Assistant Secretary of State for Human Rights and Humanitarian Affairs.

Lawyers Committee for International Human Rights
236 East 46th St
New York, NY 10017
Tel (212) 682 8564
Director: Michael Posner

The Lawyers Committee was founded in 1975 by the International League for Human Rights and the Council of New York Law Associates. In its first newsletter, *Lawyers Committee News* vol. no. 1, July 1978, it describes its activities.

The committee is concentrating on 5 areas: representing individuals such as those seeking exit visas or family reunification or asylum in the United States; preparation of complaints to international organisations detailing human rights violations in particular countries; intervening in domestic cases where international law should be applied; using domestic laws to promote human rights in foreign countries; and representation of organisations at special conferences of the United Nations.

The committee also sponsors training sessions to assist volunteer attorneys in their handling of international human rights cases.

Matters currently being dealt with are:

1) The new restrictions on Foreign Aid which have cut grants to Angolan and Ugandan students in the USA.

2) Immigration procedures, and individual immigrants to the US arriving as political refugees.

3) Monitoring the work of the Human Rights Committee of the UN's International Covenant on Civil and Political Rights.

4) Preparing a report on the human rights situation in Argentina.

5) Trying to secure an exit visa for the Vazchenko family who are at the moment in the US Embassy in Moscow.

6) Intervening on behalf of Professor Mario Zarceansky, a lawyer detained in Argentina since July 1977.

Chapter 6

MEDICINE

Medical Mobilization for Soviet Jewry
164 Main Street
Watertown, MA 02172
Chairman: Paul Appelbaum, MD

The Medical Mobilization for Soviet Jewry is a national organisation of several hundred members, now in its fifth year of efforts on behalf of Soviet Jews. Its members are health professionals working with issues they know best. It deals with denial of emigration rights and subsequent harassment of Soviet Jewish physicians, the absence of medical facilities for those imprisoned for seeking to leave the Soviet Union, the abuse of psychiatric facilities for political purposes, and the neglect of the right to treatment for those Soviet Jews who have applied to emigrate to Israel. It sends out regular mailings, issues statements to the press, arranges for resolutions at professional societies and conventions, sponsors letter and petition drives, briefs those health professionals travelling to the Soviet Union and promotes direct contact between US physicians and their oppressed colleagues in the USSR. In short, it does everything it can to gain for Soviet Jews those rights guaranteed them under accepted international law.

Bi-monthly mailings are sent out to bring members up-to-date on the precarious status of many of the people it helps, and to tell them how they can help.

Chapter 7

WRITERS AND PUBLISHERS

Inter American Press Association
141 NE Third Avenue, Suite 503
Miama, FL 33132
Tel: (305) 358 1878

The Inter-American Press Association is particularly concerned with freedom of the press and information. It is an association of newspaper publishers from Canada to Argentina. It has an active Committee on Freedom of Press and Information which represents the interests of newspaper publishers who are in difficulties because of harassment by hostile governments. The IAPA issues a newsletter and periodic reports of the state of press freedom in the countries covered.

International Freedom to Publish
Committee of the Association of American Publishers
One Park Avenue
New York, NY 10016
Tel: (212) 689 8920
Executive Director: Ms Jeri Laber
Chairman: Lawrence Hughes
President: William Morrow

The International Freedom to Publish Committee of the Association of American Publishers was formed in 1975 by American publishers who believe that those engaged in exchanging creations and ideas in written form across international borders have responsibilities to each other that go beyond the ordinary rules of international business. These publishers consider book publishing one of the most effective and peaceful means of educating the human race; they know that the greatest natural resource is the human mind and that there must be international rules so that the free flow of ideas is not destroyed.

Recognising the right of authors to create without fear of interference by government officials, the International Freedom to Publish Committee tries in every way it can to help needy writers and publishers in various

234

parts of the world survive the repressive conditions under which they live and work. This is done both publicly and privately, in talks with foreign governmental and publishing officials, in meetings with US government and opinion leaders, through articles in newspapers and magazines, though letters and telegrams of protest or support, and through invitations to foreign writers to visit the US as guests of the Committee.

The Committee holds briefings for publishers and writers who are traveling abroad and has sent out questionnaires on censorship practices in various parts of the world. The Committee carefully follows violations of the freedom of information clauses of the Helsinki Final Act and has documented cases of publishing abuse for the appropriate governmental commissions. Committee members join with other human rights groups in special campaigns and participate in human rights conferences and seminars.

The International Freedom to Publish Committee is supported by the Association of American Publishers and also receives grants from private foundations.

The Committee is currently working with the International League for Human Rights and with PEN on a publication listing 'Writers in Prison'.

PEN American Center
156 Fifth Avenue
New York, NY 10010
Executive Secretary: Mel Mendolssohn
President: Henry Carlisle
Vice Presidents: Edward Albee, Jerzy Kosinski, Bernard Malamud
Muriel Bukeyser, Theodore Solotaroff

PEN is an international association of writers. The initials stand for poets, playwrights, essayists, editors and novelists. Its basic goal (as stated) is 'to promote co-operation among men and women of letters in all countries in the interest of freedom of expression, exchange of ideas relevant to literature, and international goodwill'. (*See also* pp. 132-4.)

PEN American Center was established in 1922 in New York City, with Booth Tarkington as its first President. A tax-exempt, non-profit association, its membership is approximately 1,500 writers, editors and translators throughout the United States.

All members are bound by the terms of the charter, and pledge to uphold freedom of expression everywhere. PEN has taken increasing responsibility for writers silenced by repressive governments, many of them confined to prison. Efforts are made to provide financial help for the writer's family, retain legal assistance, send observers to the trial, petition high officials concerned with the case, mobilise prominent intellectual figures on behalf of the prisoner, and also to involve the American government, foreign diplomats, and members of the international business community in using their influence where appropriate.

III Refugees

Chapter 8

American Committee for Protection of Foreign Born — 799 Broadway, Room 239, New York, NY 10003

The American Committee for Protection of Foreign Born is concerned with the immigration rights of the foreign born, deportation, citizenship and, particularly, with political tests and discriminatory treatment. It publishes occasional reports.

American Council for Nationalities Service — 20 West 40th Street, New York, NY 10018

This is the national headquarters for local agencies which assist immigrants, refugees and the foreign born to adjust to US society. It works for a humanitarian and sound immigration policy.

Hebrew Immigrant Aid Society
200 Park Avenue South
New York, NY 10003
Tel: (212) 674 6800
Executive Vice President: Gaynor I. Jacobson

HIAS is a world-wide Jewish migration agency. For 95 years, HIAS' mandate has been the rescue, migration and resettlement of Jews from countries where they have been oppressed or endangered. Each year, HIAS helps thousands of Jewish refugees migrate from Eastern Europe, the Middle East, North Africa and elsewhere. The agency assists in family reunions and arranges for the resettlement of the refugees in Jewish communities throughout the United States, as well as in Canada, Australia, New Zealand, Western Europe and Latin America. Since its establishment, HIAS and its predecessors agencies have resettled more than 4,000,000 Jews.

In its first four decades of service, HIAS assisted more than 2,000,000 Jewish refugees to American shores. Since World War I, JIAS has taken the lead against restrictive immigration measures in Congress. As the Nazi hate campaign swung into full blast, thousands fleeing Europe were helped to escape.

HIAS met head-on with a succession of crises — Hungary and Egypt in

'56, Cuba in '58, Morocco in '61, Algeria in '62, Egypt in '67 and Czechoslovakia and Poland in '68.

HIAS operates through a global network of offices and affiliated organisations in 47 countries on six continents with world headquarters in New York City.

HIAS offers a wide variety of professional services to Jewish migrants at all stages of the migration process, which is often a lengthy and almost always complex procedure. Pre-migration planning includes processing of letters of invitation, visa documentation, consular representation and intervention, transportation, reception, reunion with family, and settlement in local communities. Post-migration services include adjustment of status, naturalization and protective service for aliens. HIAS also assists in the location of missing friends and relatives world-wide.

During 1977, HIAS provided migration services to 8,675 persons and related services to over 41,000, including aid to aliens in the US, successful location of 1,575 persons who had become separated from their relatives as a result of the holocaust, wars, revolutions and other mishaps, preliminary processing and counseling of our registered caseload in Europe, North Africa and the Middle East, and pre-migration services, among other assistance.

For 1978, HIAS estimates it will resettle 12,000 Jewish refugees and migrants world-wide. Ninety per cent of these are expected to be from the USSR, the majority of whom are expected to come to the US.

In addition, HIAS anticipates providing approximately 40,000 persons with guidance in preparing letters of invitation, counseling, post-migration and search and location assistance as well as other services.

The agency is also on the alert should trouble erupt for Jewish communities located in areas of strife and danger in Africa, Latin America and Asia.

HIAS' 1978 budget is expected to exceed $8,000,000.

Spanish Refugee Aid — 80 East Street, New York, NY 10003

The Spanish Refugee Aid, Inc, was founded in 1953 to provide material and moral support to refugees who fled Spain after the fascist takeover in 1939. It provides regular financial aid and maintains a support centre.

United States Committee for Refugees
1625 Eye Street, NW, Suite 719
Washington, DC 20006
Tel: (202) 254 8718
Executive Director: Gerald E. Connolly
Staff: Matthew J. Mitchell

The United States Committee for Refugees is a private, non-profit organisation seeking to communicate the plight of the world's millions of refugees to the American people through its many public education programmes. In its efforts to provide a non-governmental focal point for humanitarian concern in meeting the needs of a changing world's refugee situation, the Committee consults with national and international leaders, maintains close liaison with voluntary organisations, acts as an information research centre, monitors hearings and legislation of the US Congress and policies of the US Government on refuge affairs, and actively supports specialised UN agencies working to alleviate refugee problems.

The Committee produces a quarterly newsletter, *World Refugee Report*, and yearly review, the *World Refugee Survey*. The Committee also publishes occasional issue papers.

Part C

International
(Non-Governmental Organisations)

I Voluntary Organisations

Chapter 1
HUMAN RIGHTS ORGANISATIONS

Introduction

The work of the international non-governmental organisations (INGOs) is of crucial importance to all initiatives on human rights. Human rights bodies are always well-advised to keep the appropriate international bodies informed of their initiatives, both to avoid duplication of effort and for the much wider influence the INGOs are able to bring to bear as authoritative bodies capable of initiating their own enquiries, making representations to the governments in question, and where necessary lobbying the inter-governmental agencies. They also function as a clearing-house for information on human rights violations, and serve to channel information between national affiliates and other interested organisations.

The listing that follows is far from exhaustive. Further details may be obtained from the national affiliate or from the *Yearbook of International Associations*.

Amnesty International – *see* pp. 7-12, 197-8.

Fédération Internationale des Droits d'Homme – 1 avenue de la Toison d'Or, B-1060 Brussels. *President ad interim:* Marc de Kock

See UK affiliate, **Centre for Human Rights and Responsibilities**, pp. 14-15.

International Committee of the Red Cross
17 Avenue de la Paix
1211 Geneva
Switzerland

The traditional work of the Committee lies in giving protection and assistance to victims of armed conflicts and internal disorders. In 1977 visits by delegates were made to 244 places of detention, including Iran and Argentina, and some 14,000 detainees were seen. Altogether ten Latin American countries were visited, five Asian countries and Djibouti and the Yemen Arab Republic and Indonesia. The Committee recently refused to send

245

delegates to Uruguay because the authorities would not give an undertaking that there would be no witnesses present at interviews with prisoners. After making visits the ICRC submits a report to the government concerned. Two principles apply to such a report: it makes no comment on the political background to, or the reasons given for, the detention or on its justification; secondly, the report is confidential to the government. The ICRC does not publish it.

Another notable feature of the work of the ICRC is its Central Tracing Agency — first opened in 1870, then again in 1914 and in 1939 — which obtains news of soldiers in captivity, civilian internees, people who are released or repatriated, etc. In consequence the ICRC has played a vital role in re-uniting separated families. Much of this work originated in the Second World War, but although some 14 million people have already been brought together, the work continues.

The ICRC is active in promoting humanitarian law. Recently it drafted two Protocols in the 1949 Geneva Conventions on the Laws of War. The Protocols were adopted on 8 June 1977. Protocol 1 deals with the protection of victims of international armed conflicts. Article 1 extends the provisions of the Geneva conventions to 'armed conflicts in which peoples are fighting against colonial domination and alien occupation and against racist regimes in the exercise of their rights of self determination'. Article 44 conferred on guerillas the status of combatant, and, if captured, that of prisoner of war. Article 47 states, 'A mercenary shall not have the right to be a combatant or a prisoner of war'. Protection is given to the civilian population by prohibiting attacks on non-military targets and on military targets if this would cause disproportionate and incidental loss of life or injury to civilians.

Protocol 2 develops the principle contained in article 3 of the Conventions which lays down the minimum standard of treatment to be given to non-combatants in an 'armed conflict not of an international character'.

The ICRC's work relies on financial contributions from governments. The Swiss government provided 12,500,000 Swiss Francs to the ordinary budget in 1977, which was more than half the total receipts of 22,609,000 Sw. Frs. All contributions are voluntary.

International Council of Voluntary Agencies
17 Avenue de la Paix
CH-1202 Geneva, Switzerland
Executive Director: Cyril Ritchie

The International Council of Voluntary Agencies aims to provide a forum where voluntary agencies may exchange views and information on all matters and questions of common interest; and to serve as an instrument for the development, growth and improvement of voluntary agencies, and their activities. It is concerned to inform peoples, governments, inter-governmental agencies and non-governmental organisations throughout the world of the humanitarian problems to the solution or alleviation of which the voluntary agencies address themselves; to encourage the undertaking of studies and to collect, coordinate and disseminate information regarding these problems, to encourage also the establishment of national councils and other groupings of voluntary agencies; and to sponsor meetings of voluntary agencies and other bodies dealing with the afore-mentioned problems.

International Federation for the Rights of Man
27 Rue Jean-Dolent
75014 Paris, France

The International Federation for the Rights of Man was set up to disseminate in all countries the principles of justice, liberty, equality and the sovereignty of the people, principles laid down in the French declarations of the rights of man in 1789 and 1793 as well as in the Universal Declaration of Human Rights, 1948. Among other activities it makes public protests in countries where rights of man are violated; representation to public authorities to have such rights respected.

The Federation has consultative status with ECOSOC.

International Institute of Human Rights, Strasbourg
6 place de Bordeaux
67000 Strasbourg
President: Edgar Fauré

The International Institute of Human Rights, founded in 1969 by President René Cassin on his receiving the Nobel Peace Prize, is an association established according to the laws of Alsace and Lorraine. Since the death of its founder, the Institute has had as its president Edgar Faure, President of the French National Assembly. During the eight years of its existence, the Institute has asserted itself in three major directions set out in its Statutes.

Firstly, it is concerned with teaching and with the training of teachers. Since 1970, it has devoted the major part of its activities to the world-

247

wide promotion of teaching human rights at university level. Thus each year the Institute organises a Study Session intended for advanced students and professors who specialise in human rights, as well as national and international civil servants. More than 1,000 participants have come to the Sessions from more than 100 countries. In the area of teacher training, its International Training Centre for University Human Rights Teaching operates through the financial assistance of UNESCO. It has welcomed more than 150 young university teachers from 50 countries, particularly developing countries, at its five ordinary sessions and the one external session, held in Costa Rica.

Secondly, it is concerned with research in the field of human rights. In research, priority has been given to studies of the connection between human rights and the permanent forces of an organised society, which include universities, religions and the state itself. The Institute is also available for expert consultations requested by the major international organisations active in human rights. As regards universities, a worldwide survey on university teaching and research on human rights was organised in 1970-71 as a result of a contract with UNESCO. The Institute is now conducting a new survey on the teaching of human rights in faculties of Law and Political Science.

Thirdly, the Institute has been concerned to inform and involve the general public. Since its creation, it has considered that human rights should not remain solely in the hands of specialists, and it has tried to involve the public in its activities through books, cinemas and other plastic arts. Thus the Institute participated in the International Book Festival at Nice, where it presented for the first time in the world the collected books which constitute 'the minimum library on human rights'. In addition, every year the Institute organises an International Human Rights Film Festival in Strasbourg and a poster competition to illustrate the theme of the Festival.

The work of the Institute is reflected in the various publications or series of publications which appear under its auspices. Among these are the *Human Rights Journal*, the *French Yearbook of Human Rights* (it is hoped that such national yearbooks of human rights will be published in other countries) and a substantial collection of teaching materials.

International League Against Racism and Antisemitism — 40 rue de Paradis, 75010 Paris, France *President:* J. Pierre-Bloch

The aims of the League are to oppose racism and antisemitism in every possible way, and defend the right to existence and peace of victims in all parts of the world.

International League for Human Rights
777 United Nations Plaza, Suite 6F
New York, NY 10017, USA
Tel: (202) 972 9554
Chairman: Jerome Shestack

The International League for Human Rights works to develop and establish international human rights standards. It aims at the application of those guarantees of political freedom, racial and religious equality and civil liberties. The platform of the League is the Universal Declaration of Human Rights and subsequent international human rights instruments adopted by the UN, OAS, ILO and other international bodies. The test of whether a complaint will be handled is the reliability of the information that violations of internationally guaranteed rights have occurred, the importance of the issue to an identifiable and protectable category of individuals, and the usefulness of the case in developing techniques to further human rights objectives. To this end it focuses the attention of the world community on gross violations of human rights such as slavery, genocide, torture, imprisonment without trial, denial of the right to leave one's country, repression of free speech and the press, and racial and religious discrimination. It has called attention to such violations through the publication of special reports, the preparation and submission of documented complaints to governments and inter-governmental bodies, the organisation of investigative missions to countries where serious violations are reported, the despatch of international judicial observers to political trials, direct negotiation with governments, programmes to support civil liberties groups in countries throughout the world, and the organisation of publicity campaigns.

The League has been successful in helping individuals to leave countries, in re-uniting families, in securing the release of political prisoners and in getting sentences reduced and death penalties rescinded, and in reducing racial and religious persecution of all kinds.

The League has affiliates and correspondents in 76 countries and enjoys consultative status with the UN, UNESCO, the Council of Europe, the ILO and the OAS.

249

**Lelio Basso International Foundation
for the Rights and Liberation of Peoples**
and
**Lelio Basso International League
for the Rights and Liberation of Peoples**
Via Dogana Vecchia 5
Rome 00186, Italy

Lelio Basso, an Italian lawyer and politician, served as president of the Bertrand Russell Tribunal II, which was established in 1973 and focused on repression in Latin America, especially in Brazil, Chile, Uruguay and Bolivia. Following his active involvement in the Second Tribunal, Lelio Basso created the Lelio Basso International Foundation for the Rights and Liberation of Peoples (for study and research) and a parallel International League for the Rights and Liberation of Peoples (to engage in mass education and political action towards these same goals). The rationale behind these organisations is that (a) insofar as a major finding of the Second Tribunal was that political repression and the violation of the rights of individuals cannot be understood without probing the root causes – largely economic – of that repression, research and study must be devoted to those root causes; and (b) while Amnesty International, lawyers associations, leagues for human rights, all seeking to protect the rights of individuals, exist (and have United Nations recognition), nothing similar exists with regard to the rights of whole peoples, especially those of the Third World.

Following an international conference in Algiers, the Foundation and League are currently seeking to promote public debate and popular adoption of a draft 'Universal Declaration of the Rights and Liberation of Peoples', which was proclaimed on July 4th, 1976.

Among the publications of the Foundation are a monthly journal, *I Diritti dei Popoli*, and *Repression in Latin America: A Report of the First Session of the Second Russell Tribunal*, edited by William Jerman.

Survival International – *see* pp. 18-19.

Women's International League for Peace and Freedom
1 rue Varembé
1211 Geneva 20, Switzerland

The Women's International League for Peace and Freedom was established to bring together women of different political and philosophical tendencies who are united in their determination to study, make known and help abolish the political, social, economic and psychological causes of war, and to work for a constructive peace. It campaigns for disarmament; works for the protection of minorities; for the prevention of discrimination and to solve the problems of refugees and displaced persons; and it is concerned at all times to further the implementation of human rights and liberties and the peaceful settlement of disputes.

World Federation of United Nations Associations — Centre International, 3 rue de Varembé, CP54, CH-1211 Geneva 20, Switzerland *Secretary General:* Frank Field

The World Federation of United Nations Associations coordinates and promotes the activities of national UNAs in 72 countries. It runs seminars and summer schools, and works in close cooperation with other organisations concerned with the implementation of the UN Charter and the Universal Declaration of Human Rights.

See also UK affiliate, United Nations Association, pp. 19-20.

Chapter 2

CHURCHES AND RELIGIOUS ORGANISATIONS

International Association for Religious Freedom
Fischerfieldstrasse 14
D6 Frankfurt 1, Germany
Representative at UN: Dr Homer A. Jack
777 UN Plaza, New York, NY 10017, USA

The aims of the International Association for Religious Freedom are: to bring into closer union the historic liberal churches, the liberal element in all churches, and isolated congregations and workers for religious freedom; to draw into the same fellowship free religious groups throughout the world which are in essential agreement with it; to open and maintain communication with free Christian groups in all lands who are striving to unite religion and liberty; and to increase fellowship and cooperation among them.

International Catholic Migration Commission – *see* p. 271.

International Council on Jewish Social and Welfare Services – 75 rue de Lyon, 1211 Geneva 13, Switzerland

The Council exists for the exchange of views and information among members concerning the problems of Jewish social and welfare services, among them those dealing with refugees, migration and integration. It makes representations to governments and international organisations on such questions.

Lutheran World Federation
150 route de Ferney
1211 Geneva 20, Switzerland
Secretary General: Rev Carl H. Man, Jr

The Lutheran World Federation is the association of the autonomous Lutheran churches, with important missionary and educational representation throughout the world. Through Lutheran World Relief it provides help for refugee work and church-related development projects. It may be mandated by affiliated churches to intervene on behalf of members at risk. It is also active on a wide range of human rights issues and works closely with international human rights organisations.

Following its Fifth Assembly in 1970, at which it passed a series of resolutions on the question of human rights, the Lutheran World Federation has been active in the field of human rights, through representations to the South African Prime Minister, a monograph on justice in the Holy Land, a seminar in July 1976, and participation in studies on Peace, Justice and Human Rights, and Development. Alongside this an important study on Namibia has been completed.

The Lutheran World Federation has also participated in studies on human rights in the context of the World Council of Churches and the Conference of European Churches.

Pax Christi – Celebesstraat 60, Postbox 7627, The Hague 2040, Netherlands. *President:* Cardinal Alfrink (Holland) *Secretary:* Charles ter Maat

Pax Christi is a pacifist movement towards international reconciliation. Although of Catholic origins, it is non-denominational and a membership organisation, not an appointed structure of the hierarchy. It is strongly represented in Western Europe. Among it particular concerns are East-West relations, political imprisonment and conscientious objection. With its national centres it conducts campaigns and public education works.

See also **UK affiliate, Pax Christi**, pp. 63-4.

Pontifical Commission 'Iustitia et Pax'
Palazzo San Calisto
00120 Citta del Vaticano
Rome, Italy

Established in Rome in 1967 following the recommendation of the Second Vatican Council, the Pontifical Commission 'Iustitia et Pax' works 'to stimulate the Catholic Community to foster progress in needy regions, and social justice on the international scene'. Shortly afterwards, National Commissions for Justice and Peace were set up in over 60 countries. The Pontifical Commission, together with these national commissions, is known to be active on human rights issues of direct concern to the Catholic Church, although its actions are not widely publicised. It also works with other organisations, both inside and outside the church, which pursue the same goals – the specialised agencies of the UN, agencies of other churches and the major religions, religious institutes, missionary centres, research centres, etc. In addition, in 1969 the Pontifical Commission joined with the World Council of Churches to set up a working body, SODEPAX (Committee on Society, Development and Peace), which has initiated studies on Economic Development, Peace and War, and Communication. All were seen to raise essential questions about the way in which men could be dominated by other men or the possibilities which men had for ensuring a just society; and of these various studies, one on Peace in 1970 dealt explicitly with human rights.

In 1975 the Pontifical Commission published Working Paper No. 1 entitled *The Church and Human Rights*, which has a valuable introductory section on the concept of rights and duties, in respect of both individuals and groups; an account of Church teaching on these rights; and concludes by suggesting among other things a programme on education for human rights.

See also, Commission for Justice and Peace, p. 57.

World Council of Churches
P O Box 66
150 route de Ferney
1211 Geneva 20, Switzerland
Tel: (022) 333400
Telex: 23423 OIK CH
Cable: Oikumene Geneva

The World Council of Churches occupies a central position as a clearing-house for information amongst member-churches and as the forum for new attitudes and approaches by the churches to their work in such areas as development aid, education and human rights. That its proposals have on occasion proved controversial testifies to the strength of this debate and of the churches' commitment to their overseas constituencies. The WCC structures have led the way in suggesting a more active role for member-churches on human rights issues, in particular torture, political imprisonment and the right to dissent. (See above, pp. 49-51.)

The WCC disposes of considerable relief and development monies through its Commission for Inter-Church Aid to Refugees and World Service desks, just as at the national level, each Council of Churches works through its own aid agency — in the UK, through Christian Aid, which is a section of the British Council of Churches (q.v.). Similarly, the WCC Refugee Office, operating on an overall budget of US $ 775,000 (1975), gives assistance to refugees in transit. Human rights work on specific issues and cases comes under the Churches' Commission on International Affairs (*Director:* Dr Leopoldo Niilus), which has initiated an Advisory Group on

Human Rights to begin work in the summer of 1977.

The CCIA has produced a useful practical guide to the complexities of inter-governmental complaints procedures, *How to File Complaints of Human Rights Violations* (prepared by Glenda da Fonseca for CCIA, 1975), obtainable from the British Council of Churches' office in London. The WCC also publishes an *International Review of Mission*, whose July 1977 issue is devoted to human rights.

World Jewish Congress – *see* pp. 65-6.

Chapter 3

SCHOLARSHIP AID AND STUDENT ORGANISATIONS

International University Exchange Fund, *see* pp. 25-9.

International Youth & Student Movement for United Nations
5 Chemin des Iris
CH-1216 Cointrin
Geneva, Switzerland
Secretary General: Roger Manser

The International Youth & Student Movement for United Nations has member groups in 34 countries. It promotes public education amongst young people on matters connected with the UN and its work, through international seminars, study projects, etc. It is cooperative and enthusiastic in its response on human rights issues.

World Assembly of Youth — 37-41 rue d'Arlon, B-1040 Brussels, Belgium
Secretary General: Carlos Carrasco

The World Assembly of Youth has coordinating committees in 60 countries. It encourages youth activities on the basis of international understanding and is involved in human rights campaigning.

World Student Christian Federation
37 quai Wilson
CH-1201 Geneva, Switzerland

The World Student Christian Federation is an ecumenical student Christian movement, with groups in 90 countries. It coordinates the activities of its largely autonomous national affiliates, and through them runs campus education groups with a strong emphasis on Third World and human rights issues involving progressive church-related groups.

World Union of Jewish Students — *see* p. 108.

256

World University Service
5 Chemin des Iris
1216 Cointrin
Geneva, Switzerland

The World University Service exists to express and promote international university solidarity and mutual service within and between universities and centres of higher learning throughout the world; to foster the idea that the university be involved directly in the solution of problems facing society, and to resist all forms of external pressure hindering the freedom of study, teaching and research.

See also UK affiliate, **World University Service (UK)**, pp. 32-7.

II Professional Organisations

Chapter 4

LAWYERS

Centre for Human Rights: Formulation, Research and Practice
c/o Louis Edmond Pettiti
4 Square Labruyère
Paris 9, France.

Le Centre des Droits de l'Homme: Formulation, Recherche, Application Pratique has been organised by the Paris Bar with the support of, and under the auspices of, UNESCO. This is an experimental centre concerned with international human rights; it is intended to serve the members of the legal profession, and may well be a model for other regions of the world.

The Centre has three chief approaches: firstly, to develop the theory of human rights; secondly, to study cases examined by international organs for the protection of human rights; and thirdly, to promote discussion of particular themes — for example, the creation of a Statute for lawyers and judges concerning their missions as foreign observers at trials concerning the violation of human rights; and examination of the use of the doctrine of national security to justify violation of fundamental rights.

International Association of Democratic Lawyers — 49 avenue Jupiter, B-1190 Brussels, Belgium. *Secretary General:* Joë Nordmann

The International Association of Democratic Lawyers was founded in 1945 by lawyers from anti-fascist nations; it now includes members from countries of all political persuasions, having groups and correspondents in 57 countries. It meets, studies human rights problems, sends delegations to observe political trials and other alleged violations of human rights, and publishes reports, resolutions and press releases.

The IADL has consultative status with UN/ECOSOC and UNESCO.

International Commission of Jurists
109 route de Chêne
1224 Chêne-Bougeries
Geneva, Switzerland
General Secretary: Niall MacDermot

The International Commission of Jurists was founded in 1952 to realise the lawyer's faith in justice and human liberty under the rule of law. The Commission has carried out its task on the basis that lawyers have a challenging and essential role to play, working on the assumption that lawyers on the whole are alive to their responsibilities to the society in which they live and to humanity in general. It is strictly non-political; the independence and impartiality which have characterised its work for over twenty years, and which continue to do so, have won the respect of lawyers, international organisations and the international community. In its earlier years, perhaps its most important activity was to translate the general principles of the Universal Declaration of Human Rights into detailed statements of legal principles and procedures acceptable and applicable in all parts of the world. This was done by convening international conferences of lawyers representing the principal legal systems of the world to formulate in legal language the safeguards which are needed to give effect to basic human rights under the rule of law.

The Commission has published many special reports on particular situations. Among the most recent have been on 'Violations of Human Rights and the Rule of Law in Uganda' (1974), 'The Legal System in Chile' (1974), 'Report of a Mission to Uruguay' (1974) and 'The Situation of Defence Lawyers in Argentina' (1975).

The other activities of the ICJ are many. It participates in the work of UN bodies concerned with human rights by oral and written interventions, either supplying information on violations of human rights or putting forward proposals for improved procedures for implementing human rights. It sends international observers to important political trials. Defence lawyers testify to the marked improvement in the conduct of these trials when observers are present. In two cases the ICJ has been invited by the government concerned to send an observer in order to establish internationally the fairness of their procedures (in one case this object was achieved; in the other the ICJ observer was severely critical). It publishes a twice-yearly *Review*, which is distributed to some 15,000 lawyers, law libraries and lawyers' organisations throughout the world. The *Review* contains reports of recent legislation, trials and other repressive action in different parts of the world, legal articles and commentaries, basic texts, book reviews and ICJ news. The Commission also sends missions to enquire into situations concerning human rights and the rule of law and makes private interventions with governments about alleged violations of human rights. And it issues press releases on matters calling for immediate comment.

The independence of the legal profession and of the judiciary are of primary importance for maintenance of the Rule of Law; but in an increasing number of countries, and on an increasing scale, serious inroads have been made into the independence both of judges and of practising lawyers – particularly those who have been engaged in the defence of persons accused of political offences. In some countries this has resulted in a situation where it is virtually impossible for political prisoners to secure the services of an experienced defence lawyer. The ICJ has formed at its headquarters in Geneva a Centre for the Independence of Judges and Lawyers, whose objects are: to collect reliable information from as many countries as possible about the legal guarantees for the independence of the legal profession and the judiciary, any incursions which have been made into that independence, and particulars of cases of harassment, repression or victimisation of individual judges and lawyers; to distribute this information to judges and lawyers and their organisations throughout the world; and to invite these organisations in appropriate cases to make representations to the authorities of the country concerned, or otherwise take such action as they see fit to assist their colleagues.

National sections of the ICJ have been established in over 50 countries.

Justice – 2 Clement's Inn, London WC2A 2DX Tel: 405 6018. *Secretary:* Tom Sargant *Legal Secretary:* Ronald Briggs.

The British affiliate of the ICJ is Justice, who are concerned to make laws better than they are and its way of working is not by protest but by research and argument. Working committees do this work. Among the topics concerning which Justice has made recommendations are passports, immigration and complaints against statutory agencies and tribunals. Reports published include 'Freedom of Information', 'Plutonium and Liberty'.

Justice also recommends the incorporation of the European Convention on Human Rights into Britain's domestic laws, in order to secure the protection of human rights in Britain. Full details of all activities and publications are given in the informative Annual Report.

Membership stands at 1500, the largest of any of the National sections of the ICJ. Financially the office is run on a shoestring: subscriptions and fund raising events produced about £10,000 in the year to June 1978; the associated Justice Trust had an income from donations etc of about £5,750.

Chapter 5

PROFESSIONAL ORGANISATIONS

Inter American Press Association – *see* p. 234.

International Association for Cultural Freedom – 104 blvd Haussman, F 75008, Paris, France

As an organisation of intellectuals – scholars, writers, artists and men of public affairs – the association seeks to construct a bridge between the international intellectual community and those engaged in social, political and economic action; and it defends intellectual, academic and cultural freedom against infringement from any source.

International Association of University Professors and Lecturers – *see* p. 97.

International Council of Scientific Unions
51 bvd de Montmorency
75016 Paris, France
Tel: (010) 33 1 527 7702/525 0329
Telex: ICSU 63053F
Cable: ICSU Paris 16
Secretary General: Sir John Kendall
Executive Secretary: F.W.G. Baker

The ICSU, founded in 1931, is an international non-governmental organisation comprising 18 international specialist scientific unions and member organisations from 68 countries, with a wide range of political philsophies. The British affiliate is the Royal Society. The ICSU's function is to uphold the rights of all scientists throughout the world to join in international scientific activity without regard to race, religion, politics, sex or language, and to stimulate cooperation among scientists throughout the world. However, by reason of its statutory duty to respect the independence of its national members, the ICSU feels bound to avoid intervention in internal matters of discrimination.

Amongst the Council's standing committees is one devoted to the Free

Circulation of Scientists.[1] This Committee maintains a register of violations of the right of free circulation that have affected meetings of members of ICSU's family, but this is available for consultation only by ICSU organisers planning meetings in, and inviting participation from, particular countries.

If, after all other appropriate courses of action have been exhausted, participants are prevented from attending international scientific meetings, the organising body concerned may resort to a number of actions which include publicising the case and issuing formal protest statements. In a booklet giving *Advice to Organisers of International Scientific Meetings*,[2] the Committee summarises these procedures and prints a number of ICSU resolutions relating to freedom of movement for scientists.

On the thorny question of scientific emigration, the ICSU in a resolution passed in 1972 affirmed that: 'the prevention of migration of scientists from a country is an internal political question outside the terms of reference of ICSU' adding that it was 'nevertheless a serious challenge to the world scientific community'.

International Federation of Actors *see* pp. 141-2.

International Federation of Musicians – Kreuzstrasse 60, CH-8008 Zurich, Switzerland

There are 33 national musicians unions in 25 countries. In addition to dealing with strictly professional concerns such as international copyright arrangements, the International Federation of Musicians (FIM) has pressed the International Labour Office (ILO) to investigate the fate of musicians arrested in Chile and Uruguay.

See also UK affiliate, **Musicians Union**, pp. 142-3.

International PEN – *see* pp. 132-4.

International Press Institute – *see* pp. 146-7.

---

[1] *Executive Secretary:* Dr O.G. Tandberg, Royal Swedish Academy of Sciences, Roslagsvägen, Frescati S 104 05 Stockholm Tel: (08) 150 430.

[2] Available from ICSU, 51 bvd de Montmorency, 75016 Paris.

International

Inter Parliamentary Union
Place du Petit-Saconnex
1209 Geneva 28, Switzerland

The Union exchanges and maintains contact between Parliamentarians in 73 member countries, including those of the Eastern bloc and the Soviet Union. Given this spread, resolutions on human rights questions tend to be all-embracing and unexceptionable. Following establishment of a Chile Committee to enquire into the fate of missing or imprisoned deputies, a Special Committee was set up on trial basis to receive and report on such cases elsewhere — Argentina, Paraguay and Kenya among others — at the initiative of national members. The Union occasionally makes representations and sends cables and letters on human rights issues.

World Confederation of Organisations of the Teaching Professions
5 avenue du Moulin
CH-1110 Morges, Vaud, Switzerland
Tel: (021) 717467
Cable: TEACHING Morges
Secretary General: John M. Thompson

The WCOTP, which comprises 125 national teachers' unions in 75 countries, lays claim to be the most representative international organisation of teachers. It describes itself as 'an independent non-aligned political force seeking equality of opportunity through education, quality in education, economic security and the protection of civic and human rights'.

WCOTP represents teachers' interests as defined above, with UNESCO an other inter-governmental organisations. It has consistently emphasised the need for observance by member-states of commitments entered into on human rights questions, and has criticised the 'selective morality' of the United Nations when dealing with human rights issues.

In 1968 the theme of the annual WCOTP Assembly held in Dublin was 'Education and Human Rights'. It maintains a close watch on teachers in Chile, has protested at the disbanding of the Chilean teachers' unions, the detention of their leaders and the dismissal of teacher-members. WCOTP has also intervened on behalf of reachers tortured and imprisoned in connection with their union activities in Benin, and on behalf of teachers dismissed or imprisoned in connection with their union activities in other countries, including most recently Ethiopia.

In 1976 WCOTP's Constituent Federation, the International Federation of Secondary Teachers (FIPESO) acted as coordinator for a seminar on

Education and Human Rights at the Council of Europe in Strasbourg.

World Federation of Scientific Workers, *see* pp. 116-18.

World Psychiatric Association — Psychiatrische Universitätsklinik, Lazarettgasse 14, A1090 Vienna, Austria. *Secretary General:* Professor Peter Berner. *See* pp. 123-5.

Chapter 6

INTERNATIONAL UNION ORGANISATIONS AND POLITICAL PARTIES

International Confederation of Free Trade Unions – rue Montagne aux Herbes-Potapères 37.41, B-1000 Brussels, Belgium. Tel: 178085

ICFTU has affiliated trade union bodies in 91 countries (mostly pro-West). It promotes the development of trade union structures and congresses, especially in the Third World. It has set up an international Solidarity Fund to aid unionists persecuted for their activities wherever this may occur; and it passes resolutions and makes representations on human rights issues.

Liberal International – *see* p. 153.

Socialist International – *see* p. 155.

World Confederation of Labour – 50 rue Joseph II, B-1040 Brussels, Belgium

Formerly the International Federation of Christian Trade Unions, the WCL is now non-denominational. It is a loose federation of union bodies in 75 countries with orientation towards Third World development and human rights issues. It also has good contacts in Latin America.

III Refugees

Chapter 7

REFUGEES

Aid to Displaced Persons and its European Villages – 35 rue de Marche, 5200 Huy, Belgium

Aid to Displaced Persons aims to assure refugees, whatever their nationality or religion, material or moral aid in all its forms, particularly through individual sponsorship, reception centres and European villages and to forge around the refugee a chain of goodwill, a 'Europe of the Heart'.

Association for the Study of the World Refugee Problems – Landstr 64, P O Box 178, FL-9490 Vaduz, Liechtenstein

The AWR exists to promote, intensify and coordinate scholarly research in the refugee problem by mutual comparison and the exchange of results, by establishing general working principles, and by publications or any other appropriate form for spreading the results achieved.

The Association has consultative status with ECOSOC and Council of Europe.

Hebrew Immigrant Aid Society – *see* pp. 239-40.

International Catholic Migration Commission – 55 rue de Lausanne, 1202 Geneva, Switzerland. Cable: Cathicom. Dr T Stark

The Commission works to coordinate the activities of national Catholic migration organisations, represent them at international organisations and conferences, provide technical and advisory assistance to interested groups and organisations and promote international recognition of the spiritual and material rights of migrants and refugees.

International Labour Assistance
Ollenhauerstrasse 3
53 Bonn, Germany
Secretary: Richard Haar

International Labour Assistance is concerned with assisting refugees

271

(those who for defending democratic principles have been forced to find shelter abroad) and displaced persons; with taking action, as a relief organisation, in particular cases of catastrophes or social and political disturbances; and with organising relief work on behalf of children and young people.

It participates in the work of other organisations for refugees, makes housing loans and provides technical training, homes for the aged and the handicapped, financial help to students; technical services for overseas emigration; holiday homes for children and mothers; rehabilitation centre.

International Labour Assistance has consultative status with ECOSOC and UNESCO, and a working agreement with the Intergovernmental Committee for European Migration.

International Rescue Committee – 386 Park Avenue S, New York, NY 10016, USA *European Director:* 7 rue Gautier, CH-Geneva, Switzerland

The International Rescue Committee exists to assist, resettle and rehabilitate victims of totalitarian oppression and persecution and administer such relief without regard to race, nationality or religion; conduct programmes of public education regarding the situation, circumstances, needs and plight of such victims of totalitarianism for the purpose of mobilising assistance on their behalf.

International Social Service
15 rue Charles-Galland
1206 Geneva, Switzerland
Secretary General: Ingrid Gelinek
Representative at UN: Mrs M. Harris
345 East 48th Street, New York, NY 10017

The International Social Service aims to assist individuals who, as a consequence of voluntary or forced migration have to overcome personal or family difficulties, the solution of which required coordinated action in several countries. It works through its national branches, delegations or correspondents. It undertakes family and individual social enquiries across the borders of different countries and seeks to find a solution on a case-work basis to problems which arise as a consequence of migration or as a consequence of resident in a foreign country; working with groups and communities as needed, it endeavours to procure legal documents. It also conducts group and community work in certain countries to assist adaptation of immigrants, undertakes studies of underlying problems in the field of migration and collaborates closely with organisations with related interests.

It has consultative status with ECOSOC, UNICEF, the Council of Europe, UNESCO, OAS, and the ILO Special List; and it is a member of the International Council of Voluntary Agencies and the International Council on Social Welfare.

See also UK affiliate, **International Social Service of Great Britain,** pp. 180-81.

Part D

International
(Inter-Governmental Organisations)

European Commission of Human Rights
Council of Europe
Strasbourg, France
Secretary: Dr Christian Kruger

The Council of Europe was established in 1949 and has 21 states as members. (Austria, Belgium, Cyprus, Denmark, France, W. Germany, Greece, Iceland, Ireland, Italy, Liechtenstein, Luxembourg, Malta, Netherlands, Norway, Portugal, Spain, Sweden, Switzerland, Turkey, UK.) The European Convention on Human Rights and its five Protocols came into force in 1954. Under this Convention, a Commission and a Court of Human Rights were established to implement its provisions. The Committee of Ministers was also given certain powers.

The rights protected by the Convention and the First and Fourth Protocols are:
1. the right to life;
2. freedom from torture and inhuman treatment or punishment;
3. freedom from slavery, servitude and forced labour;
4. the right to liberty and security of person including the right of a detained person to be brought to trial within a reasonable time;
5. the right to a fair and expeditious trial;
6. protection against retroactivity of the criminal law;
7. the right to respect for one's private and family life, one's home and correspondence;
8. freedom of thought, conscience and religion;
9. freedom of expression;
10. freedom of assembly and association;
11. the right to marry and found a family;
12. the right to an effective remedy if one's rights are violated;
13. freedom from discrimination in respect of rights and freedoms protected in the Convention;
14. the right to peaceful enjoyment of possessions;
15. the right of parents to ensure the education of their children in conformity with their own religious and philosophical convictions;
16. the right to vote in free elections;
17. freedom of movement and freedom to choose one's residence;
18. freedom from exile and the right to enter the country of one's nationality;
19. prohibition of collective expulsion of aliens.

Complaints of violation of one or more of these rights may be submitted by individuals or groups provided they are the victims of the violation; or by a close relative of the victim, or by a lawyer authorised by the victim. However, complaints from individuals are only recognised by those states who have accepted Article 25 of the Convention. (All have done so except

Cyprus, France, Greece, Liechtenstein, Malta, Portugal, Spain and Turkey.) But this will not be effective in respect of the last four rights mentioned above unless the state concerned has both ratified the Fourth Protocol and agreed to extend Article 25 to the rights contained in it. Some states have done so, namely: Austria, Belgium, Denmark, Federal Republic of Germany, Iceland, Ireland, Luxembourg, Norway, Sweden.

Complainants should exhaust all domestic remedies before applying to the European Commission. When making a submission, the particular rights claimed to have been violated should be named; a statement of the facts and arguments and all relevant documents should be attached. Urgent applications may be given priority. Legal aid may be available.

Once all the procedures and stages have been completed (see Da Fonseca, *How to File Complaints of Human Rights Violations*), the outcome may be one of three sorts: a friendly settlement between parties; a judicial decision by the Court of Human Rights; or a decision by the Committee of Ministers.

Respect for human rights is a condition of membership of the Council. It is a feature of the Convention that an individual whose complaint is substantiated may expect redress.

Inter American Commission on Human Rights
The Organisation of American States
Washington, DC 20006

All countries of the American continents, except Canada, are members of the OAS – but Cuba was excluded in 1962. The Inter-American Commission on Human Rights was established under the OAS in 1959.

The procedures of the Inter-American Commission on Human Rights are very different from those of the European Commission. Firstly, members of the OAS have not undertaken to abide by the decisions of the Commission, and there is no provision for redress on behalf of complainants. There is no legal body, there is no procedure for conciliation and the relevant activity of the Meeting of Consultation of Ministers of Foreign Affairs is mainly confined to producing studies and recommendations. Complaints are treated as items of information and will be processed according to various procedures (*see* Glenda De Fonseca, *How to File Complaints of Human Rights Violations*). Non-governmental organisations are able to petition on behalf of individuals, and individuals themselves may succeed in lodging complaints. Glenda de Fonseca suggests that where complaints concern social or labour rights, then, assuming that the country concerned has ratified the relevant ILO convention, it would be advisable to apply to the ILO (q.v.).

However, the Commission has succeeded in reporting on torture in Brazil, illegal detention and inhumanity in Cuba, the killing of peasants by the army in Bolivia and the violations of human rights in Chile. But when the OAS failed to take any action on the report on Chile, and in fact decided to hold its June 1976 meeting in Chile, there were some sharp reactions by members of the Commission. In particular, the Executive Secretary, Dr Luis Reque, resigned and in the 1976 Sean McBride Human Rights lecture which he delivered to the annual conference of Amnesty International he said:

'The majority of the Member States of the OAS have no genuine interest in an effective Inter-American Commission on Human Rights. This lack of interest is responsible for the failure of many governments to cooperate with the Commission; replies to requests for information are delayed, incomplete reports are sent, or there is complete silence on the part of the governments. To this must be added the elimination of programmes in the field of the promotion of human rights, such as various scholarship projects and seminars. As if all this were not enough, the OAS General Secretariat has shown itself unwilling to cooperative with the Commission.'

International Labour Organization
International Labour Office
4 route des Morillons
1211 Geneva 22, Switzerland

The International Labour Organization is now one of the specialised agencies of the UN. Although concerned with the protection of labour rights in general, it also protects many basis human rights, such as freedom of association, freedom from discrimination in employment, the right to work, the right to a minimum wage, the right to collective bargaining, etc. It has adopted a large number of international standards in the form of conventions and recommendations for the protection of labour rights, among which are several dealing with human rights.

Non-discrimination and equality of opportunity and treatment form part of the ILO's declared constitutional aims. They have been dealt with specially in the Convention No 111 on Discrimination in Employment and Occupation. This Convention aims at eliminating discrimination based on political opinion, national extraction, social origin, religion, sex, colour or race and it has been ratified by 82 countries.

Other ILO Conventions dealing with human rights are:
1. Convention No 29, Concerning Forced Labour;
2. Convention No 87, on the Freedom of Association and the Protection

of the Right to Organise;
3. Convention No 98, on the Right to Organise and Collective Bargaining;
4. Convention No 105, Concerning the Abolition of Forced Labour;
5. Convention No 122, Concerning Employment Policy.

Complaints procedures are covered especially by Articles 24 and 26 of the Constitution and by reference to the Committee on Freedom of Association which deals with trade union rights generally. Only certain organisations may lodge complaints, namely occupational organisations (industrial associations of employers of workers). For a detailed explanation of the procedures, see Glenda De Fonseca, op. cit.

Recently a special committee of the ILO was set up to examine a complaint against Czechoslovakia, that many of the signatories of Charter 77 were dismissed from their jobs simply because they signed the Charter. Other recent human rights cases to be put before the ILO were: the refusal of the Soviet authorities to recognise the unofficial trade unions which are attempting to form in the USSR; a similar case against Poland concerning unofficial unions there; and a case against West Germany over the *Berufsverbot*, the policy of excluding some people from government service on political grounds.

United Nations

The Universal Declaration of Human Rights (see Appendix I) sets out the rights which member states have a duty to promote under the UN Charter. But it is not binding upon members. There are more precise and more certain procedures for implementing particular human rights in the Covenant on Civil and Political Rights (see 'UN Human Rights Committee'), in the ECOSOC resolution 1503 concerning 'consistent patterns of gross violation of human rights' (see 'UN Commission on Human Rights') and in the Conventions of the International Labour Organization (q.v.). Under the Covenant for Economic, Social and Cultural Rights, the procedure is less developed.

United Nations Commission on Human Rights
The United Nations   Palais de Nations
New York, NY 10017, USA   1211 Geneva, Switzerland
Secretary General: Kurt Waldheim

The UN Commission on Human Rights is one of the Commissions of the UN Economic and Social Council (ECOSOC). The Commission handles complaints ('communications') dealing with 'a consistent pattern of gross violations'; it does not handle complaints about individual cases unless they are tantamount to 'a consistent pattern of gross violations'. Complaints about individual, specific cases should be directed to the Human Rights Committee (q.v.) appointed under the International Covenant on Civil and Political Rights.

The members of the Commission are governments. The Sub-Commission on Prevention of Discrimination and Protection of Minorities and various ad hoc working groups service the Commission. The procedures which are followed, and the various conditions which must be satisfied if complaints are to be deemed 'admissible', are set out in Glenda de Fonseca's *How to File Complaints of Human Rights Violations*, a practical guide to intergovernmental procedures (it is published by the World Council of Churches, Geneva).

One of the main stipulations is that each complainant should have first exhausted all other remedies; however, if recourse to such remedies is, or is likely to be, ineffective or prolonged, the complaint may be admitted.

A complaint may be lodged by anyone – an individual, a group or an organisation. It should be well supported with evidence. Victims of violations, people with direct and reliable knowledge or some body with indirect knowledge but clear supporting evidence, are all likely to be regarded as important sources. The particular rights which have been violated should be named. In this connection it is helpful to refer to one or more of the UN instruments such as the UN Declaration of Human Rights (see Appendix for the text); the Convention on the Elimination of all Forms of Racial Discrimination; UN Standard Minimum Rules for the Treatment of Prisoners; the International Covenant on Economic, Social and Cultural Rights and the International Covenant on Civil and Political Rights. (These documents are available from the United Nations (Geneva or New York) in the five official languages – Chinese, English, French, Russian and Spanish.)

If a complaint is admitted, investigated and found to be substantiated, action will not necessarily be taken against the offending government. The Commission has a rather wide discretion to do what it thinks suitable, and this includes doing nothing.

In March 1978, the Commission proposed the creation of a voluntary trust fund to aid victims of human rights violations in Chile. Another resolution regarding the Covenant on Economic, Social and Cultural Rights calls for action on realising these rights. (There is as yet no committee which serves this Covenant in the way that the Human Rights Committee serves the Covenant on Civil and Political Rights.)

The ad hoc working groups have reported on Chile, the Israeli-occupied territories and Southern Africa (including Namibia and Rhodesia).

United Nations High Commissioner for Refugees
Palais de Nations
1211 Geneva, 10 Switzerland
(established by the UN)

Aims

The UNHCR has two principal functions: providing international protection for refugees, which consists in promoting a liberal application of asylum and, once this has been granted, protecting the rights of refugees in essential areas of concern such as employment, education, settlement, free movement and a guarantee that they will not be sent back to a country where their life or liberty would be threatened; and, secondly, the search for permanent solutions to the problem of refugees, by helping governments and private organisations to facilitate the agreed repatriation of these refugees and their integration into new national communities. It also provides material assistance so as to put the refugees into such a position as to meet their personal needs.

Mandate

The mandate extends as a rule to persons who for reasons other than personal convenience have left their country of origin and cannot or do not wish to return to that country and/or to avail themselves of the protection of the government of that country. Refugees meeting these conditions are entitled to the protection of the Office of the High Commissioner irrespective of their geographical location. Refugees who are assisted by other United Nations agencies, or who have the same rights or obligations as nationals of their country of residence are outside the mandate of UNHCR.

Main legal instruments concerning refugees are the 1951 Convention relating to the Status of Refugees, and the 1967 Protocol which extends provisions of the Convention to new groups of refugees. The application of these instruments is supervised by UNHCR. Other legal instruments benefiting refugees include the 1954 Convention on the Reduction of Statelessness, the 1957 Agreement and Protocol of 1973.

Activities

The main objective of UNHCR is to promote and safeguard the rights and interests of refugees. In so doing it devotes special attention to the vital question of asylum and seeks to improve the status of refugees in their country of residence through the acquisition of nationality when voluntary repatriation is not applicable. UNHCR pursues its objectives in the field of protection by promoting the conclusion of intergovernmental legal instruments in favour of refugees and encouraging governments to adopt provisions for their benefit.

United Nations Human Rights Committee
The International Covenant on Civil and Political Rights
United Nations
New York, NY 10017, USA
or
Palais des Nations
1211 Geneva, Switzerland

The Human Rights Committee was established under the International Covenant on Civil and Political Rights which came into force on 23 March 1976. It reports annually to the UN Economic and Social Council (ECOSOC). The rights covered by the Covenant are broadly the same as those laid down by European Commission on Human Rights (q.v.) in the European Convention on Human Rights. But the implementation is different.

At the moment the Committee has two main tasks. Under Article 40 it has to examine reports submitted by the states which are party to the Covenant (there are 49 of these; they are listed at the end of this entry). The reports concern measures taken to give effect to the rights recognised in the Covenant and any difficulties affecting implementation. Secondly, under the Optional Protocol it has to consider complaints from individuals who allege violations of their rights under the Covenant. Twenty states have accepted its provisions. They are:

Barbados, Canada, Columbia, Costa Rica, Denmark, Dominican Republic, Ecuador, Finland, Italy, Jamaica, Madagascar, Mauritius, Norway, Panama, Senegal, Surinam, Sweden, Uruguay, Venezuela, Zaire.

The Committee consists of 18 experts elected in their personal capacities but reflecting a fair geographical distribution.

Under Article 40 the practice is that each state is represented at the meeting which considers its report. The representative replies to questions put by Committee members. So far the representatives have cooperated and the questions put by the Committee have been wide ranging and searching. The aim is to enter into a constructive discussion with each reporting state.

Under the Optional Protocol all complaints are considered in closed sessions. Complaints are passed to the Committee by the UN Secretariat which decides how they should be treated. (Over 20,000 communications about human rights are received by the UN each year.) To be admissible the complaint must (a) not be anonymous; (b) be against a state which has accepted the Optional Protocol; (c) not be an abuse of the procedure; (d) concern violation of one of the rights laid down in the Covenant; (e) not be under consideration under any other international procedures; and the complainant must have exhausted all domestic remedies open to him. So far over twenty complaints have been made against four states.

The Covenant on Civil and Political Rights has been ratified by 51 countries (as at July 1978):

Barbados, Bulgaria, Byelorussian Soviet Socialist Republic, Canada, Chile, Columbia, Costa Rica, Cyprus, Czechoslovakia, Denmark, Dominican Republic, Ecuador, Finland, German Democratic Republic, Federal Republic of Germany, Guinea, Guyana, Hungary, Iran, Iraq, Jamaica, Jordan, Kenya, Lebanon, Libyan Arab Republic, Madagascar, Mali, Mauritius, Mongolia, Norway, Panama, Peru, Philippines, Poland, Portugal, Rumania, Rwanda, Senegal, Spain, Surinam, Sweden, Syrian Arab Republic, Tanzania, Tunisia, Ukrainian Soviet Socialist Republic, United Kingdom, USSR, Uruguay, Venezuela, Yugoslavia, Zaire.

Appendix

TEXT OF UNIVERSAL DECLARATION OF HUMAN RIGHTS

Preamble

Whereas recognition of the inherent dignity and of the equal and inalienable rights of all members of the human family is the foundation of freedom, justice and peace in the world,

Whereas disregard and contempt for human rights have resulted in barbarous acts which have outraged the conscience of mankind, and the advent of a world in which human beings shall enjoy freedom of speech and belief and freedom from fear and want has been proclaimed as the highest aspiration of the common people,

Whereas it is essential, if man is not to be compelled to have recourse, as a last resort, to rebellion against tyranny and oppression, that human rights should be protected by the rule of law,

Whereas it is essential to promote the development of friendly relations between nations,

Whereas the peoples of the United Nations have in the Charter reaffirmed their faith in fundamental human rights, in the dignity and worth of the human person and in the equal rights of men and women and have determined to promote social progress and better standards of life in larger freedom,

Whereas Member States have pledged themselves to achieve, in co-operation with the United Nations, the promotion of universal respect for and observance of human rights and fundamental freedoms,

Whereas a common understanding of these rights and freedoms is of the greatest importance for the full realization of this pledge,

Now, therefore,

The General Assembly

proclaims

THIS UNIVERSAL DECLARATION OF HUMAN RIGHTS as a common standard of achievement for all peoples and all nations, to the end that every individual and every organ of society, keeping this Declaration constantly in mind, shall strive by teaching and education to promote respect for these rights and freedoms and by progressive measures, national and international, to secure their universal and effective recognition and observance, both among the peoples of Member States themselves and among the peoples of territories under their jurisdiction.

Article 1. All human beings are born free and equal in dignity and rights.

They are endowed with reason and conscience and should act towards one another in a spirit of brotherhood.

Article 2. Everyone is entitled to all the rights and freedoms set forth in this Declaration, without distinction of any kind, such as race, colour, sex, language, religion, political or other opinion, national or social origin, property, birth or other status.

Furthermore, no distinction shall be made on the basis of the political, jurisdictional or international status of the country or territory to which a person belongs, whether it be independent, trust, non-self-governing or under any other limitation of sovereignty.

Article 3. Everyone has the right to life, liberty and security of person.

Article 4. No one shall be held in slavery or servitude; slavery and the slave trade shall be prohibited in all their forms.

Article 5. No one shall be subjected to torture or to cruel, inhuman or degrading treatment or punishment.

Article 6. Everyone has the right to recognition everywhere as a person before the law.

Article 7. All are equal before the law and are entitled without any discrimination to equal protection of the law. All are entitled to equal protection against any discrimination in violation of this Declaration and against any incitement to such discrimination.

Article 8. Everyone has the right to an effective remedy by the competent national tribunals for acts violating the fundamental rights granted him by the constitution or by law.

Article 9. No one shall be subjected to arbitrary arrest, detention or exile.

Article 10. Everyone is entitled in full equality to a fair and public hearing by an independent and impartial tribunal, in the determination of his rights and obligations and of any criminal charge against him.

Article 11. (1) Everyone charged with a penal offence has the right to be presumed innocent until proved guilty according to law in a public trial at which he has had all the guarantees necessary for his defence.

(2) No one shall be held guilty of any penal offence on account of any act or omission which did not constitute a penal offence, under national or international law, at the time when it was committed. Nor shall a heavier penalty be imposed than the one that was applicable at the time the penal offence was commited.

Article 12. No one shall be subjected to arbitrary interference with his privacy, family, home or correspondence, nor to attacks upon his honour and reputation. Everyone has the right to the protection of the law against such interference or attacks.

Article 13. (1) Everyone has the right to freedom of movement and residence within the borders of each state.

(2) Everyone has the right to leave any country, including his own, and to return to his country.

Article 14. (1) Everyone has the right to seek and to enjoy in other countries asylum from persecution.

(2) This right may not be invoked in the case of prosecutions genuinely arising from non-political crimes or from acts contrary to the purposes and principles of the United Nations.

Article 15. (1) Everyone has the right to a nationality.

(2) No one shall be arbitrarily deprived of his nationality nor denied the right to change his nationality.

Article 16. (1) Men and women of full age, without any limitation due to race, nationality or religion, have the right to marry and to found a family. They are entitled to equal rights as to marriage, during marriage and at its dissolution.

(2) Marriage shall be entered into only with the free and full consent of the intending spouses.

(3) The family is the natural and fundamental group unit of society and is entitled to protection by society and the State.

Article 17. (1) Everyone has the right to own property alone as well as in association with others.

(2) No one shall be arbitrarily deprived of his property.

Article 18. Everyone has the right to freedom of thought, conscience and religion; this right includes freedom to change his religion or belief, and freedom, either alone or in community with others and in public or private, to manifest his religion or belief in teaching, practice, worship and observance.

Article 19. Everyone has the right to freedom of opinion and expression; this right includes freedom to hold opinions without interference and to seek, receive and impart information and ideas through any media and regardless of frontiers.

Article 20. (1) Everyone has the right to freedom of peaceful aseembly and association.

(2) No one may be compelled to belong to an association.

Article 21. (1) Everyone has the right to take part in the government of his country, directly or through freely chosen representatives.

(2) Everyone has the right of equal access to public service in his country.

(3) The will of the people shall be the basis of the authority of government; this will shall be expressed in periodic and genuine elections which shall be by universal and equal suffrage and shall be held by secret vote or by equivalent free voting procedures.

Article 22. Everyone, as a member of society, has the right to social security and is entitled to realization, through national effort and international co-operation and in accordance with the organization and resources of each State, of the economic, social and cultural rights indispensable for his dignity and the free development of his personality.

Article 23. (1) Everyone has the right to work, to free choice of employment, to just and favourable conditions of work and to protection against unemployment.

(2) Everyone, without any discrimination, has the right to equal pay for equal work.

(3) Everyone who works has the right to just and favourable remuneration ensuring for himself and his family an existence worthy of human dignity, and supplemented, if necessary, by other means of social protection.

(4) Everyone has the right to form and to join trade unions for the protection of his interests.

Article 24. Everyone has the right to rest and leisure, including reasonable limitation of working hours and periodic holidays with pay.

Article 25. (1) Everyone has the right to a standard of living adequate for the health and well-being of himself and of his family, including food, clothing, housing and medical care and necessary social services, and the right to security in the event of unemployment, sickness, disability, widowhood, old age or other lack of livelihood in circumstances beyond his control.

(2) Motherhood and childhood are entitled to special care and assistance. All children, whether born in or out of wedlock, shall enjoy the same social protection.

Article 26. (1) Everyone has the right to education. Education shall be free, at least in the elementary and fundamental stages. Elementary education shall be compulsory. Technical and professional education shall be made generally available and higher education shall be equally accessible to all on the basis of merit.

(2) Education shall be directed to the full development of the human personality and to the strengthening of respect for human rights and fundamental freedoms. It shall promote understanding, tolerance and friendship among all nations, racial or religious groups, and shall further the activities of the United Nations for the maintenance of peace.

(3) Parents have a prior right to choose the kind of education that shall be given to their children.

Article 27. (1) Everyone has the right to freely participate in the cultural life of the community, to enjoy the arts and to share in scientific advancement and its benefits.

(2) Everyone has the right to the protection of the moral and material interests resulting from any scientific, literary or artistic production of which he is the author.

Article 28. Everyone is entitled to a social and international order in which the rights and freedoms set forth in this Declaration can be fully realized.

Article 29. (1) Everyone has duties to the community in which alone the free and full development of his personality is possible.

(2) In the exercise of his rights and freedoms, everyone shall be subject only to such limitations as are determined by law solely for the purpose of securing due recognition and respect for the rights and freedoms of others and of meeting the just requirements of morality, public order and the general welfare in a democratic society.

(3) These rights and freedoms may in no case be exercised contrary to the purposes and principles of the United Nations.

Article 30. Nothing in this Declaration may be interpreted as implying for any State, group or person any rights to engage in any activity or to perform any act aimed at the destruction of any of the rights and freedoms set forth herein.

Bibliography

The list of publications that follows does not attempt to be comprehensive. We have included only those books, brochures and papers which deal with general human rights and refugee topics, and have omitted the annual reports and regular publications of voluntary organisations except where these may serve as reference works on wider issues.

REFERENCE, INCLUDING PERIODICALS

Amnesty International, *AI Newsletter*, monthly, London (International Secretariat)

Amnesty International, Prisoner of Conscience Year brochures on *Journalists and Writers in Prison, Parliamentarians in Prison, Trade Unionists in Prison*, etc., AI Publications, London, 1977

Brownlie, ed., *Basic Document on Human Rights*, Oxford, 1971

Council of Europe, *European Convention on Human Rights, collected texts*, 11th ed., Strasbourg, 1976

Council of Europe, Directorate of Human Rights, *Bibliography relating to the European Convention on Human Rights*, Strasbourg, 1973

Department of Education and Science, *International Understanding: sources of information on organisations*, London, 1976

Directory of Grant-Making Trusts, Charities Aid Foundation, London, 1977 (annual)

Guardian Directory of Pressure Group and Representative Associations, ed. Shipley, 1st ed., London, 1976

Help and Action, *Newsletter in Defence of Human Rights*, occasional (BP 6, 77850 Héricy, France)

Human Rights Commission, New Brunswick, *A Bibliography for Research in Human Rights*, New Brunswick, 1972

Human Rights Internet, *Newsletter*, bi-monthly (1502 Ogden Street, NW, Washington, DC 20010, USA)

Human Rights Network, *Information on some organisations in Britain concerned with the protection of human rights*, London, 1977

IDOC-International, *Monthly Bulletin,* IDOC (International Documentation on the Contemporary Church), Rome

International Human Rights: a bibliography, 1970-76, University of Notre Dame Law School, 1977

International Institute of Human Rights, *Bibliothèque Minimum dans le domaine des droits de l'homme*, Strasbourg, 1972

National Union of Students, *Educational Charities: a guide of educational trust funds*, London, 1974

Robertson, A.H., *Human Rights in the World*, Manchester, 1972

The Human Rights Review, twice yearly, OUP/British Institute of Human Rights

Third World First, *Campaigns Bulletin*, Oxford, occasional

Union of International Associations, *Yearbook of International Associations*, annual, Brussels, 1977

United Kingdom Council on Overseas Student Affairs, *Annual Report 1976/7 and Membership List 1977/8*, London, 1977

United Nations, *Yearbook on Human Rights*, twice yearly, New York

University of Texas Law School, Tarlton Law Library, *Checklist of Human Rights Documents*, monthly, Austin, Texas

World Without War, *International Human Rights Kit*, Chicago, 1977, bibliography

GENERAL WORKS ON HUMAN RIGHTS

Amnesty International, *The Amnesty International Report 1977*, London, Dec. 1977 (annual)

Amnesty International, British Section, *Report of Trades Union Human Rights Conference, 6-8 May 1977*, London, June 1977

Bulletin of Peace Proposals, 1977/3, special issue on *Human Rights*, Oslo, 1977

Chile and the British Labour Movement, special issue of *Chile Lucha*, London, 1975

Council for Science and Society, *Scholarly Freedom and Human Rights*, London, 1977

Fabre, J., *Conscientious Objection and Human Rights*, in *Reconciliation Quarterly*, Alkmaar, Holland, December 1976

Foundation for the Study of Plural Societies, *Case-Studies on Human Rights and Fundamental Freedoms*, The Hague, 5 vols., 1975/6

General Synod of the Church of England, *Human Rights: our understanding and our responsibilities*, London, February 1977

International Confederation of Free Trade Unions, *Human and Trade Union Rights*, 11th World Congress, Mexico City, October 1975, Brussels, 1975

International Council of Scientific Unions, Committee on the Free Circulation of Scientists, *Advice to Organisers of International Scientific Meetings*, Paris/Stockholm, October 1976

International Council of Voluntary Agencies, General Conference 1976, papers on *The Voluntary Response to Situations of Conflict*, Geneva, 1976

ILO, *Trade Union Rights and their relation to civil liberties*, ILO 54th Session, Geneva, 1969

International Press Institute, *Annual Review of World Press Freedom*, London, 1976

Jacobs, F.G., *The European Convention on Human Rights*, Oxford, 1975

Law Society (UK), *Legislation on human rights with particular reference to the European Convention: comments by the Council's Law Reform Committee . . . June 1976*, Law Society, 1977

Lissner, J., *The Politics of Charity*, in *The New Internationalist*, October 1976

MacDermot, N., *The Churches and Human Rights*, CIIR, London, 1976

Minority Rights Group, *World Minorities I*, ed. Ashworth, London, 1977

Monconduit, F., *La Commission Européenne des Droits de l'Homme*, in *Aspects Européens*, E/4, Leyden, 1965

Morris, C., *The Captive Conscience*, Amnesty International British Section, London, 1977

Pontifical Commission 'Justice and Peace', *The Church and Human Rights*, Vatican, 1975

Robertson, A.H., *Privacy and Human Rights: reports and communications . . . 3rd international colloquy about the European Convention, Brussels, 1970*, Manchester, 1973

UNESCO, *Cultural Rights as Human Rights*, Expert Meeting, July 1968, *Studies and Documents on Cultural Policies 3*, Paris, 1970

United Nations, *The UN and Human Rights*, New York, 1973

United Nations, *Human Rights: a comparison of international instruments of the UN*, United Nations (UN.73.XIV.2), New York, 1973

United Nations Commission on Human Rights, *Study of the Right of Everyone to be Free from Arbitrary Arrest, Detention and Exile*, UN/ECOSOC (UN.65.XIV.2), 1964

United Nations, Division of Human Rights, *Seminar on specific problems relating to human rights in developing countries*, Nicosia, June 1969

United Nations, House of Representatives, Committee on International Relations, Sub-Committee on International Organisations, *Human Rights in the International Community and in United States Foreign Policy, 1945-76*, Washington, DC, July 1977

United Nations, House of Representatives, Committee on International Relations, Sub-Committee on International Organisations, *International Protection of Human Rights: the work of international organisations and the role of the US foreign policy . . . hearings*, Washington, DC, 1974

Wallington, P. and MacBride, J., *Civil Liberties and a Bill of Rights*, London, 1976

Whitaker, B., *Why the UN needs more muscle to guard human rights*, in *The Times*, 26 January 1977

Williams, D., *Recognition of Rights could be rewarded*, in *Overseas Development Institute Review* (1/1978), London

World Council of Churches, *How to File Complaints of Human Rights Violations: a practical guide to inter-governmental procedures*, by Glenda De Fonseca, Geneva, 1975

World Council of Churches, Commission of the Churches on International Affairs, *Droits de l'Homme apres l'Assemblee de Nairobi*, in *CCIA*

Newsletter, 1976/4, Geneva, 1976

World Federation of Scientific Workers, *Declaration on the Rights of Scientific Workers*, London, no date

REFUGEES

Legal Instruments

Convention relating to the Status of Refugees, Geneva, 28 July 1951, published in Britain as *UK Cmd 9171*, June 1954 (UK ratification 11 March 1954)

(UK) *Immigration Act 1971*, HMSO, 1971

(UK) *Statement of Immigration Rules for Control on Entry/after Entry* (separate documents for Commonwealth and non-Commonwealth citizens), 25 January 1973

HC 79, HC 80, HC 81, HC 82, January 1973

General

Lord Ashby, *Einstein was a Refugee*, World University Service (UK), 1977

Council of Europe, Parliamentary Assembly, *Report on the situation of de facto refugees*, Council of Europe Document 3642, 5 August 1975

Dansk Flygtningehjaelp, *The Refugee in Denmark*, Copenhagen, no date

France Terre d'Asile, *Dimension Européenne des Problemes d'Asile,* Paris, no date

_____ *Guide Pratique du Réfugié*, Paris, September, 1975

International University Exchange Fund, *Asylum in Europe: a handbook for refugees and exiles*, 1st edn., Geneva, 1975

_____ *Problems of Refugees and Exiles in Europe*, Geneva, 1976; Part I: *The New Refugees in Europe*, by Anne Paludan; Part II: *The Legal Aspects of the Problems of de facto Refugees*, by Dr Paul Weiss

_____ *Ten Years of Assistance to African Refugees through International Cooperation*, Geneva, 1972

Runnymede Trust, *Refugees: their status and their admission into the UK*, Briefing Paper No. 1/75, London, 1975

UK Immigrants Advisory Service, *An Outline of the Current Procedures for Refugees and Asylum-Seekers in the UK*, June 1977

_____ *Problems of de facto and Convention Refugees*, by Dr Richard Plender, London, 1976

UNHCR, *Collection of International Conventions, Agreements and other texts concerning refugees*, Geneva, 1971

UNHCR Office in London, *The Office of UNHCR and its role in UK Immigration Appeals*, by Dr Guy Goodwin-Gill, London, 1977

World University Service (UK), *Education for Refugees*, London, 1977

WUS (UK), *Third World Political Refugees in the United Kingdom*, proceedings of a conference held at the Institute of Development

Bibliography

Studies at the University of Sussex in collaboration with the World University Service (UK) in December 1977, 24p, London, 1978

Latin America

Buchan. Norman, 'Glasgow's short way with refugees', *New Statesman*, 8 March 1977
Chile Solidarity Campaign, *Campaign Against Visa Delays*, London, February, 1977
Chile Solidarity/Chile Lucha, *Chile and the British Labour Movement*, TUC Conference Report. Special issue of Chile Lucha, London, 1975
CIMADE, *De Chile à la France: exil et acceuil des réfugiés*, Paris, no date
Committee for Human Rights in Uruguay, *Uruguayan Refugees*, London, January 1977
International Commission of Jurists, *The Application in Latin America of International Declarations and Conventions relating to asylum*, Geneva, September 1975
Joint Working Group (UK), *Refugees from Chile*, London, December 1975
Pan-American Union (General Secretariat, Washington, DC), Inter-American Treaties and Conventions of Asylum and Extradition, Treaty Series, No. 34, OAS Official Records: OEA/Ser.X/1: English, Washington, DC
UNHCR, El Refugio, *Refugees from Chile*, Geneva, 1975
'We should say what we mean', leader, *The Times*, 29 January 1977
World University Service, *Chile, Argentina, Uruguay: an outline of conditions in 1977*, London, October 1977

Africa

'How the British Government forces British subjects to fight for the illegal regime in Rhodesia', joint statement by IUEF, JCWI, UKCOSA, UKIAS, WUS, London, February 1977
International University Exchange Fund, *Annual Report*, London, 1977
World University Service, *Scholarship Aid to Rhodesian Students*, London, May 1976

Unpublished

Connelly, Maureen, *The Administrative Problems of Resettlement of Individual Refugees in Britain*, University of Sussex, June 1977
International Council of Voluntary Agencies, *General Conference 1976*, papers on the role of NGOs in situations of conflict, Geneva, 1976

Index